THE SCHOLARSHIP OF TEACHING AND LEARNING
IN AND ACROSS THE DISCIPLINES

SCHOLARSHIP OF TEACHING AND LEARNING

Jennifer Meta Robinson
Whitney M. Schlegel
Mary Taylor Huber
Pat Hutchings
editors

THE SCHOLARSHIP OF TEACHING AND LEARNING
IN AND ACROSS THE DISCIPLINES

EDITED BY Kathleen McKinney

Indiana University Press
Bloomington and Indianapolis

This book is a publication of

Indiana University Press
601 North Morton Street
Bloomington, Indiana 47404-3797 USA

iupress.indiana.edu

Telephone orders   800-842-6796
Fax orders   812-855-7931

Library of Congress Cataloging-in-Publication Data

The scholarship of teaching and learning in and across disciplines /
    Kathleen McKinney, editor.
        p. cm. — (Scholarship of teaching and learning)
    Includes bibliographical references and index.
    ISBN 978-0-253-00675-2 (cl : alk. paper) — ISBN 978-0-253-00676-9
(pb : alk. paper) — ISBN 978-0-253-00706-3 (eb) 1. Education, Higher—
United States. 2. Interdisciplinary approach in education—United States.
I. McKinney, Kathleen, editor of compilation. II. Chick, Nancy L., 1968–
Difference, privilege, and power in the scholarship of teaching and learning.
LA227.4.S36   2013
378.00973—dc23
                                                              2012030703

        1   2   3   4   5   18   17   16   15   14   13

To Bob, Ben, and Claire for their love, laughter, and support,
and to my mom, the memory of my dad,
and my siblings, Davis and Maureen,
for their unwavering belief in me.

—KMc

CONTENTS

FOREWORD   **MARY TAYLOR HUBER**

Travel between the disciplinary and interdisciplinary poles of the scholarship of teaching and learning has always been exciting—sometimes easy, sometimes arduous; sometimes welcomed, sometimes feared. The tensions were evident early on, when Sherwyn Morreale and I edited an exploratory collection of essays titled *Disciplinary Styles in the Scholarship of Teaching: Seeking Common Ground* (2002). We noted then how the work "draws strength from being situated in a discipline and its particular style. But growth in knowledge also comes at the borders of disciplinary imagination," and we called attention to the "trading zones" where scholars from different fields were exchanging insights, ideas, and findings "even though the meanings and methods behind them may vary considerably among producer groups" (2–3).

As this new collection demonstrates, travel between disciplinary and interdisciplinary destinations remains a defining feature of the scholarship of teaching and learning, and gives a special flavor to the experience of engaging in the work. Yet the essays gathered here also testify to two important developments. First, there has been the emergence of a more robust "teaching commons" in higher education, where "communities of educators committed to pedagogical inquiry and innovation come together to share ideas about teaching and learning" (Huber and Hutchings 2005, x). Second, through the enriched opportunities for trade that the commons provides, we now have a core set of resources—concepts, methods, analytical strategies—that all can draw on for inquiry into learning. What does this change in the landscape mean for the role of the disciplines in this work?

There's long been agreement that disciplines are key to the scholarship of teaching and learning. This comes in part from the work's character as practitioner inquiry in the classrooms (and associated labs, field sites, and community settings) where particular courses in particular fields are taught and learned. The questions scholars ask typically focus on what and how their students are (or are not) learning about course- and field-specific subject matter, values, dispositions, and skills. And while the main goal is improvement—designing learning environments that foster better learning outcomes—there has also been a strong conviction that inquiry emerging from one setting will be of interest to faculty teaching in the same discipline in other settings, both closer to home and further away. So another defining feature of the scholarship of teaching and learning has been a commitment to making the work public—"community property" as Lee Shulman (1993) memorably put it—in ways that one's colleagues can use and build on, with the goal of bringing teaching and learning more fully into the intellectual life (and strife) of the field.

Disciplinary Styles in the Scholarship of Teaching and Learning asked first about the kinds of homes the various disciplines provided for practitioner inquiry and pedagogical debate. Essay authors from ten fields—including humanities, sciences, social sciences, and professional schools—surveyed the scene. Had conversation about educational issues been central or marginalized in the discipline's recent history? Did the discipline's forums welcome or reject pedagogical contributions? Did the field's literature have much or little to offer scholars of teaching and learning? Were there strong communities of specialists engaged in research on teaching and learning in the discipline, and if so, how did they respond to "regular" faculty who took up the scholarship of teaching and learning? Answers to questions like these, we felt, could help us understand the opportunities and challenges that scholars of teaching and learning from these different disciplines would be facing as they attempted to draw from, influence, and strengthen the culture of teaching in their fields.

In addition to these questions about the place of pedagogy in the social and intellectual life of academic fields, *Disciplinary Styles* also explored cultural and epistemological influences. It explored how the disciplines have influenced key features of the scholarship of teaching and learning—the kinds of questions physicists, historians, or engineers ask about learning, the methods they use to investigate these questions, the approaches they take towards analyzing and interpreting results, and the presentation strategies they find most persuasive. As we said, "For good or for ill, scholars of teaching and learning must address field-specific issues if they are going to be heard in their own disciplines, and they must speak in a language that their colleagues understand" (2). Chemists, physicists, and engineers are most likely to pay attention to work that's designed to produce quantitative results; literary scholars and historians may look for other things—for example, "theoretical sophistication," different "kinds of evidence," and the quality of "narrative explanation" (Calder, Cutler, and Kelly 2002, 57).

These field-specific engagements remain powerful, but it was evident, even in 2002, that the scholarship of teaching and learning could not be contained within the social and cultural or epistemological boundaries of the disciplines. Practitioners engaged in the work often found that their close disciplinary colleagues were not yet tuned in, and they sought support from colleagues in other fields engaged in similar work. Further, many found it useful, and sometimes necessary, to go outside their discipline for ideas, methods, and analytic strategies (and on occasion, collaborators) to help understand what was happening in their classrooms, or, as Sherry Linkon puts it, to "read their students' minds" (Linkon 2011). Reports from early participants in the Carnegie Academy for the Scholarship of Teaching and Learning (CASTL) testify to how scary, but also productive, these forays into foreign territory could be—for example, a chemist conducting focus groups of students and statistical analyses beyond his normal range of disciplinary expertise (see Jacobs 2000).

What has happened in the years since has been surprising. As interest in pedagogy has grown, scholars of teaching and learning have contributed to and benefited greatly from the exchange the new commons afford. Indeed, anyone who takes up the work today—especially if they do so in the company of colleagues and mentors—will soon hear about a whole range of theoretical, methodological, and pedagogical ideas that circulate in the commons and that may help them ask and answer fruitful questions about learning in their classrooms, programs, and fields. As Kathleen McKinney points out in the introductory essay to this volume, what began as a discipline-based movement (enlivened by occasional cross-disciplinary ventures) has been transformed into a lively interdisciplinary field.

The essays in this collection speak eloquently to that transformation. Here, for example, we see mathematicians, political scientists, and historians all making use of ideas and techniques from literature on the development of expertise, a literature that originated in cognitive psychology but has since made its way into the scholarship of teaching and learning through a variety of routes. Among them would certainly be the chapter on "How Experts Differ from Novices" in the widely read report from the National Research Council on *How People Learn: Brain, Mind, Experience, and School* (Bransford, Brown, and Cocking 1999). But quite a number of scholars of teaching and learning in the CASTL network were introduced to this literature through their colleagues in history, who were themselves influenced by cognitive psychologist Sam Wineburg's studies of historical thinking (see Wineburg 2001). Taking the message further afield, one of these historians, David Pace, in collaboration with psychologist and educational developer Joan Middendorf (both co-authors of the history chapter in this volume) designed an approach to classroom inquiry and instructional improvement called "Decoding the Disciplines" based on the pedagogical value of articulating aspects of expert knowledge that one would like students in one's field to master (see Pace and Middendorf 2004).

The tale of how the literature on "expertise" gained ground among scholars of teaching and learning would have many more twists and turns if fully told. The point, however, is that there has now been time for such processes of intellectual legitimation to do their magic and establish certain theoretical, methodological, and practical ideas "as something that cannot be ignored by those who define themselves, and are defined, as legitimate participants in the construction of a cognitive field" (Lamont 1987, 586). We would have to modify the force of this notion a little for the scholarship of teaching and learning, of course, because for most practitioners, it is very much a second (or third or fourth) identity—and the real test of value for something on offer in the commons is whether it gives a purchase on their questions about learning, not whether it provides entrée to this new interdisciplinary field.

Yet entrée remains an issue because, as several essays in this volume remind us, the disciplines (and subdisciplines) are differently positioned vis-à-vis the emergent "core" of the field. Speaking as a humanist, Nancy Chick expresses concern that the growing dominance of social science approaches in the scholarship of teaching and learning can leave humanists feeling left out. In fact, she argues, literary studies has much to offer: concepts that can "negotiate" the limitations of taking student writing as straightforward evidence of learning, perspectives on generalizing from single cases, an appreciation of context in assessing the relevance of conclusions, and various narrative constructs like the bildungsroman that can enrich theories of college students' moral and intellectual growth. Regan Gurung, too, though coming from the more "privileged" field of psychology, makes a case for recognizing the contributions of several subdisciplines—including perspectives on student-teacher relationships from clinical and social psychology.

Gary Poole's essay picks up on a related tension within the scholarship of teaching and learning: what counts as "real" research? With scholars of teaching and learning coming from a full range of disciplines, it is inevitable that there will be disagreements about the rigor and value of work informed by different disciplinary methodologies and epistemologies. Poole searches for a definition that will accommodate this plurality and encourage participants to respect approaches other than their own. Liz Grauerholz and Eric Main make clear how important it is to be realistic about what is possible in practitioner research and free the scholarship of teaching and learning from inappropriate methodological expectations. A similar concern undergirds Caroline Persell and Antonio Mateiro's experiments in teaching key issues in sociology, which took place outside the classroom in small focus groups of volunteers who were not their own students—a design that gives up the affordances of more familiar sociological research and indeed, of the scholarship of teaching and learning, to take advantage of the "flexibility and openness" such focus groups allow.

The paradox at the heart of the scholarship of teaching and learning is that one leaves home not to get away but to return to one's discipline enriched. As many of the projects reported here suggest, the distance traveled is less important than the insights gained. Leah Shopkow, Arlene Díaz, Joan Middendorf, and David Pace—all participants in the History Learning Project at Indiana University, Bloomington—have found that addressing bottlenecks in their students' learning by teaching the moves that experts make has led not only to better student outcomes but to "revelation about the discipline itself." Jeffrey Bernstein, adapting the "think-aloud" method used in novice-expert research to political science, emphasizes how the identification of these bottlenecks (for example, students' difficulties in understanding the "essentially conflictual nature of politics") can suggest strategic "focal points" for pedagogical inquiry and improvement.

Other benefits of engagement with the larger commons are addressed by Curtis Bennett and Jacqueline Dewar, whose interdisciplinary forays brought back think-aloud and focus group strategies to study how students approach the idea of mathematical proof and conceptual frameworks for analyzing the dimensions and levels of students' mathematical understanding. Not only did this work enable them to better "capture and preserve details of what was good and bad in student work," it enabled them to "better talk and work with people in other fields." This is no small matter. As Robinson and colleagues from a graduate-student study group suggest in their essay, "The challenges posed by multi-disciplinarity can be underestimated." Precisely because disciplinary languages contain so much that is tacit, these issues about epistemology and method are likely to spark difficult conversations again and again. Yes, leaving one's disciplinary home is worthwhile, but it can also be really hard.

As the scholarship of teaching and learning continues to mature, the opportunities (and obligations) for interdisciplinary engagement will surely increase. For starters, there will be new occasions for addressing common institutional priorities in individual work. Cheryl Albers' chapter in this volume describes a set of projects that were oriented toward elucidating a question raised by her institution's results on the National Survey of Student Engagement (NSSE): "how to promote academic challenge that will result in more learning, not just more student work." There will also be occasions for inquiry aimed more directly at program-based and institutional assessment. Lauren Scharff offers two examples: one focusing on student motivation to complete pre-class assignments in courses from different departments, the second an interdisciplinary effort to improve critical thinking skills in freshman core courses. "The inclusion of multiple disciplines" in such studies,

Scharff suggests, "will ultimately lead to both a broader understanding of the underlying factors that transcend the disciplines and a clearer realization of contextual factors that make the findings less generalizable."

The conviction that crossing disciplinary borders can yield interesting and actionable insights for teaching suggests that such travel may have power for students as well. Historian David Reichard and biochemist Kathy Takayama address this possibility in an appealing dialogue about their efforts to introduce their students to "exotic" representational styles: the poster for undergraduate history majors, and the story for those studying science. While a hard step for many students, the effort had the advantage of making more visible for them as well as their teachers the epistemologies underwriting the conventions (research papers in history, lab reports in science) of their fields. Of course, the scholarship of teaching and learning is all about making students' learning more visible (to faculty and, in fact, to students themselves). But Carmen Werder adds an interesting twist to this point. What might we learn by crossing that border between teacher and student more directly by engaging students as co-inquirers? Would their involvement help us talk less often about teaching and more often "in their terms, the terms of learning?" Would work with student collaborators, especially those "who have not yet decided on disciplinary majors," help us all communicate better "across our disciplinary streams?"

Back when Sherwyn Morreale and I were writing the introduction to *Disciplinary Styles in the Scholarship of Teaching and Learning* in 2002, we looked at the future and made a prediction: "Of one thing we can be certain. Whatever the future of the scholarship of teaching and learning, it will no longer be mostly a matter of [the disciplines engaging in] parallel play." Kathleen McKinney and the contributors to this book certainly bear us out. Of course, these essays suggest, there's much left to do to ensure a *productive* tension between the disciplinary and interdisciplinary aspects of the work: expanding the repertoire to more adequately reflect the full range of fields involved, educating colleagues about the intellectual value of practitioner inquiry, and negotiating the challenges of engaging more closely with institutional priorities—just to name a few. But we should also celebrate the success these essays document: as the theories, methods, and settings for doing the work have become more interdisciplinary, the relevance of the scholarship of teaching and learning for the disciplines has not waned, but deepened instead.

REFERENCES

Bransford, John, Ann L. Brown, and Rodney R. Cocking. 1999. *How People Learn: Brain, Mind, Experience, and School.* Committee on Developments in the Science of Learning, Commission on Behavioral and Social Sciences and Education, National Research Council. Washington, DC: National Academy Press.

Calder, Lendol, William W. Cutler III, and T. Mills Kelly. 2002. "History Lessons: Historians and the Scholarship of Teaching and Learning." In *Disciplinary Styles in the Scholarship of Teaching and Learning: Exploring Common Ground,* ed. Mary Taylor Huber and Sherwyn P. Morreale, 45–67. Washington, DC: American Association for Higher Education and the Carnegie Foundation for the Advancement of Teaching.

Huber, Mary Taylor, and Pat Hutchings. 2005. *The Advancement of Learning: Building the Teaching Commons.* San Francisco: Jossey-Bass.

Huber, Mary Taylor, and Sherwyn P Morreale. 2002. "Situating the Scholarship of Teaching and Learning: A Cross-Disciplinary Conversation." In *Disciplinary Styles in the Scholarship of Teaching and Learning: Exploring Common Ground,* ed. Mary Taylor Huber and Sherwyn P. Morreale, 1–24. Washington, DC: American Association for Higher Education and the Carnegie Foundation for the Advancement of Teaching.

Jacobs, Dennis. 2000. "A Chemical Mixture of Methods." In *Opening Lines: Approaches to the Scholarship of Teaching and Learning,* ed. Pat Hutchings, 41–52. Menlo Park, CA: Carnegie Foundation for the Advancement of Teaching.

Lamont, Michele. 1987. "How to Become a Famous French Philosopher: The Case of Jacques Derrida." *American Journal of Sociology* 93, no. 3: 584–622.

Linkon, Sherry L. 2011. *Literary Learning: Teaching the English Major.* Bloomington: Indiana University Press.

Pace, David, and Joan Middendorf, eds. 2004. *Decoding the Disciplines: Helping Students Learn Disciplinary Ways of Thinking.* New Directions in Teaching and Learning, vol. 98. San Francisco: Jossey-Bass.

Shulman, Lee S. 1993. "Teaching as Community Property: Putting an End to Pedagogical Solitude." *Change* 25, no. 6: 6–7.

Wineberg, Sam. 2001. *Historical Thinking and Other Unnatural Acts: Charting the Future of Teaching the Past.* Philadelphia: Temple University Press.

ACKNOWLEDGMENTS

Edited books, of course, are not created without contributors. Thus, I would like to thank my wonderful chapter authors for their stimulating ideas, hard work, and attention to deadlines and details.

In addition, I am grateful to Erin Frost, PhD student in English at Illinois State University, for her assistance in preparing the manuscript. Thanks also to Indiana University Press editor Rebecca Tolen, project editor Nancy Lightfoot, and all the IU Press production staff for their hard work and assistance in all phases of the birth and development of this book.

I owe a great deal to K. Patricia Cross as well as administrators and colleagues at Illinois State University for their ongoing support of the scholarship of teaching and learning and the Cross Endowed Chair in the Scholarship of Teaching and Learning. In addition, I am grateful for the many colleagues in the SOTL movement who have been an inspiration to me including Mary Huber and Pat Hutchings of the Carnegie Foundation.

Last but clearly not least, thanks go to the many unnamed students at all institutions of higher education who we study in our SOTL work, who help us conduct and understand our SOTL work, and whose learning and development we strive to enhance through our SOTL work.

Kathleen McKinney

THE SCHOLARSHIP OF TEACHING AND LEARNING
IN AND ACROSS THE DISCIPLINES

Introduction to SOTL
In and Across the Disciplines

KATHLEEN MCKINNEY

This volume explores interdisciplinarity in the field of the scholarship of teaching and learning (SOTL). A broad definition of SOTL is "systematic reflection on teaching and learning made public" (Illinois State University 2011). A range of important changes in higher education have occurred over the last two to three decades that have fed the development of this movement (McKinney 2004; McKinney 2007). For example, many higher education institutions and disciplinary organizations have renewed their focus on teaching and learning. The student body in the United States and many other nations has become increasingly diverse both demographically and in terms of preparation for postsecondary education. New instructional technologies have been quickly and widely adopted, and new research has taken place on learning and the brain. Global economic conditions have contributed to a reduction in resources available for higher education. External pressures on colleges and universities to use assessment data to determine student learning outcomes have increased. In the midst of these changes, we are reminded that we need to know much more than we do about how, why, when, and where our students learn. We cannot waste time, energy, funds, and other resources on what Lee Shulman (2001) called "the great tragedy of teaching," or the "collective amnesia" about what works and why in teaching and learning. SOTL is a way to prevent this amnesia and a means for disseminating up-to-date knowledge we can use to improve our students' learning and development.

SOTL, then, can be valuable in many specific ways. For example, SOTL can help with program assessment, program review, and accreditation; revitalize senior faculty members; facilitate new partnerships among faculty, staff, and students in and across disciplines; provide opportunities for involvement in national/international higher education initiatives; provide data to enhance institutional priorities; offer additional opportunities for research productivity and outcomes for faculty; strengthen budget requests for additional operational or personnel funds; strengthen graduate student training and the preparation of future faculty; and, most importantly, improve teaching and learning (McKinney 2006; McKinney 2007). More and more, members of the international higher education community see the need and value of SOTL and, thus, need a range of scholarly resources about SOTL from within our disciplines and across disciplinary arenas.

SOTL began, primarily, as a discipline-based movement that included few multidisciplinary conversations. Instructors in a particular discipline looked at a teaching and learning problem in a local setting usually with their own students, in their own classes, and in terms of disciplinary learning. Thus, SOTL is most often context-specific. These features were and are, in part, what separates SOTL from traditional educational research at the college and university level. It is somewhat ironic, then, that there is a movement toward greater interdisciplinarity in the field of SOTL.

SOTL is conducted in all disciplines and at all types of institutions from community colleges to small private liberal arts schools to large public research-extensive universities. In addition, SOTL is an international, multidisciplinary initiative. The status of SOTL has changed in many fields over the last few years. There are also differences among disciplines in how SOTL is conceived and ways of doing SOTL work.

An early phase of cross-discipline SOTL efforts has resulted in the creation of major international organizations that involve SOTL researchers from many disciplines (including the International Society for the Scholarship of Teaching and Learning and the Society for Teaching and Learning in Higher Education) and encouraged cross-disciplinary sharing via international conferences and publications. David Reichard and Kathy Takayama, in this volume, describe cross-disciplinary dialogue over time about student learning and SOTL projects and write that "these cross-disciplinary conversations are a defining feature of SOTL, a signature practice and methodology." Some of these conversations are around the notion of "trading zones." As Mary Taylor Huber and Sherwyn Morreale write,

> As reading—and raiding—across the fields becomes more common, as interdisciplinary conversations become more frequent, as collaborations make them more substantive, the scholarship of teaching and learning is widening what historian of science Peter Galison (1997) calls a 'trading zone' (781–884). It is this borderland that scholars from different disciplinary cultures come to trade their wares—insights, ideas, and findings—even though the meanings and methods behind them may vary considerably among producer groups (3–4).

SOTL researchers have begun to create a "teaching commons" for sharing and social change (Huber and Hutchings 2005) and to realize that some aspects of teaching and SOTL "travel" (Huber 2009) via social networks—including interdisciplinary networks.

Conversations and research about critical questions related to the disciplines and to interdisciplinary work continue to develop, raising new questions. For example, which disciplines have active, long histories of SOTL work and why? How is SOTL defined and what does it look like in such disciplines? What conditions are necessary to allow for cross- or interdisciplinary SOTL work? And, perhaps most importantly, why is interdisciplinary SOTL an important goal? SOTL writers have addressed or illustrated some of these questions in limited or specific ways (for example, Bernstein, Nowacek, and Smith 2010; Gurung, Chick, and Haynie 2009; Gurung and Schwartz 2010; Huber 2009; Huber and Morreale 2002; Hutchings, Huber, and Ciccone 2011; Kreber 2008; McKinney 2007; Nakonechny and Poole 2006; Poole, Taylor, and Thompson 2007; Smith, Nowacek, and Bernstein 2010; Takayama 2009; Tremonte 2011; Weimer 2006; Willox and Lackeyram 2009; Witman and Richlin 2007; Yakura and Bennett 2004). This volume adds to the conversation about these and related critical questions, providing a needed resource on interdisciplinarity for those interested in and engaged in SOTL.

This venture into interdisciplinary SOTL arises from at least three factors: (1) the existence of many common teaching-learning problems across disciplines, (2) the need to learn from or collaborate with colleagues in other disciplines on theories or methods for doing SOTL, and (3) the growing desire to move SOTL applications beyond the individual classroom level. All three of these factors are discussed or illustrated in chapters in this volume. As we move further in this direction and discuss pros, cons, and examples of interdisciplinary SOTL, we may also find ourselves asking, given the original nature of SOTL, at what point—if any—does such work become something other than SOTL.

For greater impact on the field of SOTL and, most importantly, student learning, we need more resources that offer examples, applications, and discussions of critical issues of SOTL in disciplines beyond our own and in interdisciplinary SOTL efforts. Such resources help broaden our horizons and encourage cross-disciplinary collaborations by sharing conceptual frameworks, methodologies, key results, and practical applications that may be useful in our own classrooms and SOTL research.

There are numerous definitions and typologies of interdisciplinary scholarship or interdisciplinarity. In *Creating Interdisciplinarity: Interdisciplinary*

Research and Teaching among College and University Faculty, Lisa Lattuca discusses a number of these and offers her own typology based on interviews with faculty engaged in interdisciplinary teaching and research. Her framework is unique in that it emerges from the reflection and voice of instructors and also encompasses a full range of types. She proposes four types of interdisciplinarity, focusing on the nature of the questions posed, though she categorizes the first type as essentially disciplinary.

(1) Informed disciplinarity—"disciplinary questions may be informed by concepts or theories from another discipline or may rely upon methods from other disciplines, but these disciplinary contributions are made in the service of a disciplinary question" (82).

(2) Synthetic interdisciplinarity—"research questions bridge disciplines. These bridging issues and questions are of two subtypes: issues or questions that are found in the intersection of disciplines and issues and questions that are found in the gaps among disciplines. . . . In both subtypes, the contributions or roles of the individual disciplines are still identifiable, but the question posed is not necessarily identified with a single discipline" (82).

(3) Transdisciplinarity—"the application of theories, concepts, or methods across disciplines with the intent of developing an overarching synthesis . . . transcend disciplines and are therefore applicable in many fields. . . . The disciplines do not contribute components, but rather provide settings in which to test the transdisciplinary approaches" (83).

(4) Conceptual interdisciplinarity—"includes issues and questions without a compelling disciplinary basis. These issues and questions can be considered either interdisciplinary or predisciplinary because they can be answered only by using a variety of disciplinary contributions . . . often implies a critique of disciplinary understandings of the issue or question" (83).

Contributors to this volume are engaged in various forms of interdisciplinary SOTL. Included in this range of work is SOTL done by one scholar in a discipline drawing on theory or methods or concepts from one or more other disciplines; related work by several scholars spanning multiple disciplines; work done by one scholar in—or of—an interdisciplinary teaching-learning setting; analysis of issues related to interdisciplinary SOTL; and faculty development efforts and institutional change that encourage and support SOTL projects and collaboration across multiple disciplines. Thus, many of the topics covered in this book fall into the categories of informed disciplinarity and synthetic interdisciplinarity, although both transdisciplinarity and conceptual interdisciplinarity SOTL are also represented.

The volume has two parts. Part 1 includes six chapters approaching inter-disciplinary SOTL issues from, primarily, a disciplinary perspective looking at the status of SOTL in a discipline and/or at an example SOTL project in a discipline. The first two chapters offer information on the status of SOTL (history of SOTL in the discipline, common teaching-learning problems, methods used to conduct SOTL, theoretical concepts, future research ideas) for two disciplines: literary studies and psychology. Readers will be able to ask similar questions about the status of SOTL in their own fields. The next four chapters in part 1 offer examples of discipline-based SOTL projects in four different fields (history, mathematics, political science, and sociology). All the authors in part 1 link their disciplinary SOTL work to other fields in some way.

Part 2 consists of seven chapters approaching key themes directly from an interdisciplinary perspective and/or presenting interdisciplinary SOTL scholarship or professional development projects. The first two chapters in part 2 discuss challenges in doing interdisciplinary SOTL. The remaining five chapters offer examples of interdisciplinary SOTL projects at the course, program, or institutional levels. These interdisciplinary efforts involve SOTL work in and across microbiology, behavioral sciences, history, physics, mathematics, sociology, education, music, business, social work, psychology, chemistry, and philosophy. SOTL work fitting the categories of transdisciplinarity and conceptual disciplinarity on student engagement, service motivation, use of technology, diversity, critical thinking, and preparing future faculty are discussed.

Each of the thirteen chapters offers innovative ideas and examples that will help improve teaching and student learning and stimulate networking among SOTL scholars. Some of the common questions and themes that run through the chapters include the following:

- What are the shared (and not shared) definitions and language for key concepts such as SOTL, evidence, cross-disciplinarity, interdisciplinarity, and research? How do disciplinary traditions influence definitions of concepts, ways of knowing in SOTL, and challenges to working with others from different disciplines?

- Are there common—across or transcending disciplines—SOTL teaching-learning problems or questions? Are there common gaps in SOTL research in higher education across disciplines?

- What are the pros and cons (and examples) of the use of disciplinary-based methods for evidence-informed SOTL? What are legitimate, valid, accepted approaches to SOTL across disciplines? Are some methods privileged over others? What, if any, problems arise when SOTL is done by researchers using unfamiliar methods from other disciplines? What are the common standards to evaluate SOTL work across disciplines? How do standards impact interdisciplinary SOTL? How are issues of context important? What does "generalizable" mean in SOTL work?

- What have contributors used from another field in their SOTL work, and how could those in another field benefit from contributors' SOTL projects? What theories or concepts are useful for SOTL in and across disciplines? Can we create transdisciplinary frameworks?

- How can we best spread and support SOTL work in and across disciplines? How do we use SOTL to enhance institutional priorities? How do we include and represent student voices in SOTL?

Contributors were encouraged to write within the styles and conventions of their own disciplines or to borrow from others. In part 1, Nancy Chick addresses how certain methods and assumptions are privileged in the cross-disciplinary field of SOTL and in ways that limit our work. She articulates the nature of SOTL in the field of literary studies by outlining what literary SOTL looks like in terms of methodology, form or genre, and content (past, present, and future). Literary scholars make meaning from student-generated texts in the same way as they do other texts. She argues further that literary SOTL scholars are, therefore, in a special position to add to the ongoing conversation about SOTL genres and impact.

Psychology has a relatively long history of SOTL work and, as a social science that involves the study of human social behavior including learning, is one of a handful of disciplines with theories and methods especially useful for SOTL projects. The chapter by Regan Gurung and Beth Schwartz offers a review of the history and current status of SOTL in the large and diverse discipline of psychology drawing on ways psychologists have been active in SOTL, past reviews of SOTL work in the discipline, and psychological concepts and research areas of use in SOTL work in any discipline and across disciplines. They end with suggestions for a future research agenda for SOTL focusing on context and the big picture.

Curtis Bennett and Jackie Dewar use work from the research in mathematics education, K–12 and postsecondary, as well as work in science education as they discuss a mathematics SOTL project on understanding proofs that they conducted as part of their Carnegie Academy for the Scholarship of Teaching and Learning (CASTL) work. They discuss the influence of other disciplines on their methods and theory. Some of the applications of their project's results and interpretation include a product that can be used in assessment of student learning at both the course and program levels in mathematics and other fields.

In the next chapter, Jeff Bernstein describes his work using think-alouds, a SOTL method used in several disciplines, to understand how novices (political science students) and experts (political science professors) understand a complex political situation—the filibuster. He reports that the novices struggle with some key political issues, including the ideas of politics as a conflict-laden arena and the tension between majority rules and minority rights. He creates broader, cross-disciplinary arguments from his work about how bottlenecks inhibit students' understanding of important disciplinary ideas as well as how we can use SOTL studies of expert and novice behaviors to create improvements in teaching, particularly how we can make explicit to our students what to do in order to break through these bottlenecks.

Bottlenecks in another discipline are the focus of the chapter by Leah Shopkow, Arlene Díaz, Joan Middendorf, and David Pace. Each explain the process by which historians describe a bottleneck to learning in one of their classes and then define, in detail, the steps that students need to master to get past the bottleneck. Each author offers specific examples of the use of this "decoding the discipline" process in one of their classes to define the specific operations that students must master and suggest practical strategies for teaching these. They also give special attention to a variety of forms of assessment in the context of "decoding the disciplines." The decoding process should be adaptable to any discipline.

Finally, sociologists Caroline Persell and Antonio Mateiro report on a SOTL project that arose from the work of an American Sociological Association task force exploring what leaders in the field of sociology think are the most important sociological understandings for students to obtain from a college-level introductory course. In this chapter, they present their efforts to engage students in, and assess the effectiveness of, several active learning strategies—potentially useful in and drawn from other disciplines— designed to teach four of the top nine understandings. These understandings were taught to small groups of students who had never taken Introduction to Sociology. Student learning was assessed using before and after questions with focus groups and student qualitative comments throughout the session.

In part 2, Gary Poole discusses a number of obstacles involved in doing interdisciplinary SOTL work. One such obstacle, he argues, is the existence of our differing research paradigms. That is, one discipline might not understand or accept what another discipline believes to be research. Poole writes about multidisciplinary, interdisciplinary, and transdisciplinary approaches. He illustrates how beliefs about the nature and purpose of research, and beliefs about the nature of knowledge, vary across SOTL investigators. Finally, he offers a possible "universal" definition of research that those doing SOTL work, in any discipline and in different contexts, might share.

Along related lines, Liz Grauerholz and Eric Main examine four assumptions about SOTL work they believe to be fallacies or myths of SOTL: the need/ability to use control groups, that SOTL research can be generalized, that common measures used to assess student learning are acceptable, and that certain pedagogical strategies emphasized by SOTL researchers are, in fact, better than others. They examine the embedded assumptions in each myth and argue that these are problematic for doing and improving SOTL work in and across the disciplines. They draw on their own disciplinary backgrounds and experiences working with faculty across disciplines to argue that these assumptions are erroneous and hamper the field of SOTL.

David Reichard and Kathy Takayama explore the impact on student learning of employing alternatives to commonly used "signature pedagogies" in their respective discipline-specific courses. Reichard explored the impact of visual modes of communicating historical research on student learning in an upper division gay, lesbian, bisexual, and transgender history course. Takayama studied how microbiology students encountered visual literacy as a component of scientific literacy. The result is a comparative and cross-disciplinary analysis assessing the pedagogical value and limitations of having students work in "unfamiliar territory." They dialogue about the role of their cross-discipline SOTL collaboration in their SOTL work and academic careers.

Jennifer Meta Robinson, Melissa Gresalfi, Tyler Booth Christensen, April K. Sievert, Katherine Dowell Kearns, and Miriam E. Zolan discuss why multidisciplinarity is indispensible to the scholarship of teaching and learning. They focus on what they refer to as the bifurcation in SOTL of relying on practitioners working within disciplines but speaking to audiences outside them. This bifurcation poses significant challenges to the development of SOTL as a field. They further discuss some of the challenges to, and offer suggestions for, collaborations across disciplines including different understandings of the same terms and ways of knowing. They do so by drawing on experiences and qualitative data from a program for preparing future faculty that brings together faculty and graduate students from four disciplines.

Two additional chapters focus on multi- or cross-disciplinary SOTL collaborations at the institutional level. Lauren Scharff argues that there are many interdisciplinary SOTL research opportunities to help us with both the generalizable and more context-specific aspects of learning across courses and disciplines. She explores two SOTL projects involving efforts across core courses in multiple departments/disciplines; both provide examples of the ways departments work independently and without collaboration, despite common goals. The projects, however, also illustrate how SOTL work can help to lower barriers and encourage interdisciplinary conversations about teaching and learning. The first project serves as an example of looking for underlying principles to explain student behaviors when using a common pedagogical technique (pre-flight assignments). The second study provides an example of an approach to assessing institutional learning outcomes across disciplines via SOTL that is designed to encourage greater "buy in" from the faculty.

Cheryl Albers reports on a group of studies focused on improving student engagement at Buffalo State College. Topics of these projects include, for example, the impact of participating in undergraduate research, service learning and students' attitudes toward individuals of diverse backgrounds, and the use of technology to reduce student anxiety for statistics. Albers uses document analysis of the project reports and interview data from the SOTL Fellows. She analyzes the challenges and benefits of this model of cross-discipline SOTL collaboration at various levels. This leads to an important discussion of context and SOTL.

Finally, Carmen Werder raises the provocative question of whether interdisciplinary SOTL work and our discussion of it are the most useful paths to take. She notes that the useful idea of signature pedagogies in the disciplines (Shulman 2005) may have led some scholars to "focus almost exclusively on their own disciplines and less on crossing disciplinary boundaries—thus posing a challenge to doing interdisciplinary SOTL work." She provides some data on the limited amount of interdisciplinary SOTL language as evidenced in titles of presentations at the 2004 and 2010 International Society for the Scholarship of Teaching and Learning conferences, and discusses some of the challenges to engaging in such work. Finally, she suggests we move from a focus on interdisciplinary SOTL toward SOTL that is "integrative learning."

Whether you are a faculty member/academic staff person teaching in a higher education setting, a graduate student, an administrator, a faculty developer, a support staff member on campus, or a staff member in a professional society, you will benefit from reading this book or offering it to others in classes or workshops. The essays will help you to understand and analyze the current status of SOTL in multiple disciplines and the implications for your own discipline, important issues in disciplinary and interdisciplinary SOTL, exemplary models of SOTL work in and across various disciplines, new networks and other resources for SOTL work, ideas for new SOTL projects based on transdisciplinary issues related to teaching and learning, the ability to view SOTL outside your discipline from your disciplinary perspective while also learning to use the disciplinary perspectives of others, and how you can move your disciplinary SOTL to various levels of interdisciplinarity.

REFERENCES

Bernstein, Jeffrey L., Rebecca S. Nowacek, and Michael B. Smith. 2010. "Collaborative Inquiry and Big Questions in the Scholarship of Teaching and Learning." *International Commons* 5, no. 3: 10–12.

Galison, Peter. 1997. *Image and Logic: A Material Culture of Microphysics.* Chicago: University of Chicago Press.

Gurung, Regan A., Nancy Chick, and Aeron Haynie, eds. 2009. *Exploring Signature Pedagogies: Approaches to Teaching Habits of Mind.* Sterling, VA: Stylus.

Gurung, Regan A., and Beth M. Schwartz. 2010. "Riding the Third Wave of SOTL." *International Journal of the Scholarship of Teaching and Learning* 4, no. 2. http://www.georgiasouthern.edu/ijsotl.

Huber, Mary Taylor. 2009. "Teaching Travels: Reflections on the Social Life of Classroom Inquiry and Innovation." *International Journal for the Scholarship of Teaching and Learning* 3, no. 2. http://www.georgiasouthern.edu.ijsotl.

Huber, Mary Taylor, and Pat Hutchings. 2005. *The Advancement of Learning: Building the Teaching Commons.* San Francisco: Carnegie Foundation for the Advancement of Teaching/Jossey-Bass.

Huber, Mary Taylor, and Sherwyn P. Morreale, eds. 2002. *Disciplinary Styles in the Scholarship of Teaching and Learning: Exploring Common Ground.* Stanford, CA: Carnegie Foundation for the Advancement of Teaching and the American Association of Higher Education.

Hutchings, Pat, Mary Taylor Huber, and Anthony Ciccone. 2011. "An Integrative Vision of the Scholarship of Teaching and Learning." *International Journal for the Scholarship of Teaching and Learning* 5, no. 1. http://academics.georgia southern.edu/ijsotl/.

Illinois State University. 2011. "The Scholarship of Teaching and Learning." http://sotl.illinoisstate.edu/.

Klein, Julie Thompson. 1996. *Crossing Boundaries: Knowledge, Disciplinarities, and Interdisciplinarities.* Charlottesville: University Press of Virginia.

Kreber, Carolin, ed. 2008. *The University and Its Disciplines: Teaching and Learning Within and Beyond Disciplinary Boundaries.* New York: Routledge.

Lattuca, Lisa R. 2001. *Creating Interdisciplinarity: Interdisciplinary Research and Teaching among College and University Faculty.* Nashville: Vanderbilt University Press.

McKinney, Kathleen. 2004. "The Scholarship of Teaching and Learning: Past Lessons, Current Challenges, and Future Visions." *To Improve the Academy* 22: 3–19.

———. 2006. "Attitudinal and Structural Factors Contributing to Challenges in the Work of the Scholarship of Teaching and Learning." In *Analyzing Faculty Work and Rewards: Using Boyer's Four Domains of Scholarship*, ed. John M. Braxton, 37–50. *New Directions for Institutional Research* (129). San Francisco: Jossey-Bass.

———. 2007. *Enhancing Learning through the Scholarship of Teaching and Learning: The Challenges and Joys of Juggling.* San Francisco: Jossey-Bass.

Nakonechny, Joanne, and Gary Poole. 2006. "The Collaboration Process in an Interdisciplinary Research Context; or, What Language Are You Speaking?" Conference of the International Society for the Scholarship of Teaching and Learning, Washington, DC. November.

Poole, Gary, Lynn Taylor, and John Thompson. 2007. "Using the Scholarship of Teaching and Learning at Disciplinary, National, and Institutional Levels to Strategically Improve the Quality of Post-secondary Education." *International Journal for the Scholarship of Teaching and Learning* 1, no. 2. http://academics.georgiasouthern.edu/ijsotl/.

Salter, Liora, and Alison Hearn. 1996. *Outside the Lines: Issues in Interdisciplinary Research.* Buffalo: McGill-Queen's University Press.

Shulman, Lee S. 2001. *Remarks.* Presented at the symposium for the Cross Endowed Chair in the Scholarship of Teaching and Learning, Illinois State University, Normal, IL. November.

———. 2005. "Signature Pedagogies in the Professions." *Daedalus* 134, no. 3: 52–59.

Smith, Michael B., Rebecca S. Nowacek, and Jeffrey L. Bernstein. 2010. *Citizenship Across the Curriculum.* Bloomington: Indiana University Press.

Takayama, Kathy. 2009. "Communities, Voices, and Portals of Engagement." *International Journal for the Scholarship of Teaching and Learning* 3, no. 2. http://academics.georgiasouthern.edu/ijsotl/.

Tremonte, Colleen M. 2011. "*Window Shopping:* Fashioning a Scholarship of Interdisciplinary Teaching and Learning." *International Journal for the Scholarship of Teaching and Learning* 5, no. 1. http://academics.georgia southern.edu/ijsotl/.

Weimer, Maryellen. 2006. *Enhancing Scholarly Work on Teaching and Learning: Professional Literature that Makes a Difference.* San Francisco: Jossey-Bass.

Willox, Ashlee Cunsolo, and Dale Lackeyram. 2009. "(Re)Considering the Scholarship of Learning: Inviting the Elephant in the Room to Tea." *International Journal for the Scholarship of Teaching and Learning* 3, no. 1. http://academics.georgiasouthern.edu/ijsotl.

Witman, Paul D., and Laurie Richlin. 2007. "The Status of the Scholarship of Teaching and Learning in the Disciplines." *International Journal for the Scholarship of Teaching and Learning* 1, no. 1. http://academics.georgia southern.edu/ijsotl/v1n1/essays/schroeder/IJ_Schroeder.pdf.

Yakura, Elaine, and Curtis Bennett. 2004. "Finding Common Ground: Collaboration Across the Disciplines in the Scholarship of Teaching." *Journal on Excellence in College Teaching* 14, no. 2/3: 135–47.

PART 1 • SOTL in the Disciplines

CHAPTER 1

Difference, Privilege, and Power in the Scholarship of Teaching and Learning: The Value of Humanities SOTL

NANCY L. CHICK

The Competing Metaphors of SOTL: The Big Tent and the Family Table

As Kathleen McKinney notes in the introduction to this volume, one path of the development of SOTL has been its expansion from primarily disciplinary inquiries toward cross-disciplinary methods and questions—as reflected in the structure of this book. While reflections on SOTL itself have appeared all along (the Carnegie publications immediately come to mind)[1] and may in fact have facilitated its development, now there is "an increased need for discussions of SOTL in *and* across disciplines" (McKinney, introduction to this volume). McKinney suggests that there is room for both and that they complement each other: it is not the case that discipline-specific and cross-disciplinary works compete with each other in a zero-sum game that only one can win. Indeed, rather than representing black-and-white visions of the field (disciplinary *or* interdisciplinary), McKinney cites Lisa Lattuca's (2001) continuum from one to the other. In theory, then, we praise the "methodological and theoretical pluralism" (Hutchings and Huber 2008, 233) of individual projects and of the field of SOTL itself, imagining an inclusive and open "big tent" (Huber and Hutchings 2005, 30).

However, despite the call to open up the field to include a variety of disciplines and cross disciplines, there is still pressure, at least in the United States, toward a fairly narrow set of approaches in SOTL that limit the methods accepted as sound and, as a result, the kind and quality of student learning we come to understand—a problem described by others in this volume (Grauerholz and Main, Poole). While many well-known SOTL leaders come from humanities backgrounds (Pat Hutchings, Randy Bass, Barbara Cambridge, Richard Gale), the on-the-ground work largely marginalizes the practices of their disciplines.[2] Gale (2005) laments the characterization of humanities perspectives as "academically 'soft'" in the larger context of higher education with its "tendency to 'harden' in order to validate, such that even the most thoughtful and rigorous of capacities can be branded as unimportant," especially if they aren't grounded in what's "rational, logical, subject to precise measurement and analysis" (5). Liz Grauerholz and Eric Main's chapter in this volume describes what they call "Fallacies of SOTL," several of which are often the source of this skepticism: the assumptions that SOTL research must use control groups, that it should (and even can) be generalizable across settings, and that quantitative measures are superior in reliability and validity. Gary Poole's chapter in this volume explores how some disciplines don't understand or even accept what another discipline considers research. In the "gatekeeper" model of multidisciplinary SOTL, humanities approaches would need another discipline, most likely a social science, to legitimize the work as real research (Garner quoted in Poole, this volume).

To illustrate, in the editors' panel at the 2009 conference of the International Society for the Scholarship of Teaching and Learning (ISSOTL), Patricia Jarvis summarized the "mistakes and pitfalls" of unpublishable work characterized by surveyed editors of a dozen SOTL journals: the methods aren't "good science," the research designs lack "empirical rigor," there's no "baseline or pre- and post-test," and the results aren't "easy to replicate" (Jarvis and Creasey 2009). Thus, while there is apparently an abundance of journals that publish SOTL (Weimer 2006; McKinney 2007), at least the dozen unidentified ones in Jarvis and Gary Creasey's study appear to very narrowly define research, SOTL, and who can participate. More recently, in a special section called "*IJ-SOTL* Reviewers: Getting SOTL Articles Published," Trent Maurer (2011) announces that "control groups and experimental design are preferable" (2). Even the two main books on how to do SOTL (McKinney 2007; Gurung and Schwartz 2009), while offering some encouragement and validation of the range of methods used by different disciplines, include statements in their project design descriptions that suggest that the disciplinary backgrounds equipped for SOTL are limited. McKinney's chapter on project design defends subjectivity against expectations of objectivity, supports methodological pluralism, and briefly covers a wide range of methods; however, the chapter's second paragraph begins, "*As in any good scholarship involving empirical data,* the research question guides the methodology within the constraints of practical realities and ethical guidelines" (emphasis added; 67). The italicized language comes from the scientific method, and many humanities scholars would say that they do not use "empirical data" but instead "evidence" (or some other term). Also, the research question alone shouldn't guide methodology (there is more than one valid way to answer a question): the researcher's disciplinary background should also come into play in SOTL, as recommended by Charles Glassick, Mary Taylor Huber, and Gene Maeroff (1997) and Mick Healey (2000). Even further, Regan Gurung and Beth Schwartz's book for SOTL beginners—despite earlier nods to the multidisciplinary nature of SOTL—devotes one of five chapters to "the main statistical analyses needed to conduct SOTL," giving us "the tools and the know-how to assess teaching and learning" (145). The chapter is even titled "Is It Significant? Basic Statistics." The book seems to suggest that without statistics, an SOTL project, its methods, or its conclusions won't be considered significant. In isolation but even more so taken together, these instances suggest that SOTL doesn't welcome the valuable ways in which many scholars—especially those in the humanities and fine arts—are trained to conduct research, make meaning, and demonstrate knowledge.

Even within my own discipline of literary studies, a closer inspection of our journals shrinks the potential outlets for literary SOTL. For instance, although the National Council of Teachers of English (NCTE) seems to offer obvious choices, *Research in the Teaching of English* publishes education research, *College English* publishes primarily disciplinary research and very little on pedagogy or classroom research, and *Teaching English in the Two-Year College* is limited to a specific type of institution. *PMLA*, the journal of the Modern Language Association (MLA), privileges disciplinary research virtually to the exclusion of pedagogy. *Pedagogy* is arguably the premiere SOTL journal for our discipline, yet it's also the one Randy Bass and Sherry Lee Linkon (2008) note as lacking in examples of strong disciplinary methodologies: most of its articles present general descriptions of student learning, rather than close readings of student texts—our discipline's methodology and evidence of learning.

Conferences are typically more receptive venues that encourage multiple perspectives, yet an analysis of the first six ISSOTL conference programs reveals that only 10 percent of all sessions (panels, papers, posters, workshops, or plenaries) were about humanities-based SOTL projects, issues, or classrooms, and less than 1 percent were literature-based ones (Chick 2009). It's unclear if this minimal presence is due to reviewers rejecting SOTL in such areas as inadequate, submissions that are not good enough for acceptance, potential presenters shying away from such conferences, a dearth of literary teacher-scholars studying their students' learning, or some combination. Whatever the cause, there is reason to be confused and even nervous about humanities scholars' place at the public SOTL table—a metaphor recalling Lee Shulman's warning that SOTL should not become a "family table," one with "familiar faces" and conversations, one that's too "insular" (Chick 2006,

7). This is not to suggest that the SOTL tent or table shouldn't have standards; instead, I encourage a critical examination of what and whose standards we apply, who they mark as inferior, and on what grounds. I argue that there is an invisible norm in the field of SOTL that needs closer interrogation.

Understanding and Responding to Differences in SOTL

This criticism of SOTL scholars who identify strongly with their disciplines (especially those from the humanities and fine arts) is evocative of Peter McLaren's (1995) four multicultural theories, or four different and progressively more complex ways of thinking about difference and diversity: conservative, liberal, left-liberal, and critical.[3] Conservative multiculturalism promotes assimilation with "whiteness as [the] invisible norm" and other cultural groups as mere "'add-ons' to the dominant culture" because they lack the values necessary to being an American (McLaren 1995, 49). Liberal multiculturalism, on the other hand, assumes equality among all cultures but is subtly undergirded by the conservative's normalized whiteness in its assertion that "we're all the same" and that identifying differences is racist in itself. The left-liberal view focuses on differences between groups, differences resulting from singular, static, essentialist, inherent elements of "a primeval past of cultural authenticity" (51). Finally, critical multiculturalism challenges the previous three, calling attention to specific differences "*between* and *among* groups" that emerge from the complex interplay between "history, culture, power, and ideology" (McLaren's emphasis; 53).

Concerns about the disciplines in SOTL lead me to McLaren's theories of difference and culture for a variety of reasons. First, both are about the controversies of contested, hierarchical identities in a landscape of limited resources and rewards. After all, our disciplines are our intellectual and academic cultures: our experiences of knowing and being known, seeking and making meaning, valuing and being valued. The competitive environment in higher education in which opportunities, resources, and rewards affect groups differently, particularly men and women, is already documented for SOTL (McKinney and Chick 2010).

Translating McLaren's perspectives to SOTL, a conservative SOTL scholar would promote a narrow definition of SOTL (including its questions, methods, evidence, and genre) as the norm, suggesting that variations lack important qualities of SOTL. A liberal SOTL scholar would claim Huber and Pat Hutchings's "big tent" definition of the field but resist attention to any disciplinary differences on the assumption that SOTL is beyond the disciplines and such attention would create hierarchies among approaches. The left-liberal SOTL scholar would assert that good SOTL must be discipline-specific, using a narrow conception of each discipline's approaches, which have little in common with others.' Finally, a critical SOTL scholar would resist the tendency to normalize a few approaches to invisibly exclude, delegitimize, erase, or homogenize disciplinary identities. This SOTL scholar invokes the differing approaches between and even within many disciplines. (For instance, English encompasses the very different approaches of composition, literary studies, creative writing, and sometimes linguistics; geography includes the natural scientists in physical geography and the social scientists of cultural geography.) This view also acknowledges that differences may arise from the experiences of developing an identity within a field in specific national, regional, institutional, and even subdisciplinary or specialty contexts, rather than a simple, singular common background.

The normalized privileging of control groups, experimental designs, pre- and post-tests, and the specific language accompanying "scientific rigor" strikes a chord of the conservative and liberal approaches, as if there's only one way to make and reflect meaning, as if there's only one language—like an English-only nation in which those who more naturally use other languages should disappear into the proverbial melting pot. Even the universally accepted criticism of text-heavy posters and PowerPoint slides resonates with this perspective, since text is what most humanities disciplines highly value. If disciplinary perspectives are how scholars do their daily work, make meaning, think about the world, and interpret their experiences and those of others, they can't simply deny them or change them—nor would they want to. Nor should they have to. However, much like the invisibility of the norm of whiteness described in Peggy McIntosh's (1989) classic "White Privilege: Unpacking the Invisible Knapsack," those who practice the widely accepted SOTL methods are probably unaware of the privileging of their approaches at the expense of those with strengths and expertise in other backgrounds and those who value and speak through other methods. It's not a matter of ill intent; it's a matter of invisibility.

Many humanities and fine arts SOTL scholars describe their frustration as if they're being asked to "pass" as social scientists, invoking the language of light-skinned blacks who must deny their complex racial identities to assimilate into the dominant white society. The parallel is how these scholars mimic the dominant methodologies and genres rather than freely expressing their own backgrounds and their more familiar ways of seeking, making, and articulating meaning. The danger for these SOTL scholars is that—because of their different backgrounds, strengths, and worldviews—they may not do it well. Hutchings and Huber (2008) describe the fear of "amateurs" (239) as one explanation for the resistance to SOTL research outside the narrow definition.[4] As academics and disciplinary experts, we don't like playing the amateur any more than others like to see the work of the amateur, especially when it's held up to represent the quality of the field.

To return to McLaren's framework for understanding responses to difference, while two approaches would define SOTL through a narrow, dominant perspective (explicitly for the conservatives, implicitly for the liberals), a left-liberal SOTL scholar would suggest that we should remain entrenched in our disciplinary questions, methods, and audiences. This view is guided by the essentialist assumption that we're bound by static, simplified disciplinary backgrounds. The potential for this kind of disciplinary segregation probably explains concerns about creating "silos" or "tribes" within SOTL, groups resistant to collaborating across campus, varying approaches, or sharing findings with each other (presenting and publishing only in disciplinary venues), as if there is no common ground. The worry is that discipline-focused work (for example, decoding the disciplines [see Shopkow's chapter in this volume], threshold concepts, or signature pedagogies) isolates and segregates, reflecting cautions against students focusing on singular disciplinary learning, which would inhibit "intellectual empathy and tolerance" (Nelson 1999, 174). When I hear such concerns at SOTL conferences when conferees gather or present by disciplinary groups, I'm reminded of Beverly Tatum's (1997) interrogation of the question "Why are all the black kids sitting together in the cafeteria?" in the book by that name. She notes that the "tone of voice implied what usually remained unsaid, 'And what can we do to solve this problem?'" (xvii). While the questioners may be uncomfortable with what they perceive as self-segregated "tribes,"[5] Tatum points out that the groups originate from feeling "invalidated," so members are "more likely to turn to someone who will understand their perspective" (59–60). "Joining with one's peers for support in the face of stress is a positive coping strategy," she notes, and (here, replacing her words for the black teenagers in her study to humanities SOTL scholars) "connecting with one's [disciplinary] peers in the process of [SOTL] identity development is important and should be encouraged" (69). Whether disciplinary grouping in SOTL is a stage in the development of a new field is unclear but worth pursuing.

Finally, McLaren's critical SOTL scholar would advocate for an alternative approach to the field, one that explicitly acknowledges and validates the role of disciplinary background in how scholars approach SOTL. The questions asked about student learning, research designs, and notions of rigor, evidence, and going-public genres are all influenced in very real ways by what we've learned in our education, our academic conversations, our prior scholarship, and our current interests. Huber and Sherwyn Morreale (2002) compare SOTL to a "borderland [in which] scholars from different disciplinary cultures come to trade their wares" (3–4), invoking the metaphor at the heart of Gloria Anzaldúa's *Borderlands/La Frontera: The New Mestiza* (1987). Anzaldúa describes the residents of a borderland "at the confluence of two or more genetic streams, with chromosomes constantly 'crossing over'" in positive terms: "rather than resulting in an inferior being, [this experience] provides hybrid progeny, a mutable, more malleable species with a rich gene pool . . . a new *mestizo* consciousness . . . a consciousness of the Borderlands" (77). Again, as Huber and Morreale suggest, this metaphor is perfect for SOTL as we bring our rich disciplinary identities to create "a plural personality" that "operates in a pluralistic mode" (79)—language that invokes that much-discussed "methodological and theoretical pluralism" (Hutchings and Huber 2008, 233). Also, unlike the melting pot in which individuality disappears into something more monolithic, the borderland is a "synthesis" in which the parts are still visible (79).[6] This perspective is similar to Lattuca's synthetic interdisciplinarity in which, regardless of research question, the disciplines are still "identifiable," perhaps through conceptual frameworks, methodologies, and/or types of evidence (2001, 82 quoted in McKinney's introduction in this volume). More descriptive than the "big tent" or the "family table," the borderland metaphor encourages all of us (not a few) to bring our disciplinarity with us in all its richness and complexity as we inhabit a territory that's even richer and more complex as a result.

In sum, a critical SOTL scholar would assert that all disciplines have something to bring to the table (Shulman 2004, Tatum 1997), or valuable wares to sell under the big tent (Huber and Hutchings 2005), or strong genes to contribute to the borderlands (Anzaldúa 1987). In this book's spirit of "sharing conceptual frameworks, methodologies, key results, and practical applications that may be useful in our own classrooms and SOTL research" (McKinney, introduction in this volume), it's worth explaining what the humanistic disciplines bring to that table, tent, and gene pool.

Understanding a Humanities Approach: What We Bring to SOTL

In this section, I unpack the following approaches as part of my broader effort to seek more than disciplinary "tolerance," which connotes "something one had for a bad job or a bad smell or a nightmare relative who visited once a year" (Wypijewski 1999, 67). Instead, I hope to show the value of humanities scholars in scholarship of teaching and learning. Rather than attempting to encompass all of the humanities and extend perhaps too far outside of my own strongest frameworks (and thus assuming the role of the amateur), I draw from literary studies as a case study in humanities-based SOTL. Many cross-disciplinary venues and conversations (statewide, regional, and international conference presentations, for example) have confirmed that the practices I'm most familiar with aren't limited to my specific field but are also used in an array of humanities disciplines, and perhaps beyond. I do, however, encourage scholars across the humanities to contribute to this discussion from their varied and specific frameworks as well.

The presence of literary scholars in SOTL is one that plenty might define as weakly disciplinary: in addition to concerns about how seriously literary SOTL will be taken by those outside the discipline, criticisms of the ways in which literary scholars have written about teaching and learning aren't hard to find from within the discipline, either. Mariolina Salvatori (2002) looks back at the problematic tradition of teaching anecdotes, which are focused solely on the teacher, "'experiential and instinctive,'" context-bound, and "untheorizable" (297, 302). John Guillory (2002) notes that many of these pedagogical publications are "less conceptually developed" and lack the "measure of sophistication" (164–65) of our disciplinary scholarship. Bass and Linkon (2008) review five years of a premiere literary SOTL journal and note that the focus is again on the instructor and rarely on the products of learning or the students' work. They conclude that, although the methods of literary studies are in fact well suited to SOTL, "*literary scholars are not yet fully applying the methods of the discipline,*" revealing how we marginalize our own practices within this work (Bass and Linkon's emphasis; 260). Perhaps we, too, often have acted the amateur, forging ahead with unfamiliar but widely accepted methods, instead of drawing from our positions as experts with relevant and valuable disciplinary skills and principles. Indeed, some of the discipline's most applicable methodologies and its fundamental principles about texts, as well as others that don't fit into the limits of a single chapter, illustrate how well suited we are as SOTL scholars.

Close Reading: Our Strongest Methodology

Bass and Linkon (2008) broadly define "close reading" as literary scholars' primary practice that foregrounds "the careful analysis of the individual text" and "prioritize[s] the text and the act of reading . . . from fairly well-defined theoretical standpoints that influence [scholars'] assumptions about what matters in texts as well as what kinds of secondary data to consider in the research process" (247). Robert Scholes's (1985) classic notion of "textual competence" also reflects this systematic process of "*reading, interpreta-*

tion, and *criticism*" (Scholes's emphasis; 24). Sheridan Blau (2003) usefully translates these fundamental skills into a disciplined series of questions that make our moves more meaningful to scholars in other areas: reading, or "'What does it say?' translates in all other fields into 'What are the facts?'" Interpretation or "'What does it mean?' translates to the question, 'What inferences can be drawn from the facts?'" Criticism can be thought of as "'So what?'" and "'What applications does it suggest?' and 'What theory does it generate or challenge?'" (52). In thinking again about textual competence, Scholes (2002) wonders if "What we actually mean by 'close' reading may be distant reading—reading as if the words belonged to a person at some distance from ourselves in thought and feeling . . . before they can be seen as words . . . that need to be read with close attention" (166). His revision of the signature practice in our discipline points to the critical distance literary scholars use to recognize valid, evidence-based meanings within the written text rather than relying on the lenses of a more subjective, relativistic set of reader expectations, projections, or life experiences. Perhaps Scholes's clarification of the reader's role in close/distant reading is a cousin to the scientist's valuing of objectivity.

Imagine looking closely at a student paper, discussion posting, paragraph, or specific passage and asking carefully, mindfully, "What does it say? What are the facts expressed by the student? What does it mean, or what inferences can we fairly and intelligently draw from these facts? And so what? What applications do these meanings suggest? What theory do they generate or challenge?" Applying this careful, rigorous, close, and distant analysis to student texts would lead to multilayered considerations of their demonstrations of learning and sometimes, more importantly, when their learning falls short. Social scientists may loosely compare the literary scholar's meaning-making process of close reading to Barney Glaser and Anselm Strauss's process of grounded theory (1967), an inductive, iterative, systematic process of analyzing and reanalyzing data (or text) to build toward a theory (or interpretation, or our process of meaning making). For instance, in a project documenting novice practices and misconceptions in introductory literature courses, closely reading three sets of writings from approximately seventy-five students over several semesters revealed something significant and meaningful in how the students described and did literary analysis:

> The metaphorical language students used reveals a way of thinking about literary analysis as an act of violence from which pleasure needs guarding: "take apart," "tear up," "dissect," "breaks apart," "pick apart," "dismantle," and other attacks on the texts suggesting that

that this type of analysis will ruin the reading experience for them. (Chick, Hassel, and Rybak 2012, 15)

In this repeated use of similar language, we now understand—and can respond more effectively to—some of students' resistance to literary analysis: they view our practices as antithetical to their preferences for reading for pleasure, escapism, and fun, and they see literary scholars as "cold, heartless, soulless, and at odds with what's valued off campus" (14). Without identifying this language, we wouldn't as fully understand why students resist in our introductory courses, and we certainly wouldn't know how to handle that resistance.

Fundamental Principles about Texts: The Question of Evidence

Using these skills of close reading honed over years of practice, literary scholars value texts that are meaningful, multilayered, and context-rich. Written text is our language, our site for finding evidence of meaning, our way of making meaning, and what we value most. Whatever the genre, we recognize these writings as much more than a plot or what is denotatively written on the page, as is suggested by Scholes's central practices described above. Writing also encodes specific personal, historical, and cultural contexts, as well as the larger circumstances of the human condition. Literary SOTL scholars approach student-generated texts in the same way—as documents that can reveal much about moments of thinking and learning within their contexts of a classroom, an institution, a region, and what may be called the student condition. The implications of this approach to student work suggest a great deal about how seriously we take our students and their written work and is one of many ways for SOTL to honor the student voice.

Student texts are also rich sources of evidence of gradations of learning, not just as they represent students' thoughts but also as they represent their exact, unparaphrased, unaltered language. In this context, students' word choices, their syntax, their stops and starts (especially in the case of informal or unpolished writing), and their mistakes are all potentially meaningful, depending on the research question. Consider, in this example of our SOTL practice, a sophomore-level literature course in which a small group of students tries to understand the Theodore Roethke poem "My Papa's Waltz," a seemingly simple poem that is actually full of ambiguity, complexity, and ambivalence, as the adult speaker recalls his experiences as a young boy dancing with the abusive father he loved. The students in the group note that the rhythm of the poem "sound[s] like a waltz" because "It is an up-beat rhyme scheme, but is it fitting because we assume that he [the son] is being beaten"

(Chick, Hassel, and Haynie 2009, 412). To us, their use of a period instead of a question mark at the end of the question isn't just a punctuation error; it suggests "a lack of confidence with their questioning of the text and with their observation of this tension between the poem's form [its rhythm] and meaning [parental abuse]" (Chick, Hassel, and Haynie, 2009, 412). We read this moment in the student text as their "beginning to struggle with the complexities of the poem" while being "still unable to create meaning through this struggle." We saw not error but students moving from overly simplistic readings toward more sophisticated ones, and we developed tools for how to nudge students in this direction while they're in this moment of struggle.

As described earlier, this process and our focus on student writing—and what may appear as small, insignificant, or accidental details to those from other approaches to student work—may draw skepticism from those outside the field. The challenge, though, isn't simply misrecognition by those outside of our field; as Bass and Linkon document, close reading done poorly becomes "*diegesis*" or "'telling'" rather than "'showing,'" presented as scholars' generalizations about the texts of student learning without the direct textual evidence that builds a convincing argument or without the theoretical foundation that positions the analysis within a larger, more meaningful context to extend it beyond a single classroom (254). Unfortunately, space limitations in our publications (especially the ones that come out in print and are understandably less flexible with word counts) often limit our ability to include the actual passages documenting our close readings, so we have to present our conclusions alone. As Bass and Linkon suggest, we should prioritize such inclusion in the future to show its richness and value as evidence. As with any methodology, when done well, the results are meaningful and convincing.

When we apply our disciplinary skills, we take a serious, disciplined, and systematic look at what others may cast off as anecdotal evidence: unreliable, unrepresentative, decontextualized, and atheoretical. It is useful to situate these four primary concerns about literary SOTL within long-standing disciplinary concepts, conversations, and values. First, focusing on student writing as evidence of learning may be questioned as unreliable; however, as Blau (2003) explains, literary scholars don't seek certainty (or even believe it's possible) but instead "evidentiary reasoning" (51), or logical argument based on "compelling interpretive evidence . . . located in the words of the text or in the world from which the text emerges" (51–52). In other words, unlike the *apparent* certainty of some quantitative approaches, humanities SOTL doesn't strive for or result in "'truth' but the reasoned search for truth," as we "grow uncertainty" and experience "humility in the face of complexity" (Slouka 2009, 37). Rather than treating student writings (or any writings) as sacred texts that speak for themselves, literary scholars are proficient at acknowledging and negotiating the limitations of these texts through that process of close reading. Three fundamental concepts in literary study may be useful here: intentional fallacies, first-person narratives, and dramatic irony.

The fundamental literary error called the intentional fallacy, or locating the meaning of "a work of art by the author's expressed or ostensible intention in producing it" (Harmon and Holman 2009, 293), limits literary scholars' overreliance on students' self-reports of learning, whether in surveys or in their first-person narratives. The basic literary approach to all first-person narratives, such as Mark Twain's *The Adventures of Huckleberry Finn,* is one of caution and skepticism about the speaker's reliability. In literary study, unreliability isn't a matter of dishonesty or lying; more often, it's the possibility that the narrator "may be in error of his or her understanding or report of things" (Harmon and Holman 2009, 569). The potential for a difference between what students say they've learned and what they document in their application of learning calls for this skill in SOTL scholars. In our field, we call this gap between what the speaker understands and what the reader understands "dramatic irony," or the acknowledgment that the "words or acts of a character [or here, student] may carry a meaning unperceived by the character but understood by the audience [here, instructor or SOTL scholar]" (Harmon and Holman 2009, 177). Through our familiarity with the intentional fallacy, first-person point of view, and dramatic irony, literary SOTL scholars would thus consider novice or apprentice learners limited in their abilities to directly self-report what they understand (or don't) and look also to their actual performances of understanding for further evidence.

Related to Scholes's idea of distant or critical reading, we thus at once validate the layers of meaning of written text (professional or student-generated) while also recognizing its limits in its literal or surface meanings. In other words, the gap between what the speaker or writer *intends* in the text and what is *actually written* is itself a source of meaning—as in the example above with the absence of a question mark in the students' hesitant questioning of the poem. Dawn Skorczewski's (2000) analysis of students' clichés also reminds us that what may appear as simple thoughts in student writing may disguise more complex thinking and represent their developing abilities to express more precisely what they're learning. For now, they may be retreating into linguistic "safe houses" while struggling through such complexity. Diane Fallon (2006) similarly describes a "metastable state [in learning] where they truly are striving for complexity, but then revert to another position that feels more comfortably aligned with, or less challenging to, the value system and past experiences they've brought with them to the classroom" (413). While her study focuses on learning about diversity, this moment of struggle and retreat—rhetorically, cognitively, and sometimes emotionally—applies to an array of learning experiences at the heart of SOTL investigations.

In an illustration that may resonate across the disciplines, in the study described earlier about introductory literature students' practices and mis-conceptions, the student writings were full of expressions of what we call "interpretive relativism," such as claims that "there is no right or wrong answer" in interpretation (Chick, Hassel, and Rybak 2012, 26). While some readers may dismiss these familiar statements as students' failing to under-stand the value of what the text actually says, we came to some different conclusions. First, we recognized that many of the students in these classes are at the developmental stage of assuming that all opinions are equal, what William Perry (1968) calls multiplicity, so they may need support and direct instruction that all interpretations aren't in fact equal and that some are wrong. More precisely, we realized that the students didn't quite mean that interpretation is a free-for-all. Instead, through their writings about and applications of interpretation, we observed that, whereas before they had assumed the professor and the author are the only ones who know what a text means, students were "beginning to claim agency and authority over the text, but they're not yet comfortable taking that authority away from others. They also may be misstating the idea of multiple interpretations, representing multiple as infinite as they revel in their newfound but overstated authority" (26). Reading closely what students say *and* how they interpret allowed us to see through what others may dismiss as simplistic thinking.

Issues of generalizability or what social scientists might call a "small N" are also familiar to literary scholars, though the connection between this scientific benchmark and our own disciplinary values isn't self-evident. Some literary scholars boldly proclaim a universal human experience, as William Faulkner did in his Nobel Prize acceptance speech (1949) when he said that any writer worth his salt writes about "the old verities and truths of the heart, the old universal truths lacking which any story is ephemeral and doomed." This humanistic belief in universal human experiences may explain why the case study approach, or focusing on the learning of a single student as rele-vant to the learning of many students, would be meaningful to us. At the same time, with the rise of multicultural literature and subsequent canon debates, others in our field are skeptical of claims of representativeness and general-izability. In fact, many resist the notion of generalizability out of discomfort with the idea that single individuals (characters or writers) can be held up as representative of an entire group that's far more complex and multifaceted than any single individual. So while literary scholars regularly employ the disciplinary skill of analyzing and understanding people through what's documented in written texts (compare to Breithaupt's explanation of teaching his students about "the analysis of a culture through a text" [Ardizzone, Breithaupt, and Gutjahr 2004, 53]), this work is done methodically and tempered by the specific, explicit contexts in which the texts were written. In our article (Chick, Hassel, and Haynie 2009) about a lesson study project on helping students recognize and interpret complexity and ambiguity in literary texts, we describe a specific interaction between two students (411), an interaction and set of writings that were to us obviously grounded in their specific contexts of a rural Wisconsin classroom populated by students of traditional and nontraditional ages, men and women, mostly working but also some middle classes, and those taking their first literature class with others who were very well read. Due to space limitations and editorial feedback, we had to cut out much of this contextual analysis—but cutting other parts of our publication and prioritizing our efforts to clarify and apply these principles we value in our field to our SOTL work would mitigate some of the apprehension about our methods. In fact, Grauerholz and Main, in this volume, argue that "the concept of generalizability of results across settings" is "inappropriate to SOTL literature" because the variables are too numerous between and even within institutions. In other words, "teaching methods" (and I would add "learning moments") are "cultural practices that only become meaningful when seen in relation to larger social contexts." Situating our SOTL projects explicitly within rich details of specific contexts, rather than arguing for generalizability, would be a more authentic approach for our discipline and, according to Grauerholz and Main, for SOTL in general.

When literary SOTL scholars present findings about teaching and learning without any context, we fall short on two fronts. First, we don't provide enough information for others to assess the relevance of our conclusions, exacerbating the criticism of our work as too narrow or not rigorous enough. Next, we revert to a literary approach popular from the 1930s to the 1960s called New Criticism, which most in our discipline have recognized as an incomplete way of viewing texts: it treats a text "as if it were written in a vacuum," which makes its perspective "inherently flawed" because each work "is always an artifact of the culture that produced it" (Brown and Yarbrough 2005, 214). In modern literary approaches, we situate texts in their biographical, historical, geographical, socioeconomic, gendered, racial, and cultural contexts. Bass and Linkon note that an important function of close reading is to "offer new insights on a more broadly defined subject: a literary or cultural period, a genre or set of related texts, a theoretical concept" (247). In other words, unlike the misconception that we simply offer decontextualized readings of words on a page, "the examination of text occurs within and gains significance only when it is embedded in inquiry, engages with theory, and generates an argument that is useful to other readers" or "offers ways of reading and thinking about texts that can be adapted and applied to other texts and even to other subjects" (247–48). In using our disciplinary approaches in SOTL, then, we should remember to be explicit as we apply the same considerations to our students' texts.

Finally, in the four main concerns about our methods, claims about SOTL in general and our work in particular being atheorized or untheorizable remind literary scholars—who, ironically, participate in a field criticized from inside and out for being obsessed with theory—to be explicit about our conceptual frameworks when studying student texts as well. We have a wealth of theorists from which to draw, from feminist, Marxist, and New Historicist scholars who would help us look more closely at our classrooms as microcosms of power, history, ideology, identity, and even story. In addition, even some of our most fundamental narrative concepts in literary study would provide useful conceptual frameworks for understanding student learning. The bildungsroman, for example, is a "novel that deals with the development of a young person, usually from adolescence to maturity" (Harmon and Holman 2009, 65). Understanding student writing through the lens of some of these stories and the literary scholarship on the bildungsroman would be useful companions with the more widely known SOTL work on cognitive development by Perry (1968), Mary Field Belenky and her colleagues (1986), Marcia Baxter Magolda (2004), and John Bransford, Ann Brown, and Rodney Cocking (2000). Literary scholarship on the *Künstlerroman*, or an "apprenticeship novel in which the protagonist is an artist struggling . . . toward an understanding of his or her creative mission" (Harmon and Holman 2009, 308) would also illuminate the study of disciplinary learning, especially in light of SOTL's adoption of the constructivist language of "cognitive apprenticeship."

Imagine using such narratives and the scholarship written about them to theorize and understand our students' learning and lives. The bildungsroman stories in Toni Cade Bambara's "The Lesson," Twain's *Adventures of Huckleberry Finn*, or Sarah Orne Jewett's "The White Heron" offer different narratives of resistance, for example. How might they lend a framework for understanding resistance in courses with challenging content, specifically given the different kinds of resistance each character voices? Or imagine Toni Morrison's *Sula* providing a framework for how information is interpreted differently by different people—and often misinterpreted. How might this novel provide a theoretical framework for analyzing students' reading practices, for instance? Or any number of journey narratives, from Herman Melville's *Moby-Dick* to Morrison's *Song of Solomon,* might frame our approach to the development of student understanding. (Some are solitary journeys, others have guides and helpers; they all have obstacles, and there are often tangents or side trips on the journey.)

. . .

In this chapter, I support McKinney's (2005) assertion that SOTL should have its standards while also raising questions about what standards we apply to SOTL, whom they privilege and whom they disadvantage, and on what grounds. Without sacrificing the goal of high-quality research, other chapters in this volume remind us that we can't limit SOTL's conception of research to our own narrow practices (Poole) and we have to think more critically about the invisible norms and assumptions that have often been taken for granted as truth (Grauerholz and Main). We should all take a close look at how we think about difference, privilege, and power in the field of SOTL; we're all seeking the same goal of understanding and improving student learning. As SOTL becomes increasingly interdisciplinary or welcomes more interdisciplinary work, now is the time to think about such issues.

NOTES

Thank you to my dear colleagues Holly Hassel and Katie Kalish for serving as early readers of this chapter and for their helpful feedback.

1. See, for instance, Boyer's *Scholarship Reconsidered* (1990), Hutchings's *Opening Lines* (2000), Shulman's *Teaching as Community Property* (2004, containing essays published earlier), and Huber and Hutchings's *The Advancement of Learning* (2005).

2. The Obama effect (Marx, Ko, and Friedman 2009), the idea that one visible exception to a stereotype will mitigate the effects of that stereotype for others, is certainly a myth in SOTL.

3. As with any metaphor, there are limits to the comparison. The limits here are significant: I don't mean to trivialize or co-opt the lived and daily oppressions of people of color but instead to invoke the human responses to differences so effectively articulated by McLaren.

4. This resistance to amateur SOTL, while it seems to sometimes disguise disciplinary bias rather than criteria for quality, also strikes me as ironic, given the fact that "amateur" is nearly synonymous with "novice" but without the recognition of the developmental process or potential to learn. Perhaps the use of amateur instead reflects the concern that these SOTL scholars lack the inclination or ability to advance—but again, advance to what? Drawing from constructivist notions of knowledge, novices will start with what they know, so if the goal of the field is to grow, it must allow practitioners to start with what they know (disciplinary approaches) before they can experiment with and become fluent in less familiar, more pluralistic approaches. Again, like Tatum's (1997) exploration of the phenomenon of cultural

aggregation, this disciplinary loyalty and identity exploration may be a necessary stage in development.

5. Again, note the language here and how it invokes race and/or culture.

6. The metaphor is also appropriate because Anzaldúa is describing a mestiza, a woman—and as McKinney and Chick (2010) have documented, SOTL is largely women's work. Anzaldúa's metaphor is so rich and so significant to SOTL that an entirely new piece could be written about SOTL—its struggles, its successes, its future—through this lens.

REFERENCES

Anzaldúa, Gloria. 1987. *Borderlands/La Frontera: The New Mestiza*. San Francisco: Aunt Lute Books.

Ardizzone, Tony, F. Breithaupt, and P. C. Gutjahr. 2004. "Decoding the Humanities." In *Decoding the Disciplines: Helping Students Learn Disciplinary Ways of Thinking*, ed. David Pace and Joan Middendorf, 45–56. San Francisco: Jossey-Bass.

Bass, Randy, and Sherry Lee Linkon. 2008. "On the Evidence of Theory: Close Reading as a Disciplinary Model for Writing about Teaching and Learning." *Arts and Humanities in Higher Education* 7: 245–61.

Belenky, Mary Field, Blythe McVicker Clinchy, Nancy Rule Goldberger, and Jill Mattuck Tarule. 1986. *Women's Ways of Knowing: The Development of Self, Voice, and Mind*. New York: Basic Books.

Blau, Sheridan D. 2003. *The Literature Workshop: Teaching Texts and Their Readers*. Portsmouth: Heinemann.

Boyer, Ernest L. 1990. *Scholarship Reconsidered: Priorities of the Professoriate*. Stanford, CA: Carnegie Foundation for the Advancement of Teaching.

Bransford, John D., Ann L. Brown, and Rodney R. Cocking, eds. 2000. *How People Learn: Brain, Mind, Experience, and School*. Washington, DC: National Academy Press. http://books.nap.edu/openbook.php?isbn=0309070368.

Brown, James S., and Scott D. Yarbrough. 2005. *A Practical Introduction to Literary Study*. Upper Saddle River, NJ: Pearson/Prentice Hall.

Chick, Nancy. 2006. "From Community Property to Public Property: Shulman Challenges CASTL Participants to Fill in Moats and Lower Drawbridges." *International Commons* 1: 7.

———. 2009. "In Search of the Humanities in (IS)SOTL: A Panel of the ISSOTL Interest Group for the Humanities." Panel presentation at the conference of the International Society for the Scholarship of Teaching and Learning, Bloomington, Indiana, October 22–25.

Chick, Nancy L., Holly Hassel, and Aeron Haynie. 2009. "'Pressing an Ear Against the Hive': Reading Literature for Complexity." *Pedagogy: Critical Approaches to Teaching Literature, Language, Composition, and Culture* 9: 399–422.

Chick, Nancy L., Holly Hassel, and Chuck Rybak. 2012. "'All They Want to Do': Novice Practices and Misconceptions in Literary Studies." Under review.

Fallon, Diane. 2006. "'Lucky to Live in Maine': Examining Student Responses to Diversity Issues." *Teaching English in the Two-Year College* 33: 410–20.

Faulkner, William. 1949. Nobel Prize acceptance speech. http://nobelprize.org /nobel_prizes/literature/laureates/1949/faulkner-speech.html.

Gale, Richard. 2005. "Aesthetic Literacy and the 'Living of Lyrical Moments.'" *Journal of Cognitive Affective Learning* 2: 1–9.

Glaser, Barney, and Anselm Strauss. 1967. *The Discovery of Grounded Theory.* Chicago: Aldine.

Glassick, Charles E., Mary Taylor Huber, and Gene I. Maeroff. 1997. *Scholarship Assessed: Evaluation of the Professoriate.* San Francisco: Jossey-Bass.

Guillory, John. 2002. "The Very Idea of Pedagogy." *Profession:* 164–71.

Gurung, Regan A. R., and Beth M. Schwartz. 2009. *Optimizing Teaching and Learning: Practicing Pedagogical Research.* Malden: Wiley-Blackwell.

Harmon, William, and Hugh Holman. 2009. *A Handbook to Literature.* Upper Saddle River, NJ: Pearson/Prentice Hall.

Healey, Mick. 2000. "Developing the Scholarship of Teaching in Higher Education: A Discipline-Based Approach." *Higher Education Research and Development* 19: 169–89.

Huber, Mary Taylor, and Pat Hutchings. 2005. *The Advancement of Learning: Building the Teaching Commons.* San Francisco: Carnegie Foundation for the Advancement of Teaching/Jossey-Bass.

Huber, Mary Taylor, and Sherwyn P. Morreale, eds. 2002. *Disciplinary Styles in the Scholarship of Teaching and Learning: Exploring Common Ground.* Stanford, CA: Carnegie Foundation for the Advancement of Teaching and the American Association of Higher Education.

Hutchings, Pat, ed. 2000. *Opening Lines: Approaches to the Scholarship of Teaching and Learning.* Menlo Park, CA: Carnegie Foundation for the Advancement of Teaching.

Hutchings, Pat, and Mary Taylor Huber. 2008. "Placing Theory in the Scholarship of Teaching and Learning." *Arts and Humanities in Higher Education* 7: 229–44.

Jarvis, Patricia, and Gary Creasey. 2009. "Strengthening SOTL Research: The Voices of Journal Editors." Featured session presentation at the conference of the International Society for the Scholarship of Teaching and Learning. Bloomington, Indiana. October 22–25.

Lattuca, Lisa R. 2001. *Creating Interdisciplinarity: Interdisciplinary Research and Teaching among College and University Faculty.* Nashville: Vanderbilt University Press.

Magolda, Marcia Baxter. 2004. *Making Their Own Way: Narratives for Transforming Higher Education to Promote Self-development.* Sterling: Stylus.

Marx, David M., Sei Jin Ko, and Ray A. Friedman. 2009. "The 'Obama Effect': How a Salient Role Model Reduces Race-Based Performance Differences." *Journal of Experimental Social Psychology* 45: 953–56.

Maurer, Trent W. 2011. "On Publishing SOTL Articles." *International Journal for the Scholarship of Teaching and Learning* 5: 1–2.

McIntosh, Peggy. 1989. "White Privilege: Unpacking the Invisible Knapsack." *Peace and Freedom* July/August: 10–12.

McKinney, Kathleen. 2005. "Response to Hanson's 'The Scholarship of Teaching and Learning—Done by Sociologists: Let's Make That the Sociology of Higher Education.'" *Teaching Sociology* 33: 417–19.

———. 2007. *Enhancing Learning through the Scholarship of Teaching and Learning: The Challenges and Joys of Juggling.* San Francisco: Jossey-Bass.

McKinney, Kathleen, and Nancy Chick. 2010. "SOTL as Women's Work: What Do Existing Data Tell Us?" *International Journal for the Scholarship of Teaching and Learning* 4, no. 2: 1–14. http://academics.georgiasouthern.edu/ijsotl/v4n2.html.

McLaren, Peter. 1995. "White Terror and Oppositional Agency: Towards a Critical Multiculturalism." In *Multiculturalisms,* ed. David Theo Goldberg, 45–74. Cambridge: Blackwell.

Nelson, Craig E. 1999. "On the Persistence of Unicorns: The Trade-off between Content and Critical Thinking Revisited." In *The Social Worlds of Higher Education: Handbook for Teaching in a New Century,* ed. Bernice A. Pescosolido and Ronald Aminzade, 168–184. Newbury Park, CA: Pine Forge Press.

Perry, William. 1968. *Forms of Intellectual and Ethical Development in the College Years: A Scheme.* New York: Holt, Rinehart, and Winston.

Salvatori, Mariolina Rizzi. 2002. "The Scholarship of Teaching: Beyond the Anecdotal." *Pedagogy* 2: 297–310.

Salvatori, Mariolina Rizzi, and Patricia Donahue. 2005. *The Elements (and Pleasures) of Difficulty.* New York: Pearson Longman.

Scholes, Robert. 1985. *Textual Power: Literary Theory and the Teaching of English.* New Haven: Yale University Press.

———. 2002. "The Transition to College Reading." *Pedagogy* 2: 165–72.

Shulman, Lee S. 2004. *Teaching as Community Property: Essays on Higher Education.* San Francisco: Jossey-Bass.

Skorczewski, Dawn. 2000. "'Everybody Has Their Own Ideas': Responding to Cliché in Student Writing." *College Composition and Communication* 52: 220–39.

Slouka, Mark. 2009. "Dehumanized: When Math and Science Rule the School." *Harper's,* September.

Tatum, Beverly Daniel. 1997. *Why Are All the Black Kids Sitting Together in the Cafeteria? And Other Conversations about Race.* New York: Basic/Perseus Books.

Weimer, Maryellen. 2006. *Enhancing Scholarly Work on Teaching and Learning: Professional Literature that Makes a Difference.* San Francisco: Jossey-Bass.

Wypijewski, JoAnn. 1999. "A Boy's Life." *Harper's,* September.

CHAPTER 2

Contributions from Psychology: Heuristics for Interdisciplinary Advancement of SOTL

REGAN A. R. GURUNG AND BETH M. SCHWARTZ

Psychology is a field that incorporates information from biology, sociology, anthropology, and philosophy, among others, in the study of human behavior. Psychology is also a field that has long paid attention to teaching and learning. In fact, one of the fathers of psychology in America, Harvard psychologist William James, gave a talk to teachers in 1892 (James 1899/2006) in which he demonstrated how psychology could be best used to help students learn. Whereas most disciplines can take an historic look at the development of the scholarship of teaching and learning within that discipline (Chick, Haynie, and Gurung 2012; Gurung, Chick, and Haynie 2009), few disciplines can really lay claim to the science of teaching and learning as can the discipline of psychology. In particular, a number of areas within the discipline of psychology explicitly study learning and the processes that foster it. Furthermore, given that psychology is in many ways transdisciplinary, the ways that SOTL in psychology draws from its subdisciplines models how one could make SOTL more interdisciplinary in general.

In this chapter, we will first review the theoretical foundations of learning and then explore how and when SOTL really got its start in psychology. We will summarize the current state of SOTL in the field showing how it is cross-disciplinary and illustrating how SOTL findings within the field are applicable to all classrooms regardless of discipline. We end by discussing interdisciplinarity in the context of psychology.

Theoretical Foundations of Learning and Psychology

Psychology is a natural home for work on SOTL as many areas in psychology have contributed directly to our understanding of learning. Cognitive and educational psychologists (Bjork and Bjork 2011; Halpern et al. 1998; Halpern and Hakel 2002) have made major contributions to studies of teaching and learning and recently clinical and social psychologists have weighed in (Gurung and Burns 2011; Prieto and Meyers 1999). The roots of these contributions go all the way back to the work of the original learning theorists.

Both learning theory and behavior theory were instrumental in shaping the study of learning over the past century. Learning theorists (sometimes referred to as behaviorists) focused on the role of the environment on learning processes, and how changes in behavior are evidence of learning. Cognitive psychology emerged from, and in response to, a number of early schools of psychology including structuralism, functionalism, and behaviorism. As a cognitive psychologist, one approaches learning with a focus on a person's own mental activities rather than on the environment. As opposed to the learning theorists, who were interested in the environmental change that led to behavioral changes as an indicator of learning, cognitive psychologists were interested in what each learner brings to the situation and the new knowledge created.

To further address the history of learning in the field of psychology, we could start with when psychologists began to study the content and processes of the mind. The history of the scientific study of the mind often begins with the work of Ivan Pavlov, a Russian physiologist. His initial focus on the digestive system of animals led to what he called "psychic reflexes," a learned response once a new stimulus was paired with food. This serendipitous discovery led Pavlov to devote the rest of his career to understanding the formation of these "reflexes." He was fascinated by the potential of gaining a better understanding of what he called the laws of the mind. By studying the observable association of the stimuli he called the conditioned and unconditioned stimulus and the resulting response, Pavlov's research led to what was believed to be an objective science of learning, with a focus on observable stimulus-response associations. In other words, one can understand learning without taking into account processes taking place in the mind. This is often referred to as the "black box" or "blank slate" approach to learning, and it is the core of the behaviorist learning perspective first expressed by John B. Watson in 1913 (Benjamin 2008).

From there, psychologists continued to study learning and began to examine more complex behaviors beyond the simple stimulus-response associations. At the turn of the century, Edward Thorndike proposed the *law of effect*, which helped to explain the trial-and-error mechanism underlying behaviors that are more likely to occur again. At this point learning was not only discussed in the context of classical conditioning but also instrumental learning. Psychologists examined how learning is influenced by environmental factors, and much of the research focused on animal learning, still with an understanding that learning can be best understood without the need to examine mental processes that take place.

Clearly the internal processes are too important to ignore. The mental representation of the information that led to the associations created should also be examined to understand the processes underlying learning. However, lack of technology made direct study of the mind difficult. The use of introspection by Wilhelm Wundt in Germany and Edward Tichener in the United States (Schacter, Gilbert, and Wegner 2011, 8) was thought to allow a window into these mental processes. However, this method was fraught with methodological issues that created problems with both reliability and validity. Many mental processes were not part of our conscious experiences and therefore could not be reported through introspection. To gain ground in scientific communities, psychologists attempted to distance themselves from the method of introspection, which led to behaviorism, the study of the observable, dominating the field.

It was not until the middle of the twentieth century that psychologists such as Edward Tolman moved away from the notion that only observable behaviors should be examined. Developments in technology and information processing opened the way to what is known as the cognitive revolution. Psychologists once again were willing to focus on the unobservable workings of the mind and those studying learning began to recognize the important distinction between performance and learning. The cognitive approach directed psychologists to examine the determinants of learning and memory, with an emphasis on understanding the acquisition of knowledge in humans. This theory of learning included the understanding that the learner plays an active role, with a goal of understanding internal processes that gather, modify, store, and retrieve information. In other words, learning takes place even in the absence of observable behaviors. Cognitive psychology attempts to gain a better understanding of how people perceive, learn, remember, and think about information, all processes we must take into account in the field of the scholarship of teaching and learning.

In order to provide a complete explanation of the learning process, both the environmental influences and the underlying cognitive and physiological mechanisms must be considered. Those in the field of psychology understand the theoretical connection between the scholarship of teaching and learning and the historical context of learning within the field; however, there still exists a lack of understanding of how the scholarship of teaching and learning is applicable to all areas of psychology as well as other academic disciplines. Although the science of pedagogy has roots in the fields of learning theory and cognitive psychology, gaining a better understanding of how one's pedagogical choices can influence student learning outcomes is important in all fields. The theories of learning developed by cognitive theorists can provide guidance in educational settings, with empirical evidence to provide pedagogical change that could enhance retention of material, and learning and studying strategies for students to improve their understanding of material and performance on assessments that follow.

The State of SOTL in Psychology

Following in Ernest L. Boyer's (1990) footsteps in which he set the stage for academics to reconsider the definition of scholarship, Diane F. Halpern et al. (1998) attempted to broaden the construct of scholarship in psychology to include activities that investigate pedagogy and student learning. Halpern et al. provided the field of psychology with a "paradigm for the twenty-first century" (1292)—a five-part definition of scholarship that included (a) original research, (b) integration of knowledge, (c) application of knowledge, (d) the scholarship of pedagogy, and (e) the scholarship of teaching in psychology. There have been significant developments within the field of psychology that widen the scope of this original paradigm and include questions about interdisciplinary and cross-disciplinary work in SOTL. Not only do different areas of psychology (for example, social psychology) explicitly address SOTL questions specific to that discipline, but there is also a growing use of methodologies and results from different academic areas (for example, computer science), methodologies typically not used in psychological research. Over the twelve years since Halpern et al.'s conceptualization, there has been a spate of writing identifying the fruits of such labors.

A task force of the Society for the Teaching of Psychology (division 2 of the American Psychological Association) conducted a survey to ascertain the degree to which psychology departments and the institutions of higher education that house them have enacted the scholarship of teaching (Gurung, Ansburg, Alexander, Lawrence, and Johnson 2008). Findings regarding departmental and institutional support for SOTL presented a mixed picture. The field of psychology seems to recognize SOTL better than higher education as a whole (that is, when compared to the results seen in a survey of higher education by Huber and Hutchings 2005). For example, 60 percent of the survey respondents reported having colleagues involved in SOTL, and 78 percent reported that departmental policies encourage SOTL. That said, doing pedagogical research is clearly not without obstacles for psychologists. Three-quarters of survey respondents did not view SOTL as part of their normal scholarship activities, and likewise 75 percent of the participants indicated they do not understand what constitutes SOTL. Recent publications (for example, Gurung, Chick, and Haynie 2009; Gurung and Schwartz 2009) including a special issue on SOTL in the journal *Teaching of Psychology* (Smith and Buskist 2008) should help alleviate the definitional confusion. For example, Jessica Irons and William Buskist (2008) compared different definitions of SOTL and provided suggestions on which would be most beneficial to use.

A number of recent reviews and meta-analyses provide insight into the wide breadth and exact nature of SOTL being done in psychology. More importantly, they provide us with key items for future research agendas. Peden and Wilson-VanVoorhis (2009) reviewed back issues of the *Teaching of Psychology* (2003–2007) and made many observations about the state of SOTL in psychology. They observed that the 2007 guidelines for learning outcomes in psychology suggest how to think like a psychologist, but they do not articulate how to teach it. Most SOTL shows that lecture is still the default mode of instruction, and Peden and Wilson-VanVoorhis propose that instructors integrate critical thinking skills with content material. They stress the importance of more SOTL connecting skills and ideas, something they argue that traditional lecture courses do not achieve.

In a slightly different vein, Thomas Tomcho and Rob Foels (2008) conducted a meta-analysis of 197 studies published in the *Teaching of Psychology* from 1974 to 2006. They found that, on average, studies evidenced a medium effect size across types of learning outcomes. The majority of SOTL reviewed focused on teaching activities. Given the effectiveness of the published teaching activities, the authors suggested that researchers should address the (a) potential confounding role of teacher rapport, immediacy, and alliance in evaluating teaching effectiveness; (b) ethics of teaching activity development; and (c) appropriateness of using course grades to assess teaching activity effectiveness (286). In a content analysis of the same years of content, Tomcho and Foels identified fifteen general teaching strategies in 681 teaching activity articles and coded each strategy's potential impact on student development of scientific inquiry skills. Tomcho and Foels found that authors of articles reviewed had consistently used learner-centered strategies and significantly increased their use of active evaluation strategies. In perhaps the granddaddy of meta-analyses, and SOTL that would be hard to replicate, John Hattie (2009) analyzed over 800 meta-analyses of studies relating to achievement (a meta-meta-analysis as it were) and listed 131 factors that influence learning. He identifies three emergent themes: the best teachers communicate clear learning intentions and criteria for success, use multiple teaching strategies that emphasize student perspectives in learning, and seek feedback regarding the effectiveness of their teaching and provide feedback to students regarding the effectiveness of their learning (Hattie 2011, 134–37).

Most recently, Daniel Bernstein et al. (2010) and Stephen Chew et al. (2010) provide comprehensive pictures of what is known about the processes surrounding teaching and learning and provide general models that can guide future pedagogical research. These two examples show a rare form of SOTL involving theory building and provide models worthy of replication in other disciplines. Bernstein et al. suggest that to meet the challenges associated with accepting responsibility for learning rather than just providing access to resources and coherent presentation of material, teachers can gain much from psychology's successful scientist-practitioner model of preparation for clinical, counseling, and school psychology. Chew et al. present a comprehensive, empirically based process to guide the selection and implementation of teaching strategies including both a model of teaching that can guide this process and a set of examples of how the model can be used to accomplish learning goals.

Subdisciplinary Contributions to SOTL: Cognitive Psychology

Within the field of psychology, cognitive psychology is the next major contributor to studies of teaching and learning (after or perhaps parallel to the area of educational psychology). Cognitive scientists, who offer well-researched principles of learning and memory, have only recently begun to get involved in classroom research (Metcalfe 2006). The theoretical characteristics of metacognition (for example, thinking about the process of thinking) have dominated research since the 1960s; however, only recent research has focused on educational application. According to Douglas F. Hacker, John Dunlosky, and Arthur C. Graesser (2009), researchers convinced of the educational relevance that metacognitive theory has for teachers and students are shifting their attention from the theoretical to the practical, from the laboratory to the classroom. A number of lab studies have explicitly demonstrated the benefits of monitoring one's thinking about learning (for example, Dunlosky and Nelson 1997; Koriat and Bjork 2005) and cognitive research on metacognition is now beginning to move into the classroom (for example, Metcalfe 2006). Metacognitive theory can help teachers create classroom environments that foster flexible and creative, strategic learning (Borkowski and Muthukrishna 1992). This research suggests students will benefit from teachers who indeed use knowledge of metacognitive processes to facilitate learning (see Dunlosky and Lipko 2007; Hacker, Dunlosky, and Graesser 2009; Metcalfe and Greene 2007).

Akin to metacogntion, there are many cognitive concepts that can apply to teaching and learning across all disciplines. Some include temporal spacing (Cepeda, Pashler, Vul, Wixted, and Rohrer 2006), using self-generation rather than reading (Slamecka and Graf 1978), multimodal and contextual variability, spaced practice (Bahrick and Hall 2005; Pashler, Zarow, and Triplette 2003), corrective feedback (Butterfield and Metcalfe 2001), and repeated testing (Roediger and Karpicke 2006). The concept of "desirable difficulties" (Bjork and Bjork 2011, 58) recommends spacing rather than massing study sessions, interleaving rather than blocking practice on separate topics, varying how to-be-learned material is presented, reducing feedback, and using tests as learning events—all based on findings from the cognitive psychology literature. Many cognitive concepts have explicit pragmatic implications. For example, because research has shown that retrieval produces robust mnemonic benefits that exceed those of additional study (Kang, McDermott, and Roediger 2007), testing (that is, requiring retrieval) may be an especially effective method for improving learning (Karpicke and Roediger 2008; McDaniel, Anderson, Derbish, and Morrisette 2007; McDaniel, Roediger, and McDermott 2007). Cognitive psychologists recommend that instructors quiz more often in their courses (Pashler et al. 2007). Work such as this has led to the development and testing of specific strategies for students (for example, the "3R" read-recite-review strategy, McDaniel, Howard, and Einstein 2009).

As is evident, cognitive psychologists have made explicit attempts to ensure that work from the cognitive laboratory is considered in the classroom. Perhaps one of the best examples can be seen in a special issue of the *New Directions for Teaching and Learning* series dedicated to "Applying the science of learning to university teaching and beyond" (Halpern and Hakel 2002). While research from the tradition of cognitive psychology identifies core principles that constrain how people learn, they often lack application studies in the classroom; the recommendations for teaching that have emerged from this tradition do not always work (Daniel and Poole 2009). What works in the lab does not always directly succeed in the classroom (Gurung, Ansburg, Alexander, Lawrence, and Johnson 2009).

Although researchers have started taking cognitive science into the classroom (for example, McDaniel and Einstein 2005; Metcalfe 2006; Roediger and Karpicke 2006), the theory and practice suggested by research is not yet fully applicable to teachers and learners. Many of the recommendations from controlled lab studies have yet to be translated into practices for the classroom. Furthermore, as much as the areas of educational and cognitive psychology have a monopoly on SOTL, researchers in these areas primarily treat the classrooms of others as their laboratory (educational psychology) or primarily work in the lab (cognitive psychology). The pedagogical research we advocate, SOTL, puts one's own classroom, teaching, and learning under the microscope (see also Smith 2008).

Clinical psychology was the first to follow in the footsteps of educational and cognitive psychology. Although clinical psychology does not at first seem to be as relevant to learning as the areas of education and cognition (relevant almost by definition), it is an area that is perfectly primed to contribute to our understanding of pedagogy as more clinical psychologists have been working in applied areas. Clinical psychologists noted the parallel between the client-therapist dyad and the student-teacher. Loreto R. Prieto and Stephen A. Meyers (1999) introduced the concept of the scientist-practitioner-educator in the psychology teaching assistant (TA) training literature to extend a counseling model (the Boulder model) to teaching. This model views teaching as a professional practice and identifies the need for theory-driven, evidence-based teaching of psychology (Prieto and Meyers 2009; see also Snyder 2005).

At the American Psychological Association National Conference on Undergraduate Education in Psychology, Bernstein et al. (2010) offered an expanded view of teacher training, suggesting that the discipline of psychology needs to recognize teaching as a form of professional practice, requiring sufficient preparation to perform competently and ethically and with training beginning at the graduate level. Similar to the basic call for scholarly teaching, Prieto and Meyers (2009) advanced the notion that training in psychology should adopt the scientist-educator model (similar to the Boulder model of scientist-practitioner for clinical practice) that involves theory-based teaching, continuous reflection on teaching practices, application of evidence-based instructional strategies, and multifaceted evaluation of teaching and learning outcomes. Using the language of clinical psychology, the authors suggest that the essential preparation for a scientist-educator qualified to teach at all levels and in all kinds of settings should include a deep knowledge of core psychology, course work in teaching and learning, supervised practicum experience in teaching, and learning how to reflect on and evaluate teaching in a scholarly, theory-driven manner. Supporting this point, Prieto and Meyers (2009) advocate the use of social psychological theory to help explain the effects of TA training (for example, social cognitive approaches such as self-efficacy). Social psychologists are taking this work many steps further to push for the explicit use of social psychological theory and theorizing in pedagogical research.

SOTL Ideas from the Social Psychology of Teaching and Learning

The newest area of psychology to take on SOTL is social psychology. A recent call for using social psychology in pedagogical research was made in 2009 at a Claremont College Applied Social Psychology Symposium that led to a volume of edited articles (Mashek and Hammer 2011a). There was one significant voice raised earlier. A special issue of the *Journal of Social and Clinical Psychology* edited by Snyder (2005) opened "a new turf for the interface of social and clinical psychology" (1). Master teachers portrayed a variety of perspectives on college teaching and student learning. Three explicitly made the case for a greater use of social psychological work (Halpern and Desrochers 2005; Hammer 2005; Smith 2005). There are a variety of SOTL research studies in this area that can inspire future research across disciplines.

Elizabeth Hammer (2005) provided perhaps the most explicit link between social psychological concepts and teaching, good starting points for the application of social psychological research in realms such as classroom management (for example, group dynamics, decision-making, and social norms), explaining student behavior (for example, attributional biases), and the delivery of information (for example, persuasion, 4). She focused on research in the area of interpersonal relationships as it applies to student-teacher relationships, especially research on attributional styles, ego depletion, and relationship styles. These social psychological theories can help instructors from any discipline get better insight into the behavior of their students and perhaps shape their own SOTL.

In the same issue, Halpern and Stephan Desrochers (2005) went so far as to call education "applied social psychology" (51). They suggest applying cognitive psychology research to student-centered learning to help apply social psychological principles. Specifically, they discuss the problem of anonymity in classes and suggest countering it by increasing individual responsibility, accountability, and social comparison. In order to foster a commitment to learning, Halpern and Desrochers draw on equity and reciprocity theory and using contracts. Similar to Hammer (2005), they also invoke attribution theory and self-handicapping to help understand both faculty and student behavior.

Perhaps someone who has written the most about the link between social psychology and the classroom is Randolph A. Smith (2005; 2008). In his piece in the 2005 special issue discussed previously, he identifies a wide array of social psychological concepts that are applicable to SOTL (for example, fundamental attribution error, social categorization, overjustification effect). He shows, for example, how a concept such as self-handicapping helps explain why students may not read assignments or study for exams, how the self-serving bias explains why students believe they have performed better than they really have, and how belief perseverance explains why it is hard to change the beliefs students bring to class. Of note is that many of the studies cited by Smith (2005) were lab-based even though they addressed issues relating to the classroom.

Given the variety of obvious, and some not so obvious, ways social psychological theories and concepts are applicable to the classroom, many faculty probably unconsciously use social psychological concepts about which they have read in their teaching. We urge any faculty interested in SOTL to take advantage of recent resources that make social psychological theories easily digestible (for example, Mashek and Hammer 2011a; Mashek and Hammer 2011b) and consequently ready for use in any disciplinary SOTL. Many different conceptualizations illustrate the interactions between faculty, students, and classroom situations (see Chew et al. 2010; Entwistle 2009; Gurung and Schwartz 2009). There is probably no silver bullet or single factor that will make our students learn better. Pedagogical research, as any other research, can try to limit the factors studied, but especially when studying learning in a classroom, as it is happening, we have to acknowledge all the different factors that are possibly playing a part. The main players involved are the teacher, student, the interaction between the two, and the environment in which they exist. We briefly review SOTL in some of these areas as exemplars that can be used by faculty in different disciplines for their own SOTL.

Beyond the methodological contributions of social psychology, both in terms of rigor, design complexity, and inventiveness, there are many aspects of the teaching-learning relationship that can be better understood using social psychology. There are elements such as the textbook and course design that can be treated in their own right, but are also under the jurisdiction of the instructor. Although social psychology may have once proclaimed a focus exclusively on the situation, leaving personal characteristics to the purview of personality psychology, today social psychology succeeds best when taking the interactional approach. Behavior and learning are clearly functions of both the person and the situation. The classroom is perhaps one of the most powerful situations with its own specific expectations for behavior and social psychology's focus on the situation is helpful. That said, the most recent reviews of factors influencing learning suggest that characteristics of both the instructor and the student contribute the lion's share of the variance in predicting learning (Hattie 2009).

Much of psychological SOTL work has focused on characteristics of the teacher. Passionate, knowledgeable, organized instructors are well evaluated by their students and the students of such instructors say they learn more

(Bain 2004). Research suggests that there are "ideal" instructor character-istics: Kimberly Epting and colleagues (Epting, Zinn, Buskist, and Buskist 2004), for example, found that students' ideal professor was accessible, per-sonable, flexible, and explicit about course policies. There are many social psychological factors that can help predict how an instructor will perform and how her students will learn, and how she will be evaluated. Right out of the gate, the research on thin slices of behavior suggests that what we do in class in the first five seconds or so can determine how we are rated at the end of the semester (Ambady and Rosenthal 1992; Babad, Avni-Babad, and Rosenthal 2004). Add to this the recent finding that this first impression may even be influenced by an electronic communication sent out before class begins (Wilson, Stadler, Schwartz, and Goff 2009) presses for a close look at how first impressions of a class and an instructor can be modified. What does your syllabus say about you? How does your dress that first day set the tone? These are examples of explicit questions social psychological findings make all of us across disciplines ask as we teach and prepare to teach.

The first day of class is ripe with social psychological phenomena that influence learning and provide a good illustration of why social psychology is important. Paying attention to impression formation in general and the volumes of research on the processes therein can help those first days in the classroom tremendously. There are also many more phenomena that pertain to the first day that can also influence the rest of the semester. For example, Gurung and Vespia (2007) had 861 undergraduate students complete an online questionnaire rating their instructors. Students were equally spread across class years and from different majors. The authors used multiple regression analyses and found that likeable, good-looking, well-dressed, and approachable teachers had students who said they learned more, had higher grades, and liked the class better, supporting research on teacher immediacy (Wilson et al. 2009). Results revealed several significant predictors of partici-pants' class performance and self-reported learning, including student (for example, GPA), course (for example, difficulty), and instructor (for example, likeability) variables. By far the strongest single predictor of self-reported learning, and a significant predictor of self-reported grades, however, was the likeability of the professor. Likeability, in turn, was predicted by instruc-tor attractiveness, approachability, and formality of dress, along with student attendance, participation, and self-reported class difficulty. Attractiveness accounted for the largest proportion of unique variance. Social psychologi-cal research consistently finds that people equate beauty with goodness and believe attractive individuals possess numerous positive qualities but few negative attributes (Weeden and Sabini 2005). Clearly this finding maps onto classroom life as well and can be used in many different disciplines.

Social psychology can also help solve major recurrent classroom problems in easy ways and provide key factors to be tested in multidisciplinary SOTL. Many instructors are asked for their lecture notes; others are peeved by students using their computer laptops in class for nonacademic purposes. Too many students use their phones to send and receive text messages. Some students show more extreme classroom incivilities (Boice 2000). Just saying no does not always work. Justifying why you are making a request does. In a classic study, Langer (1975) had experimenters try to cut into a line of people waiting to use a copy machine. When the experimenters said, "Excuse me, I have five pages, may I use the copy machine?" only 60 percent of the people in line agreed. When the experimenter added a justification, "because I have to make some copies" even that statement of obvious fact resulted in 93 percent compliance. When we ask students not to do something (for example, "please do not use any laptops"), adding a simple justification such as "Carrie Fried (2008) shows that students who use laptops in class do not learn as well/score as highly as those who do not use computers" drives compliance up to 100 percent. Most importantly, the justification also drives complaining down to zero. That is social psychology in action.

The major concepts of social psychology pertain to both an instructor's performance and how a student learns: self-concept, self-esteem, self-efficacy, self-fulfilling prophecy, social comparison, and confirmation bias, to name but a few (Gurung and Burns 2011). Similarly, we know that there are a number of psychological factors that predict student learning such as motivation, conscientiousness, and self-efficacy (Gurung and Schwartz 2009). One of the most influential books on teaching, Parker Palmer's *The Courage to Teach* (1998) describes how it is critical for a teacher to know themselves well and teach to their strengths. Palmer suggests that techniques, even though they can be learned, are not the hallmarks of a good teacher to the extent that character is. Whereas Palmer is an inspiration to many, his book and many of its ilk do not provide tangible footholds for rigorous study and exploration for developing a theory of good teaching and learning. The good news is that many of the social psychological terms listed in the preceding sentences underlie what Palmer and many others (for example, Bain 2004; Brookfield 2009) allude to in reference to what makes skillful teachers. Unfortunately, very little pedagogical research has explicitly used these concepts to drive design and hypothesizing. We hope this book and this chapter change this status. Instructors from any field should take a cue from social psychology and closely examine the situational factors that could influence learning. How does the classroom seating arrangement influence student interaction in the class you teach? Does it vary for upper- or lower-level students? How does the framing of the questions of your assignment make a difference? What are ways you can curb classroom incivilities and foster learning?

Many of the same social psychological concepts (for example, self-handicapping) also influence student behavior. Students often chuckle and nod their heads in disbelief when hearing that participants in Stanley Milgram's (1963) classic obedience study continued just because the experimenter said "the experiment must continue." They often fail to notice the extent to which they also do things just because the professor asks them to. Of course many instructors would like students to do more of what they are told (for example, read the book), and perhaps there are answers in studies of obedience. In like vein, we can use research on phenomena such as the false consensus effect and social norming to decrease inappropriate behaviors. Do students text message in class because they think it is normative to do so? Do students overestimate how many other students text in class and so feel more comfortable doing it? Do students falsely believe that everyone else in class thinks texting is appropriate? These questions are all answered by research in social psychology. The strategy of changing social norms has been used to reduce smoking in general (Ahern et al. 2009) and in college communities (Gurung 2010), so perhaps it can be used to change classroom behavior including how students study. The false consensus effect, the tendency to attribute one's own views to others, can also be a powerful explanatory force. In a recent study, Magdalena Wojcieszak and Vincent Price (2009) assessed the association between individual views on several issues such as the death penalty, gun regulation, and teaching morality in public schools. They found that there was a correlation between personal and perceived opinion and that those who strongly favored the three policies estimated public support to be higher than do those who are unfavorable or moderate. Studies such as this one provide a good model for how to study our students' attitudes and design ways to change their behaviors. But again, apart from a few studies such as the one described above, little to no pedagogical research explicitly uses social psychological theories and concepts to understand student learning save perhaps for some work in sociology.

An Interdisciplinary Model of SOTL

In many ways, psychology is a hub science (Cacioppo 2007). Kevin Boyack and colleagues quantified the patterns of scientific influence within and across the sciences based on citation data from more than a million journal articles appearing in 7,121 natural and social sciences journals published in 2000 (Boyack, Klavans, and Börner 2005). Eight different approaches to quantifying citation patterns were used to ensure structural accuracy, where accuracy means that journals within the same subdiscipline were grouped together and groups of journals that cite each other were close to each other. Additionally, new visualization techniques were used to generate a two-dimensional spatial map of the sciences based on each metric. Finally, the validity of these maps was compared using two different accuracy measures. The best measures converged on the landscape of scientific influence. The resulting mapping of science provides a visual depiction of where each scientific discipline is, what is around it, what its relationships are to neighboring disciplines, and how strong its impact is on neighboring disciplines. Not surprisingly, given scientific specialization over the past century, contemporary sciences no longer originate from a single source. Instead, seven hub sciences—areas that seemed central to a variety of theorizing and research—were identified: mathematics, physics, chemistry, earth sciences, medicine, psychology, and the social sciences. Psychology emerged as one of the hub disciplines of science. This empirically derived centeredness also maps on the theoretical transdisciplinariness described above and suggests that the theories in this hub could serve SOTL in the many disciplines that link to the hub and indirectly connect to it beyond.

For a broader interdisciplinary approach to SOTL, psychology has been instrumental in answering the need for better, more integrated, theoretical work that crosses disciplinary boundaries. Pat Hutchings (2007) depicted "the role of theory in the scholarship of teaching and learning as the elephant in the room" (1). For example, cognitive psychologists and social psychologists are nicely taking theoretically driven lab work and applying it to the classroom (Bjork and Bjork 2011, 56–62; Gurung and Burns 2011). Going beyond this call for theory is the need to situate all the myriad studies of pedagogical research in a common context (Gurung and Schwartz 2009). We are all trying to understand how students learn best. Although tests of individual class activities and techniques are important, it is now time for us to look at the big picture. What are the different factors that influence learning? How do the results of a smaller-scale study contribute to the bigger pictures of learning? Bernstein et al. (2010) and Chew et al. (2010) provide comprehensive pictures of what is known about the processes surrounding teaching and learning from across the discipline of psychology and provide general models that can guide future research. Similarly, Duane Shell and colleagues (Shell, Brooks, Trainin, Wilson, Kauffman, and Herr 2010) take concepts from the cognitive, motivation, and neurobiological sciences and use them to set out a unique theory of learning. These are exactly the endeavors that more pedagogical researchers need to be aware of and use to position their own research.

REFERENCES

Ahern, J., Sandro Galea, A. Hubbard, and S. L. Syme. 2009. "Neighborhood Smoking Norms Modify the Relation between Collective Efficacy and Smoking Behavior." *Drug and Alcohol Dependence* 100, no. 1–2: 138–45.

Ambady, Nalini, and Robert Rosenthal. 1992. "Thin Slices of Expressive Behavior as Predictors of Interpersonal Consequences: A Meta-analysis." *Psychological Bulletin* 111, no. 2: 256–74.

Babad, Elisha, Dinah Avni-Babad, and Robert Rosenthal. 2004. "Prediction of Students' Evaluations from Brief Instances of Professors' Nonverbal Behavior in Defined Instructional Situations." *Social Psychology of Education* 7, no. 1: 3–33.

Bahrick, Harry P., and Linda K. Hall. 2005. "The Importance of Retrieval Failures to Long-Term Retention: A Metacognitive Explanation of the Spacing Effect." *Journal of Memory and Language* 52: 566–77.

Bain, Ken. 2004. *What the Best College Teachers Do.* Cambridge, MA: Harvard University Press.

Benjamin, Ludy. T. 2008. *History of Psychology: Original Sources and Contemporary Research.* Malden, MA: Blackwell.

Bernstein, Daniel J., William Addison, Cindy Altman, Debra Hollister, Meera Komarraju, Loreto Prieto, Courtney A. Rocheleau, and Cecilia Shore. 2010. "Toward a Scientist-Educator Model of Teaching Psychology." In *Undergraduate Education in Psychology: A Blueprint for the Future of the Discipline,* ed. Diana F. Halpern, 29–45. Washington, DC: American Psychological Association.

Bjork, Elizabeth L., and Robert A. Bjork. 2011. "Making Things Harder on Yourself, but in a Good Way: Creating Desirable Difficulties to Enhance Learning." In *Psychology and the Real World: Essays Illustrating Fundamental Contributions to Society,* ed. Morton A. Gernsbacher, Richard W. Pew, Leaetta M. Hough, and James R. Pomerantz, 56–64. New York: Worth.

Boice, Robert. 2000. *Advice for New Faculty Members.* Needham Heights, MA: Allyn and Bacon.

Borkowski, John G., and Nithi Muthukrishna. 1992. "Moving Metacognition into the Classroom: Working Models and Effective Strategy Teaching." In *Promoting Academic Competence and Literacy in School,* ed. Michael Pressley, Karen R. Harris, and John T. Guthrie, 477–501. San Diego: Academic.

Boyak, Kevin W., Richard Klavans, and Katy Börner. 2005. "Mapping the Backbone of Science." *Scientometrics* 64, no. 3: 351–74.

Boyer, Ernest L. 1990. *Scholarship Reconsidered: Priorities of the Professoriate.* San Francisco: Jossey-Bass.

Brookfield, Stephen D. 2009. *The Skillful Teacher: On Technique, Trust, and Responsiveness in the Classroom.* San Francisco: Jossey-Bass.

Butterfield, Brady, and Janet Metcalfe. 2001. "Errors Committed with High Confidence are Hypercorrected." *Journal of Experimental Psychology: Learning, Memory, and Cognition* 27, no. 6: 1491–94.

Cacioppo, John T. 2007. "Psychology as a Hub Science." *APS Observer* 20.

Cepeda, Nicholas J., Harold Pashler, Edward Vul, John T. Wixted, and Doug Rohrer. 2006. "Distributed Practice in Verbal Recall Tasks: A Review and Quantitative Synthesis." *Psychological Bulletin* 132, no. 3: 354–80.

Chew, Stephen L., Robin M. Bartlett, James E. Dobbins, Elizabeth Yost Hammer, Mary E. Kite, Trudy Fey Loop, Julie Guay McIntyre, and Karen C. Rose. 2010. "A Contextual Approach to Teaching: Bridging Methods, Goals, and Outcomes." In *Undergraduate Education in Psychology: A Blueprint for the Future of the Discipline,* ed. Diane F. Halpern, 95–112. Washington, DC: American Psychological Association.

Chick, Nancy, Aeron Haynie, and Regan A. R. Gurung. 2012. *Exploring More Signature Pedagogies.* Sterling, VA: Stylus.

Daniel, David B., and Debra A. Poole. 2009. "Learning for Life: An Ecological Approach to Pedagogical Research." *Perspectives on Psychological Science* 4, no. 1: 91–96.

Dunlosky, John, and Amanda R. Lipko. 2007. "Metacomprehension: A Brief History and How to Improve Its Accuracy." *Current Directions in Psychological Science* 16: 228–32.

Dunlosky, John, and Thomas O. Nelson. 1997. "Similarity between the Cue for Judgments of Learning (JOL) and the Cue for Test Is Not the Primary Determinant of JOL Accuracy." *Journal of Memory and Language* 36, no. 1: 34–49. doi: 10.1006/jmla.1996.2476.

Entwistle, Noel. 2009. *Teaching for Understanding at University: Deep Approaches and Distinctive Ways of Thinking.* London: Palgrave Macmillan.

Epting, Kimberly L., Tracy E. Zinn, Colin Buskist, and William Buskist. 2004. "Student Perspective on the Distinction Between Ideal and Typical Teachers." *Teaching of Psychology* 31, no. 3: 181–83.

Fried, Carrie B. 2008. "In-Class Laptop Use and Its Effects on Student Learning." *Computers and Education* 50, no. 3: 906–14.

Gurung, Regan A. R. 2010. *Health Psychology: A Cultural Approach.* San Francisco: Cengage.

———. 2009. Applying Method to (Seeming) Madness: Doing SOTL in Your Class. In *Essays from Excellence in Teaching,* ed. Steven A. Meyers and Jeffrey R. Stowell, 16–18. http://teachpsych.org/ebooks/eit2008/index.php.

Gurung, Regan A. R., Pamela I. Ansburg, Patricia A. Alexander, Natalie Kerr Lawrence, and David E. Johnson. 2008. "The State of the Scholarship of

Teaching and Learning in Psychology: A National Perspective." *Teaching of Psychology* 35, no. 4: 249–61.

Gurung, Regan, A. R., and Kathleen Burns. 2011. "The Social Psychology of Teaching and Learning" In *Social Psychology and Teaching,* ed. Elizabeth Yost Hammer and Debra Mashek, 1–31. Malden, MA: Wiley-Blackwell.

Gurung, Regan A. R., Nancy L. Chick, and Aeron Haynie. 2009. *Exploring Signature Pedagogies: Approaches to Teaching Disciplinary Habits of Mind.* Sterling, VA: Stylus.

Gurung, Regan A. R., and Beth M. Schwartz. 2009. *Optimizing Teaching and Learning: Practicing Pedagogical Research.* Malden, MA: Blackwell.

Gurung, Regan A. R., and Kristin M. Vespia. 2007. "Looking Good, Teaching Well?" *Teaching of Psychology* 34, no. 1: 5–10.

Hacker, Douglas J., John Dunlosky, and Arthur C. Graesser. 2009. *Handbook of Metacognition in Education.* New York: Routledge/Taylor and Francis Group.

Halpern, Diane F., and Stephan Desrochers. 2005. "Social Psychology in the Classroom: Applying What We Teach as We Teach It." *Journal of Social and Clinical Psychology* 24, no. 1: 51–61.

Halpern, Diane F., and Milton D. Hakel. 2002. *Applying the Science of Learning to the University and Beyond: New Directions for Teaching and Learning.* San Francisco: Jossey-Bass.

Halpern, Diane F., Daniel W. Smothergill, Mary Allen, Suzanne Baker, Cynthia Baum, Deborah Best, Joseph Ferrari, Kurt F. Geisinger, Eugene R. Gilden, Maureen Hester, Patricia Keith-Spiegel, Nicholas C. Kierniesky, Thomas McGovern, Wilbert J. McKeachie, William F. Prokasy, Lenore T. Szuchman, Ross Vasta, and Kenneth Weaver. 1998. "Scholarship in Psychology: A Paradigm for the Twenty-first Century." *American Psychologist* 54, no. 5: 1292–97.

Hammer, Elizabeth Y. 2005. "From the Laboratory to the Classroom and Back: The Science of Interpersonal Relationships Informs Teaching." *Journal of Social and Clinical Psychology* 24, no. 1: 3–10.

Hattie, John. 2009. *Visible Learning: A Synthesis of Over 800 Meta-Analyses Relating to Achievement.* London: Routledge.

———. 2011. "Strategies to Enhance Teaching and Learning in Higher Education." In *Empirical Research in Teaching and Learning: Contributions from Social Psychology,* ed. Debra Mashek and Elizabeth Y. Hammer. Malden, MA: Wiley-Blackwell, 130.

Huber, Mary T., and Pat Hutchings. 2005. *The Advancement of Learning: Building the Teaching Commons.* San Francisco: Jossey-Bass.

Hutchings, Pat. 2007. "Theory: The Elephant in the Scholarship of Teaching and Learning Room." *International Journal for the Scholarship of Teaching and Learning,* 1, no. 1. http://academics.georgiasouthern.edu/ijsotl/2007_vini.htm.

Irons, Jessica G., and William Buskist. 2008. "The Scholarship of Teaching and Pedagogy: Time to Abandon the Distinction?" *Teaching of Psychology* 35, no. 4: 353–57.

James, William. 1899/2006. *Talks to Teachers on Psychology and to Students and Some of Life's Ideals.* New York: Metropolitan Books/Henry Holt.

Kang, Sean H. K., Kathleen B. McDermott, and Henry L. Roediger III. 2007. "Test Format and Corrective Feedback Modify the Effect of Testing on Long-Term Retention." *European Journal of Cognitive Psychology* 19: 528–58.

Karpicke, Jeffrey D., and Henry L. Roediger III. 2008. "The Critical Importance of Retrieval for Learning." *Science* 319: 966–68.

Koriat, Asher, and Robert A. Bjork. 2005. "Illusions of Competence in Monitoring One's Knowledge during Study." *Journal of Experimental Psychology: Human Learning and Memory* 31, no. 2: 187–94.

Langer, Ellen. 1975. "The Illusion of Control." *Journal of Personality and Social Psychology* 32: 311–28.

Mashek, Debra, and Hammer, Elizabeth Yost. 2011a. *Empirical Research in Teaching and Learning: Contributions from Social Psychology.* Malden, MA: Wiley-Blackwell.

———. 2011b. *Social Psychology and Teaching.* Malden, MA: Wiley-Blackwell.

McDaniel, Mark A., J. L. Anderson, M. H. Derbish, and N. Morrisette. 2007. "Testing the 'Testing Effect' in the Classroom." *European Journal of Cognitive Psychology* 19: 494–513.

McDaniel, Mark A., and Gilles O. Einstein. 2005. "Material Appropriate Difficulty: A Framework for Determining When Difficulty Is Desirable for Improving Learning." In *Experimental Cognitive Psychology and its Applications,* ed. A. F. Healy, 73–85. Washington, DC: American Psychological Association.

McDaniel, Mark A., Daniel C. Howard, and Gilles O. Einstein. 2009. "The Read-Recite-Review Strategy: Effective and Portable." *Psychological Science* 20, no. 4: 516–22.

McDaniel, Mark A., Henry L. Roediger III, and Kathleen B. McDermott. 2007. "Generalizing Test Enhanced Learning from the Laboratory to the Classroom." *Psychonomic Bulletin and Review* 14: 200–206.

Metcalfe, Janet. 2006. "Principles of Cognitive Science in Education." *Association for Psychological Science Observer.* http://www.psychologicalscience.org/observer/getArticle.cfm?id=1950.

Metcalfe, Janet, and Matthew Jason Greene. 2007. "Metacognition of Agency." *Journal of Experimental Psychology: General* 136: 184–99.

Milgram, Stanley. 1963. "Behavioral Study of Obedience." *Journal of Abnormal and Social Psychology* 67: 371–78.

Palmer, Parker J. 1998. *The Courage to Teach: Exploring the Inner Landscape of a Teacher's Life.* San Francisco: Jossey-Bass.

Pashler, Harold, Patrice M. Bain, Brian A. Bottge, Arthur Graesser, Kenneth Koedinger, Mark McDaniel, and Janet Metcalfe. 2007. *Organizing Instruction and Study to Improve Student Learning: A Practice Guide* (NCER 2007–2004). Available from the U.S. Department of Education, Institute of Education Sciences, National Center for Education Research web site, http://ies.ed.gov /ncee/wwc/pdf/practiceguides/20072004.pdf.

Pashler, Harold, Gregory Zarow, and Baylor Triplett. 2003. "Is Temporal Spacing of Tests Helpful Even When It Inflates Error Rates?" *Journal of Experimental Psychology: Learning, Memory, and Cognition* 29: 1051–57.

Peden, Blaine F., and Carmen R. Wilson-VanVoorhis. 2009. "Developing Habits of the Mind, Hand, and Heart in Psychology Undergraduates." In *Exploring Signature Pedagogies: Approaches to Teaching Disciplinary Habits of Mind*, ed. Regan A. R. Gurung, Nancy L. Chick, and Aeron Haynie, 161–82. Sterling, VA: Stylus.

Prieto, Loreto R., and Steven A. Meyers. 1999. "Effects of Training and Supervision on the Self-Efficacy of Psychology Graduate Teaching Assistants. *Teaching of Psychology* 26, no. 4: 264–66.

———. 2009. "A Scientist-Educator Model of Psychology TA Training." In *State-of-the-Art Practice for Training Psychology Teaching Assistants,* chaired by L. R. Prieto and S. A. Meyers. Symposium presented at the annual meeting of the American Psychological Association, Toronto, CA.

Roediger, Henry L., and Jeffrey D. Karpicke. 2006. "Test-Enhanced Learning: Taking Memory Tests Improves Long-Term Retention." *Psychological Science* 17, no. 3: 249–55.

Schacter, Daniel L., Daniel T. Gilbert, and Daniel M. Wegner. 2011. *Psychology.* New York: Worth.

Shell, Duane F., David W. Brooks, Guy Trainin, Kathleen M. Wilson, Douglas F. Kauffman, and Lynne M. Herr. 2010. *The Unified Learning Model: How Motivational, Cognitive, and Neurobiological Sciences Inform Best Teaching Practices.* New York: Springer.

Slamecka, Norman J., and Peter Graf. 1978. "The Generation Effect: Delineation of a Phenomenon." *Journal of Experimental Psychology: Human Learning and Memory* 4: 592–604.

Smith, Randolph A. 2005. "The Classroom as a Social Psychology Laboratory." *Journal of Social and Clinical Psychology* 24, no. 1: 62–71.

———. 2008. "Moving Toward the Scholarship of Teaching and Learning: The Classroom Can Be a Lab, Too!" *Teaching of Psychology* 35, no. 4: 262–66.

Smith, Randolph A., and William Buskist. 2008. "The Scholarship of Teaching and Learning in Psychology." *Teaching of Psychology* 35, no. 4: 247–48.

Snyder, C. R. 2005. "Teaching: The Lessons of Hope." *Journal of Social and Clinical Psychology* 24, no. 1: 72–84.

Tomcho, Thomas J., and Rob Foels. 2008. "Assessing Effective Teaching of Psychology: A Meta-Analytic Integration of Learning Outcomes." *Teaching of Psychology* 35, no. 4: 286–96.

Weeden, Jason, and John Sabini. 2005. "Physical and Attractiveness and Health in Western Societies: A Review." *Psychological Bulletin* 131, no. 5: 635–53.

Wilson, Janie H., Jonathan R. Stadler, Beth M. Schwartz, and Dennis M. Goff. 2009. "Touching Your Students: The Impact of a Handshake on the First Day of Class." *Journal of the Scholarship of Teaching and Learning* 9, no. 1: 108–17.

Wojcieszak, Magdalena, and Vincent Price. 2009. "What Underlies the False Consensus Effect? How Personal Opinion and Disagreement Affect Perception of Public Opinion." *International Journal of Public Opinion Research* 21, no. 1: 25–46.

CHAPTER 3

SOTL and Interdisciplinary Encounters in the Study of Students' Understanding of Mathematical Proof

CURTIS BENNETT AND JACQUELINE DEWAR

For students working toward a major in mathematics, learning to appreciate the need for proof and learning to create and write proofs present significant challenges. Much as using the scientific method through hypothesis confirmed by experiment is how scientists discover new information, making conjectures and trying to prove them is how mathematicians discover new results. Unfortunately, whereas the scientific method is a major part of K–12 science education, by 1989, mathematical proof was marginalized in the high school curriculum (Greeno 1994). The 2000 National Council for the Teaching of Mathematics standards have remedied this problem somewhat (Hanna 2000), but many students begin college thinking that mathematics is simply a set of techniques, formulas, and theorems that others have discovered, rather than thinking of mathematics as a creative discipline where new information is being discovered daily.

These misconceptions about mathematics add to the challenge of developing mathematics majors' understanding of the crucial role of and need for proof. The college and university mathematical community has been addressing this problem in many ways for some years. Not surprisingly, students' understanding of proof has been the subject of many studies. The many misconceptions students have about what constitutes a proof were detailed and categorized by Gureshon Harel and Larry Sowder (1998). Students from secondary school through college have major difficulties with the tasks of proof construction and proof validation (Weber 2001; Selden and Selden 2003). In a study by Angel Recio and Juan Godino (2001), less than 50 percent of 204 beginning students at the University of Córdoba (Spain) produced a substantially correct proof of an elementary number theory statement, and 40 percent relied solely on empirical evidence.

As experienced college mathematics instructors, we were drawn to investigating the level of understanding of proof our students had at critical points in our mathematics curriculum and then to identifying the learning experiences that promoted growth in student understanding of proof. Toward these goals, we conducted think-alouds with twelve students in which they first investigated and then attempted to prove a simple conjecture from number theory while speaking all of their thoughts out loud so that the thoughts could be transcribed. We also surveyed students and faculty on the nature of mathematics and held a focus group in which students reflected on their learning experiences in mathematics. To describe accurately the results revealed by the think-alouds, we were prompted to develop a typology of mathematical knowledge that, in part, draws on a typology of scientific knowledge (Shavelson 2003). Our typology includes six cognitive and two affective components. Looking at the student responses in detail, we were able to identify markers of progress for students in several of the components. This led us to expand our typology into a two-dimensional description of mathematical *knowledge* and *expertise* by drawing on Patricia Alexander's (2003) model of domain learning. The end result was the development of a taxonomy of mathematical knowledge and expertise that took us far beyond answering our first research question.

An analysis of the student responses regarding what learning experiences contributed to their development of understanding of the role of proof in mathematics suggested an answer to our second research question. It seems that an introductory two-semester workshop course sequence on problem solving and writing in mathematics (henceforth referred to as "the workshop course") was most significant in their development, surprisingly, more so than a sophomore course dedicated to mathematical proof.

Our investigation prompted us to use qualitative research methodologies foreign to most mathematicians. We can report that, as mathematicians, the experience of investigating SOTL questions with methods and skills drawn from social science proved useful in unexpected ways and led us to other endeavors and connections in our careers.

The Research Study: Developing the Questions

Our experience and work during 2003–2004 when we were selected as scholars in the Carnegie Academy for the Scholarship of Teaching and Learning (CASTL) program led to the results reported in this chapter. The broad theme for that year's call for CASTL scholars was liberal education and we had applied with "paired projects" that were going to examine different aspects of the question *How does mathematics contribute to liberal learning?*

Initial evidence gathered from a survey of mathematics students and faculty interested both authors in exploring more deeply the role that the workshop course played in the development of students' mathematical knowledge and what moves them from a reliance on examples to an understanding of and desire for proof. As one author began to focus on the role of the workshop course in this transformation as well as how knowledge gained in the workshop course was being applied more broadly, the other examined the evolution of student understanding of proof throughout the major. Using shared data from surveys, think-alouds, interviews and focus groups, it became apparent that the workshop course Dewar helped to develop, taught for the previous four years, and that Bennett was studying, plays a central part in helping students at LMU learn the essential role of proof. By the midpoint of the year-long study, these investigations had become inseparably intertwined.

Answering the First Question:
What Is the Evolution of Student Understanding of Proof?

Our study was cross-sectional in that it took a snapshot of students in the major during 2003–2004. We began with a survey on proof and problem solving administered to fifty students (forty-two mathematics majors and eight computer science majors) enrolled in mathematics courses. This same survey was subsequently administered to sixteen full-time mathematics faculty.

The first finding related to students' acceptance of empirical evidence as proof from the survey was that after four semesters in the major, student responses to the following question become very similar to faculty responses:

Respond on a five-point Likert scale ranging from Strongly Disagree to Strongly Agree: *If I see five examples where a formula holds, then I am convinced that formula is true.*

The percentage of students indicating a willingness to accept empirical evidence as proof, as evidenced by answering "Agree" or "Strongly Agree" to this survey question, declined from 44 percent to 9 percent as they moved through the major. By comparison, one of the sixteen faculty surveyed indicated they would find five examples convincing.

While we were disappointed that nearly one in ten upperclassmen would still be convinced by empirical evidence, we were more than surprised when one of the faculty gave what we considered to be an "incorrect" response to "Five examples convinces me." When asked for an explanation of his response, the faculty member stated, "'Convinced' does not mean 'I am certain' to me, so whenever I am testing a formula/conjecture, if it works for about five cases, then I try to prove that it's true," as the reason for his "wrong" answer.

So early in our investigation we discovered for ourselves a fact well known to researchers in the social sciences, namely, quantitative data obtained from a Likert scale response to a survey question will not completely reveal a respondent's thinking.

In order to learn more about what our students think about proof and how willing they are to accept a small number of favorable examples (empirical evidence) of a statement as proof, we employed think-aloud methodology as they worked on a mathematical task we provided. Think-aloud protocols are a psychological research method that elicits verbal reports from research participants while they are performing a task. As is common in this methodology, we audiotaped and later transcribed these verbal reports. Because mathematical work often involves exploratory computations, we made pencil and paper available for subject use. Evidence gathered included both what subjects said as well as what they wrote down about each question or task in the protocol. We also asked and recorded what courses or other learning experiences they said helped them answer a question or complete a task. Initially the subjects were twelve mathematics majors, spanning our curriculum from first semester in the major through to six months after graduation. Later on a faculty member was recruited to serve as an "expert" subject for the think-aloud protocol.

The following mathematical situation was used in the think-aloud protocol.

Please examine the statements: For any two consecutive positive integers, the difference of their squares:

(a) is an odd number,

(b) equals the sum of the two consecutive positive integers.

What can you tell me about these statements?

This was the same statement used by Recio and Godino (2001, 83) to investigate student proof strategies and what reasons might underlie their choices of nondeductive methods. In their study at the University of Córdoba (Spain), proving this and other statements was presented as a written task to several hundred incoming freshman, whereas initially we presented it as a statement to investigate and only later gave directions to try to write a proof. Another difference was that our twelve subjects spanned our curriculum from its very beginning through just after graduation.

Recio and Godino (2001) developed a 1 to 5 numeric rubric intended to differentiate between students who relied on examples (category 2) and students who relied on definitions or general results to develop partially (category 4) or substantially correct (category 5) proofs (86). On their scale, category 1 indicated an answer that is very deficient (confused or incoherent).

We found that, in contrast to Recio and Godino's results, where 40 percent of the students relied on empirical evidence, all of our students realized that empirical proofs were insufficient, and all attempted to make some sort of general argument, or at least expressed concern that their argument was not general enough. However, only two of the twelve students we interviewed were beginning freshmen and thus only they were comparable to the subjects in the Córdoba study. Of those two, one produced a very deficient proof, but did so by trying to appeal to general definitions and restating the desired conclusions.

One of our goals was to see how students' understanding of proof evolved in the major. Because, relative to proof, there are three critical courses in our curriculum, we assigned levels to students' progression in the major relative to these courses as defined in the first two columns in table 3.1. We were then able to display our students' proof performance by level in the major. Each "X" in the table denotes the proof performance of a single student at the indicated level. As table 3.1 shows, all but one student placed in the top two of Recio and Godino's (2001) five categories of performance, with seven of the twelve students placing in the top category.

We discovered that Recio and Godino's proof performance rubric, designed to distinguish between students using empirical proof schemes and students using deductive proof schemes, did not suffice for an in-depth analysis of the multifaceted work that we were able to document with the think-aloud transcripts. We required a system that would allow us to describe the following:

- A Level IV student asked an insightful question about whether the order of the numbers in the subtraction mattered, and consequently, demonstrated both uncertainty and high interest, ultimately producing a partially correct answer.

- A Level I student exhibited advanced mathematical thinking in coming up with a novel and valid geometric interpretation but wasn't able to write down a polished proof.

- A Level III student made a poor strategic choice to use an advanced method. Then he gave up after being stuck for less than two minutes in the middle of the proof, saying he really couldn't see it, couldn't figure it out. He lacked the confidence needed to deal with the uncertainly of how to proceed.

- After finishing a reasonably well-written proof, a Level III student reflected that it probably needed refining because it didn't

TABLE 3.1. Level of Progression in the LMU Math Major Curriculum vs. Proof Performance Category of the Twelve Think-aloud Subjects

Level	Progression in the LMU Math Curriculum	Proof Performance Categories				
		1	2	3	4	5
0	Prior to the workshop course	X			X	
I	Completed workshop course the preceding semester				X	X
II	Completed the proofs course the preceding semester					XX
III	Completed a real analysis course the preceding semester				X	XX
IV	Completed a real analysis course a year earlier				X	X
V	A graduate from the preceding year					X

sound very good, but she thought it got the job done and she wasn't interested in spending any more time on it. So lack of interest inhibited her from doing a better job.

Confidence appeared as a factor in our expert's performance as well. Initially, he expressed trepidation at being asked to be our "expert," especially since we had described the problem as coming from number theory, which was not his field. However, when pressed into service, he displayed a sense of assurance as he moved through the tasks. He used language carefully, made a smooth and unprompted transition from investigating to proving, and wrote a clear and correct proof that employed proper definitions, notation, organizational features, complete sentences, and detailed algebraic steps. In sum, then, these think-alouds on proof gave us compelling illustrations of the various types of knowledge, strategic processing, and motivation required to produce a correct and well-written proof. They showed how additional knowledge may sometimes result in poorer overall performance and that a student could exhibit both expert and novice behavior during the same task. They also indicated that affects such as confidence and interest could influence student performance.

The Development of the Taxonomy

Our desire to describe the rich detail of these think-aloud performances both in terms of the types of knowledge they document and the levels of expertise exhibited in different types of knowledge led us to develop a mathematical knowledge-expertise taxonomy (see table 3.2). This taxonomy has two dimensions. The first dimension consists of a typology of mathematical knowledge that includes six cognitive and two affective components. The six cognitive components were adapted and extended from a typology of scientific knowledge developed in response to calls for national K–12 science assessment (Shavelson 2003, 10). Richard Shavelson developed his typology of scientific knowledge, in part, to make the point that multiple-choice testing does not accurately assess the complete spectrum of scientific knowledge we want K–12 students to attain by graduation. The second dimension describes student progression toward proficiency using the language of a K–12 classroom-based theory of expertise development (Alexander 2003).

The Mathematical Knowledge Dimension

The descriptions provided by Shavelson (personal communication) for the six types of scientific knowledge—factual, procedural, schematic, strategic, epistemic, and social—were readily adapted to mathematical knowledge. For example, epistemic knowledge, or how one decides if a statement is true in the discipline, changed from *the scientific method* to *proof.* Social knowledge, which refers to the disciplinary ways for communicating truth or knowledge, became the accepted rules of exposition for writing proofs that observe the norms and conventions of mathematical discourse. The last two components, epistemic and social knowledge, were the content core of our think-aloud investigation; namely, how do students know something is true and how do they communicate that knowledge. The first four cognitive components encompass the knowledge and strategic processing portions of Alexander's (2003) model, which we will describe in the next section, after examining two influential affects.

Our think-alouds indicated that in addition to these six cognitive components of knowledge, two affective components, interest and confidence, influenced students' performance. Interest plays an important role in moving students toward proficiency (Alexander 2003, 10) and is often cited as a motivating factor in learning (Bain 2004; Harel 2008). Confidence is less frequently considered, but we concur with Schoenfeld (1985) that it plays a very important role in students' willingness to persist on a task.

The Mathematical Expertise Dimension

To describe our students' growth in understanding of proof, we turned to Alexander's (2003) model of domain learning (MDL). MDL is a perspective on expertise theory that arose from studies of K–12 student learning in academic domains, such as reading, history, physics and biology. MDL does not see someone as either a novice or an expert but rather is concerned with the journey from novice to expert. It looks at three stages of learning. The initial stage is *acclimation* wherein the learner is orienting to a complex, unfamiliar domain. The next stage is *competence,* and the final is *proficiency.* Occupants of this last stage are characterized by having a depth and breadth of knowledge, a mastery of methodologies, and an ability to contribute new knowledge to the field. MDL focuses on three components that play a role in the journey toward expertise in academic domains: knowledge (which roughly corresponds to factual and procedural knowledge in our typology), strategic processing (corresponding to schematic, strategic and, potentially, epistemic knowledge) and interest (one of the affective components). Alexander's work was applied to K–12 teaching and learning, with competence in academic domains seen as an attainable goal for most high school graduates. When MDL is applied to the academic domain of mathematics, given the specialized knowledge, advanced heuristic knowledge, and high interest of an expert mathematician, reaching that level of expertise is unrealistic for all but the most exceptional of collegiate mathematics majors. Our adaptation of MDL allows us to describe performance on mathematical tasks across our typology of mathematical knowledge components. To illustrate how it applies, we will describe in more detail the three stages of learning in the epistemic and social knowledge components.

A student in the acclimation stage of epistemic knowledge would often depend solely on examples to test the truth of a statement or rely on external authority to validate a claim. Students at this stage would be likely to respond that to be certain of a statement they would ask a professor or look in a book. Students moving through this stage are beginning to recognize that a conjecture with a valid proof cannot have counterexamples, and they might be skeptical of the validity of a statement having seen only five examples where it holds. In contrast, students at the competence stage in epistemic knowledge will still use examples but then will express a desire for a proof in order to be certain. These students recognize that a general proof applies to special cases. They are also more strongly aware that a proven conjecture cannot have counterexamples, at least in specific cases of proofs they have seen. Collegiate mathematics students at the proficient level in the epistemic

TABLE 3.2. Mathematical Knowledge-Expertise Taxonomy

AFFECTIVE	ACCLIMATION	COMPETENCE	PROFICIENCY
Interest	Students are motivated to learn by external (often grade-oriented) reasons that lack any direct link to the field of study. Students have greater interest in concrete problems and special cases than abstract or general results.	Students are motivated by both internal (e.g., intrigued by the problem) and external reasons. Students still prefer concrete concepts to abstractions, even if the abstraction is more useful.	Students have both internal and external motivation. Internal motivation comes from an interest in the problems from the field, not just applications. Students appreciate both concrete and abstract results.
Confidence	Students are unlikely to spend more than 5 minutes on a problem if they cannot solve it. Students don't try a new approach if first approach fails. When given a derivation or proof, they want minor steps explained. They rarely complete problems requiring a combination of steps.	Students spend more time on problems. They will often spend 10 minutes on a problem before quitting and seeking external help. They may consider a second approach. They are more comfortable accepting proofs with some steps "left to the reader" if they have some experience with the missing details. They can start multi-step problems but may have trouble completing them.	Students will spend a great deal of time on a problem and try more than one approach before going to text or instructor. Students will disbelieve answers in the back of the book if the answer disagrees with something they feel they have done correctly. Students are accustomed to filling in the details of a proof. They can solve multi-step problems.

COGNITIVE	ACCLIMATION	COMPETENCE	PROFICIENCY
Factual	Students start to become aware of basic facts of the topic.	Students have working knowledge of the facts of the topic but may struggle to access the knowledge.	Students have broad knowledge about the topic and quick access to that knowledge.

COGNITIVE	ACCLIMATION	COMPETENCE	PROFICIENCY
Procedural	Students start to become aware of basic procedures. Can begin to mimic procedures from the text.	Students have working knowledge of the main procedures. Can access them without referencing the text but may make errors or have difficulty with complex procedures.	Students can use procedures without reference to external sources or struggle. Students are able to fill in missing steps in procedures.
Schematic	Students begin to combine facts and procedures into packets. They use surface level features to form schema.	Students have packets of knowledge that appropriately tie together ideas with a common theme, method, or proof.	Students have put knowledge together appropriately in packets, tied together with common themes, methods, and/or proofs. Those packets include multiple or rich representations of the topic.
Strategic	Students use surface-level features of problems to choose between schema, or they apply the most recent method they learned.	Students choose schema to apply after considering just a few heuristic strategies. Students are slow to abandon a nonproductive approach.	Students choose schema to apply after considering many different heuristic strategies. Students self-monitor and abandon a nonproductive approach for an alternate.
Epistemic	Students begin to understand what constitutes "evidence" in the field. They begin to recognize that a valid proof cannot have a counterexample. They are likely to believe based on 5 examples; however, they may be skeptical.	Students are more strongly aware that a valid proof cannot have counterexamples. They use examples to decide on the truth of a statement but require a proof for certainty.	Students recognize that proofs don't have counterexamples, are distrustful of 5 examples, see that general proofs apply to special cases, and are more likely to use "hedging" words to describe statements they suspect to be true but have not yet verified.
Social	Students will struggle to write a proof and include more algebra or computations than words. Only partial sentences will be written, even if they say full sentences. Variables will seldom be defined, and proofs lack logical connectors.	Students are likely to use an informal shorthand that can be read like sentences for writing a proof. They may employ connectors but writing lacks clarity often due to reliance on pronouns or inappropriate use or lack of mathematical terminology.	Students write proofs with complete sentences. They use clear, concise sentences and employ correct terminology. They define all variables and use logical connectors correctly.

domain recognize that truth is decided by proof, and that given a valid proof, there can be no counterexample. When they see that they have been given a special case of a proven result, they know they can apply the general result to the particular case. Students proficient in the epistemic domain will refuse to take five examples as evidence of truth and take care to make distinctions between proven and conjectured statements. In fact, we observed our faculty "expert" carefully using hedging language, words and phrases like "conjecture," "plausible," and "seem to be true," to describe statements he was considering until he arrived at a proof.

In applying these stages, a lack of knowledge in one of the components might affect the ability of a student to progress in another. Surprisingly, however, an increase in knowledge in one component might hamper a student in another. For example, one of the students in our study showed poor strategic knowledge on the think-aloud due to his possessing a greater factual knowledge about mathematical induction as a method of proof. This notion of backwards motion in understanding is reminiscent of many other theories of learning. In particular, Jean Piaget's (1970) work on accommodation argues that making room for new ideas that do not fit with previously held notions may cause students to temporarily regress in their understanding of something (708). Susan Pirie and Tom Kieren (1989) and Ed Dubinsky (1991) also argue that accommodating new ideas will cause students to go through a retrenchment of their understandings. In addition, the assignment of a stage of expertise is often very particular to the aspect of the task under consideration or to the person being examined. A student may exhibit proficiency relative to some knowledge components and acclimating traits on others. The acclimating to proficient continuum presented in table 3.2 is describing typical college mathematics majors rather than professional mathematicians as a whole.

In the social knowledge component, acclimating students will struggle to write a proof. Most will write down very few words, even though in a think-aloud they might actually say the words and use full sentences. If they employ algebraic expressions in their proofs, the variables will probably not be explicitly defined for the reader. Their written proof will lack logical connectors, careful definitions, equal signs, and organizational labels or features such as centering equations. Students in the competence stage may write using an informal mathematical shorthand notation that can be read as full sentences. They may employ connectors but their writing will lack clarity, often because pronouns or other non-mathematical language such as, "it works," are substituted for accurate mathematical terminology. Writing clear, concise sentences, employing logical connecters and using mathematical terminology accurately are markers of proficiency, as are defining and using variables appropriately and formatting writing for easy reading.

Answering the Second Question: What Promotes Student Understanding of Proof?

Having our mathematical knowledge-expertise taxonomy in hand, the next stage of the analysis was to understand what activities helped students understand the role of proof in mathematics. As part of our think-aloud protocol, we asked students to reflect on what coursework or learning experience they felt helped them complete the task to investigate the statement and write a proof. On the question of what helped them investigate the statement, five of our twelve students cited the workshop course, three cited the sophomore-level proofs course, while the rest cited their previous math experience, often explicitly mentioning pre-college experiences. When asked what experiences or courses helped them with the proof-writing portion of the think-aloud investigation, six of the twelve students explicitly mentioned the workshop course, four students mentioned the proofs course, two students mentioned high school geometry (typically the only high school course where proofs are encountered), two other students mentioned high school algebra (which is where they would have thought about squaring numbers, as required by the problem in the think-aloud), one student mentioned the real analysis course (used in our demarcation of "levels" in the mathematics major curriculum), and one student simply mentioned a "variety of courses." Curiously, despite the fact that students typically refer to the proofs course in the curriculum as "Proofs," that answer was given less often than the workshop course. Moreover, if we consider only those students who were beyond the first two years of the major, when they take the workshop and proofs courses, then four of six students mentioned the workshop course, while only two of them referred to the proofs class.

At this point, a few words should be said about the two courses. The proofs course is a sophomore-year course in which students learn to write mathematical proof. Typically the course progresses through a variety of proof techniques, and the students learn to create and write proofs using each of these techniques. This course is frequently referred to as a transition course or sometimes a bridge course; that is, a course in which students transition from solving exercise-type problems in calculus to creating proofs. Learning to create proofs and to write them well are challenging bottlenecks in mathematics (Middendorf and Pace 2004). Our taxonomy captures both sides of this threshold, as collegiate mathematics courses up to and including calculus tend to focus on the factual, procedural, and schematic knowledge domains, whereas the later courses focus much more directly on the strategic, epistemic, and social knowledge domains.

On the other hand, the workshop course on problem solving and writing mathematics was developed at Loyola Marymount University to address a serious problem with student retention. Statistics gathered between 1987 and 1991 showed that 30 percent of students who declared a mathematics major failed to complete it. Of those who left the major, 73 percent had dropped it by the end of their sophomore year. In 1991, 43 percent of the fourteen freshmen told their advisors they were leaving the major. To address this problem, in 1992 the department introduced the workshop course with these four components: mathematical problem solving, mathematical writing/communicating, mathematical careers, and the culture of mathematics. After the introduction of the workshop course, the dropout rate for students taking both semesters of the course was nearly halved (Dewar 2006). Other effects of the workshop course reported by Dewar (2006) included improvement in problem solving skills, study skills, and providing more complete mathematical arguments as well as increased motivation to pursue a career in mathematics.

What the student responses from our study suggested, however, is that in addition to improving the retention rate in the major, the workshop course also apparently provides a better introduction to the epistemology of mathematics. Certainly the fact that the two students who had completed the workshop course but not the proofs course placed in the top-performing categories on the think-aloud (table 3.1) provides some support for this claim, but we must note that one of the students who had not yet taken the workshop course also performed well. However, further reflection on the nature of the two courses provides a different kind of support for the claim of the significance of the workshop course in aiding students' progress in understanding mathematical proof. The very design of the proofs course suggests that a professor can easily address the stated objectives of that course by teaching the factual, procedural, and schematic knowledge domains of writing proofs along with the social knowledge domain, without really addressing the epistemological domain. Indeed, one of the distinctions in the philosophy of mathematics is the role of proof. For a constructivist, proofs are constructed, and as such are the method of discovery of mathematics. For a mathematical Platonist, however, theorems are discovered and proven (although again often discovered via proof). Thus when teaching from a Platonist perspective, it is quite common for students to get a perspective that mathematics progresses in a "definition, theorem, proof" model (Davis and Hersch 1981), meaning that the students see proof primarily as a way of showing something already known to be true rather than as a way of discovering whether something is true. By contrast, the workshop course focuses students on the epistemological questions brought up by problem solving and then explaining their answers to those problems. Certainly the work of Schoenfeld (1985) on problem solving suggests that proof-based classes by themselves do not necessarily help students learn to use proof as a method of problem solving. These insights combined with our students' responses and performance reinforce the plausibility of the conclusion that the workshop course plays an important role in developing student understanding of proof.

The Taxonomy Viewed from the Perspective of Other Disciplines and Levels

In the years following its development, we have presented the taxonomy and its development to interdisciplinary audiences both on and off campus. Faculty from disciplines as disparate as computer science, education, and music have told us that it resonated both with their disciplinary work and their teaching. On our own campus, a cadre of our computer science colleagues have drawn upon the work in a number of ways. These include citing it in their scholarly work (Dionisio, Dickson, August, Dorin, and Toal 2007) and informing their development of a departmental assessment plan. Among the tasks in developing an assessment plan for their department was producing a curriculum and outcomes map in which each outcome is designated as being introduced (I), developed (D), or mastered (M) in each course (Loyola Marymount University Office of Assessment 2011). Ideas from the taxonomy played into their production of these maps. According to one colleague, "Seeing the [taxonomy] was an eye-opener and helped in assessment and curriculum development." This colleague referenced the taxonomy when reflecting on his teaching during a speech given on the occasion of his receiving the university teaching award.

Because our computer science colleagues have not yet produced a version of the taxonomy for their discipline, we cannot describe how they went about it. We can, however, offer some suggestions about how one might approach such a task. We believe that any taxonomy of disciplinary knowledge-expertise should include both cognitive and affective components, as there is a growing body of evidence of the impact that affect has on learning (Krathwohl, Bloom, and Masia 1964; McLeod 1994; Nuhfer 2005). On the cognitive side, an investigation paralleling ours would begin with an exploration of the disciplinary method used to produce new knowledge in the field. Another resource to draw on for developing a taxonomy would be Middendorf and Pace's decoding the disciplines work surrounding bottlenecks (Middendorf and Pace 2004), a topic treated in the chapters by Bernstein and Shopkow and colleagues in this volume.

We would expect any taxonomy to contain components that reflect in some way elements in Bloom's taxonomy, as ours does (factual, conceptual and procedural knowledge, application, and creating new knowledge). In addition, what we now know about "learning and the brain" suggests organization of knowledge into schema is key to learning in a discipline (Leamnson 1999, 11–22; Zull 2002). How one confirms and then communicates new knowledge are other elements to consider including. Insights gained from surveys or interviews with students and faculty, focus groups, close examination of student work on carefully crafted tasks, and think-alouds will assist in the selection of elements for the knowledge dimension and in the formulation of the descriptions of levels of expertise. Clearly, both deep disciplinary understanding and social science methodologies will be critical to the development of a taxonomy, regardless of the discipline being investigated and described.

We close this section with a few observations about connections between our taxonomy for collegiate-level mathematical knowledge and expertise and related ideas in elementary education. Only after completing the taxonomy did we realize that the cognitive components of the knowledge dimension relate to significant work in K–8 mathematics education research. In fact, our six cognitive components encompass the five strands of K–8 mathematical proficiency (conceptual understanding, procedural fluency, strategic competence, adaptive reasoning, and productive disposition) delineated in the National Research Council's publication *Adding It Up: Helping Children Learn Mathematics* (Kilpatrick, Swafford, and Findell 2001, 116). We now view the taxonomy as an extension of *Adding It Up*'s intertwined strands of elementary school mathematical proficiency to the development of mathematical proficiency in the undergraduate mathematics major (Kilpatrick, Swafford, and Findell 2001, 117).

Challenges Emanating from the Interdisciplinary Nature of SOTL Work

Our investigation encountered two major challenges arising from the interdisciplinary nature of SOTL work. One arises from unfamiliarity with the methodologies often employed in SOTL work and the other from the need to link discoveries to a literature and body of work or ideas that will almost certainly lie partially within and partially outside of the researcher's "home" discipline.

Traditionally trained mathematics faculty would have lots of experience with using student performance on tests, quizzes, or assignments to measure student understanding. They might have used course or program completion rates or student surveys as other ways of gathering data about student performance. But few mathematics faculty would be familiar with focus groups, interviews, or think-alouds as methods for gathering deeper and more nuanced looks at student understanding, let alone have experience in analyzing the qualitative data generated by these methods. Thus collecting and interpreting qualitative data can be a real hurdle for mathematicians interested in doing SOTL work.

As investigators on this SOTL project, we fit much of the profile above. While both of us had some prior experience in working on mathematics-education projects, neither one of us was particularly comfortable or well versed in collecting or analyzing qualitative data. One investigator had been coached by a qualitative analyst in a previous SOTL project (Bennett and Yakura 2003, 135). However, neither of us had any prior experience conducting "think-alouds." We were especially fortunate to have access to experienced social science researchers and Carnegie mentors during our 2003–2004 year as CASTL scholars. These colleagues and advisors provided both encouragement and suggested resources (Silverman 2001, 64–69; Ericsson and Simon 1993, 167) to undertake the collection and analysis of qualitative data.

Once the evidence was gathered, other problems arose. In particular, making an effective analysis of what qualitative evidence suggests is a complicated process. In our case, reading and rereading the transcripts of these think-alouds did little to help us at first because we lacked a proper taxonomy for our analysis. As stated earlier, the Recio and Godino rubric was insufficient for our purposes because it was not designed to deal with the in-depth data that we had collected from the think-alouds. Moreover, in looking at the mathematical literature on proof and problem solving, we were unable to find any taxonomies that spoke to our data.

Serendipitously, Richard Shavelson, a Stanford University professor of education, visited our campus as a Sigma Xi lecturer. His talk on assessing K–12 student learning in science included a taxonomy of scientific knowledge that clearly demonstrated how national assessment methods focused on facts and procedures and left out critical aspects of scientific learning. A later conversation with Shavelson convinced us we could adapt the six components in the taxonomy in a meaningful way to meet our needs. In that same conversation, we expressed our frustration with our inability to describe accurately the range of our students' performance, from novice to expert, on different aspects of the think-aloud task. He suggested we look at the work of Patricia Alexander, an education scholar, on models of domain learning. While mathematics was one of the areas to which Alexander applied her model of domain learning, she focused on K–12 mathematics, which effectively meant that the idea of understanding proof was left out of her discussion. However, we were able to build off of Alexander's work in terms of looking towards a progression of knowledge that would make sense to teachers of college mathematics and allow us to express our findings from the think-aloud. In her progression model, Alexander also identified an affective component of learning that motivated student improvement, namely, interest. In our initial reading of our data, we had seen that interest was an important aspect of student performance, and Alexander's work prompted us to include it as one of the components of knowledge. More important than this addition of interest, however, was the recognition that our taxonomy could and should include not just cognitive domains but affective ones as well. Thus, important to our moving forward with our SOTL investigation was the lucky chance of an interdisciplinary connection.

Recognizing that we wanted to develop a taxonomy was a real breakthrough and an unexpected outcome of our intertwined projects. It took us out of the realm of the two most common types of SOTL investigations as characterized by Pat Hutchings (2000) in the introduction to *Opening Lines*. We had moved from simply seeking to answer a "What works?" and a "What is?" question to a theory-building question in our own discipline with applications to other disciplines. This made our work both more challenging and more rewarding.

Once we understood that we wanted to develop a two-dimensional taxonomy, issues of doing qualitative work arose again. To develop the taxonomy, we needed to look for markers denoting each of the twenty-four cells across both dimensions (table 3.2). One author's previous experience helped with this; however, we still found it important to consult with researchers who had more experience with such analysis. And in some cases, cells were filled in by relying on the disciplinary and pedagogical content knowledge we had derived from our combined total at the time of nearly fifty years of teaching collegiate-level mathematics.

Final Reflections

We close with some final reflections on the rewards of doing SOTL work. Personally and professionally, we have both found this investigation, like most SOTL investigations, to be energizing and rewarding. We have argued elsewhere (Bennett and Dewar, 2012) that SOTL promotes more reflective teaching and improved teaching effectiveness. It is common for the details of what was good and bad in student work from previous semesters to fade from an instructor's memory. But reflecting on student work from a SOTL perspective helps faculty capture and preserve those details. By asking and answering SOTL questions, faculty can find out how well their students are learning and get insights for making improvements in their classrooms. The taxonomy itself now influences how we think about and analyze the failures we encounter in our teaching, and it helps us make choices about selecting learning outcomes.

This work has had a positive impact on our work outside our classrooms as well. It has informed subsequent work we were asked to undertake for program level assessment and university accreditation. And, as we mentioned in an earlier section, it has assisted our computer science colleagues in their departmental assessment efforts.

Learning to use methods of investigation and discovery that are quite different from mathematical methods was a challenge. Yet this effort has proven worthwhile for it has given us a greater understanding of other disciplinary methods and fields. Consequently this SOTL experience has enabled us to talk and work more knowledgeably with colleagues in other disciplines, assisting us in interdisciplinary work beyond SOTL. In particular, it provided important foundational knowledge for one of us to become involved in cross-discipline faculty development work. It has also allowed us to work more centrally at our university in expanding awareness of and resources for SOTL, as we have made allies in other disciplines.

Beyond our institution, this particular investigation has enabled us to make connections with researchers in mathematics education and science education across the United States. It also provided us with background and confidence to develop a four-hour workshop on the scholarship of teaching and learning in mathematics that has been offered several times at the national mathematics meetings. This, in turn, has led us to organize SOTL paper sessions at subsequent meetings and to invitations to speak about SOTL on panels aimed at junior faculty. The total experience has enriched our knowledge about teaching and learning, expanded our professional connections, and enabled us to have an impact on our own institution, the larger mathematical community, and the interdisciplinary SOTL movement.

REFERENCES

Alexander, Patricia. 2003. "The Development of Expertise: The Journey from Acclimation to Proficiency." *Educational Researcher* 32, no. 8: 10–14.

Bain, Ken. 2004. *What the Best College Teachers Do.* Cambridge: Harvard University Press.

Bennett, Curtis D., and Jacqueline Dewar. 2012. "An Overview of the Scholarship of Teaching and Learning in Mathematics." *PRIMUS: Problems, Resources, and Issues in Mathematics Undergraduate Studies,* 22, no. 6.

Bennett, Curtis D., and Elaine K. Yakura. 2003. "Finding Common Ground: Collaboration Across the Disciplines in the Scholarship of Teaching." *Journal on Excellence in College Teaching* 14, no. 2/3: 135–47.

Davis, Phillip J., and Reuben Hersch. 1981. *The Mathematical Experience.* Boston: Birkhauser.

Dewar, Jacqueline M. 2006. "Increasing Math Majors' Success and Confidence through Problem Solving and Writing." In *Educational Transformations: The Influences of Stephen I. Brown,* ed. Frances Rosamond and Larry Copes, 101–121. Bloomington, IN: AuthorHouse.

Dionisio, John David N., Caskey L. Dickson, Stephanie August, Philip M. Dorin, and Ray Toal. 2007. "An Open Source Software Culture in the Undergraduate Computer Science Curriculum." *ACM SIGCSE Bulletin* 39, no. 2: 70–74.

Dubinsky, Ed. 1991. "The Constructive Aspects of Reflective Abstraction in Advanced Mathematics." In *Epistemological Foundations of Mathematical Experiences,* ed. Leslie P. Steffe, 160–87. New York: Springer-Verlag.

Ericsson, K. Anders, and Herbert A. Simon. 1993. *Protocol Analysis: Verbal Reports as Data.* Cambridge: MIT Press.

Greeno, James. 1994. "Comments on Susanna Epp's Chapter." In *Mathematical Thinking and Problem Solving,* ed. Alan H. Schoenfeld, 270–78. Hillsdale, NJ: Lawrence Erlbaum Associates.

Hanna, Gila. 2000. "Proof Explanation and Exploration: An Overview." *Educational Studies in Mathematics* 44, no. 1/2: 5–23.

Harel, Guershon. 2008. "What Is Mathematics? A Pedagogical Answer to a Philosophical Question." In *Proof and Other Dilemmas: Mathematics and Philosophy,* ed. Bonnie Gold and Roger A. Simons, 265–90. Washington: Mathematical American Association.

Harel, Gureshon, and Larry Sowder. 1998. "Students' Proof Schemes: Results from Exploratory Studies." In *Research in Collegiate Mathematics Education III,* ed. Alan H. Schoenfeld, Jim Kaput, and Ed Dubinsky, 234–83. Providence, RI: American Mathematical Society.

Hutchings, Pat, ed. 2000. *Opening Lines: Approaches to the Scholarship of Teaching and Learning.* Palo Alto, CA: Carnegie Foundation for the Advancement of Teaching.

Kilpatrick, Jeremy, Jane Swafford, and Bradford Findell, eds. 2001. *Adding It Up: Helping Children Learn Mathematics*. Washington, DC: National Academy Press.

Krathwohl, David R., Benjamin S. Bloom, and Bertram B. Masia. 1964. *Taxonomy of Educational Objectives*. Vol. 2, *Affective Domain*. New York: David McKay.

Leamnson, Robert. 1999. *Thinking about Teaching and Learning: Developing Habits of Learning with First Year College and University Students*. Sterling, VA: Stylus.

Loyola Marymount University Office of Assessment. 2011. "Curriculum and Outcome Maps." http://www.lmu.edu/about/services/academicplanning /assessment/Assessment_Resources/Curriculum___Outcome_Maps.htm.

McLeod, Douglas B. 1994. "Research on Affect and Mathematics Learning in *JRME*, 1970 to Present." *Journal for Research in Mathematics Education* 25, no. 6: 637–47.

Middendorf, Joan, and David Pace. 2004. "Decoding the Disciplines: A Model for Helping Students Learn Disciplinary Ways of Thinking." In *Decoding the Disciplines: Understanding Student Thinking and Learning*. ed. David Pace and Joan Middendorf, 1–12. Vol. 98, *New Directions for Teaching and Learning*. San Francisco: Jossey-Bass.

Nuhfer, Ed. 2005. "De Bono's Red Hat on Krathwohl's Head: Irrational Means to Rational Ends." *National Teaching and Learning Forum* 14, no. 5: 7–11.

Piaget, Jean. 1970. "Piaget's Theory." In *Carmichael's Manual of Child Psychology*, vol.1 r(3d ed.), ed. Paul H. Mussen, 703–23. New York: Wiley.

Pirie, Susan, and Tom Kieren. 1989. "A Recursive Theory of Mathematical Understanding." *For the Learning of Mathematics* 9, no. 3: 7–11.

Recio, Angel M., and Juan D. Godino. 2001. "Institutional and Personal Meanings of Mathematical Proof." *Educational Studies in Mathematics* 48, no. 1: 83–99.

Schoenfeld, Alan H. 1985. *Mathematical Problem Solving*. Orlando: Academic Press.

Selden, Annie, and John Selden. 2003. "Validation of Proofs Considered as Texts: Can Undergraduates Tell Whether an Argument Proves a Theorem?" *Journal for Research in Mathematics Education* 33, no. 1: 4–36.

Shavelson, Richard. 2003. "Responding Responsibly to the Frenzy to Assess Learning in Higher Education." *Change* 35, no. 1: 10–19.

Silverman, David. 2001. *Interpreting Qualitative Data: Methods for Analyzing Talk, Text, and Interaction*. London: Sage.

Weber, Keith. 2001. "Student Difficulty in Constructing Proofs: The Need for Strategic Knowledge." *Educational Studies in Mathematics* 48, no. 1: 101–19.

Zull, James E. 2002. *The Art of Changing the Brain: Enriching the Practice of Teaching by Exploring the Biology of Learning*. Sterling, VA: Stylus.

CHAPTER 4

Plowing through Bottlenecks in Political Science: Experts and Novices at Work

JEFFREY L. BERNSTEIN

As a political scientist, I am a fortunate participant in the scholarship of teaching and learning field. Scholars in some disciplines face a stark divide between their disciplinary research—what Ernest Boyer (1990) called the scholarship of discovery—and their scholarship of teaching and learning work. For example, biologists studying the behavior of certain amino acids gain no leverage from that research on increased understanding of how their students learn biology, nor does their research on teaching and learning inform their work on amino acids. In my case, however, the line between "teaching" and "research" is blurrier. Research on how students form their political beliefs and build knowledge and skills as political actors (for example, Bernstein 2008; Niemi and Junn 1998) fits loosely under the umbrella of political socialization. This subfield of political science is concerned with how individuals learn about politics and get socialized as participants in the system. While the subfield's impact on the discipline has waned since the 1960s and 1970s, studying how people learn politics can be placed under the tent of disciplinary research more so than studying how people learn in most other fields.

The political science classroom, then, can become a useful laboratory for investigating how students make sense of the political world. To that end, this chapter uses methodologies of the scholarship of teaching and learning, and theoretical constructs derived from that field, to explore how students become (or do not become) sophisticated political actors. It focuses on what it looks like when novice government students confront a critical aspect of American politics—the use of the filibuster in the United States Senate—and what it looks like when their professors (the experts) confront it.[1] What can we learn from the behavior of the experts that informs how we should teach novices? To preview the findings, I identify two particular theoretical perspectives that the professors bring to the task that are not possessed by the novices—an understanding of politics as an arena laden with seemingly intractable conflicts, and of the tensions between majority rule and minority rights. A rich understanding of these perspectives is essential to understanding how political scientists study a political system.

I begin with a theoretical discussion of expert-novice work in the scholarship of teaching and learning and with a treatment of the concept of bottlenecks; both concepts are drawn from a range of academic disciplines outside my own yet significantly buttress the discussion in the chapter. I then outline my study, which explores how experts and novices overcome (or fail to overcome) the bottlenecks, leading each to understand one critical concept (the role and use of the filibuster in the U.S. Senate) quite differently. I present evidence drawn from think-aloud exercises—a method drawn from another discipline—conducted with students and from interviews with faculty colleagues to support my argument. I conclude by discussing implications of this work for classroom practice and for the study of teaching and learning more generally.

Theoretical Background

Experts and Novices

One of the best explanations of the scholarship of teaching and learning is provided in David Pace's (2004) classic article "Amateurs in the Operating Room." Pace argued,

> At the core of the entire project of a scholarship of teaching and learning is the belief that disciplinary thinking is crucial to learning. Therefore, a central goal of this work is to define as clearly as possible the kinds of thinking that students typically have to do in each academic field and to devise strategies for introducing students to these mental operations as effectively as possible. (1179)

This chapter is motivated by Pace's conceptualization of the scholarship of teaching and learning. If I am able to unpack how my students "do" political science, and how the way they do political science can be improved (compared to how an expert does it), I can better structure my classes to build these skills; this is similar to the approach Shopkow et al. use in this volume.

In this approach, *process* is central. Robert Bain (2000, 333) argues that our focus ought be on the thinking processes inherent in our disciplinary work: "By making visible the "invisible" cognitive work of historians, scholarship in history-specific cognition creates a richer, more nuanced picture of cognition than linear lists of skills or general taxonomies of thought." These perspectives, drawn from the field of history, are central to my work in the discipline of political science, which unfortunately lacks the body of work that teachers of history enjoy. Thus, while the work presented in this chapter is done almost entirely within political science, it is inherently interdisciplinary work. By borrowing the think-aloud method from other disciplines, most notably history and mathematics, I make use of the methodological trading zone (see Huber and Hutchings 2005) that characterizes the scholarship of teaching and learning.

While I borrow from outside my discipline for this rich theoretical literature on teaching and learning, importing the literature proves surprisingly easy. It is true that a central tenet of the scholarship of teaching and learning is that teaching and learning look different across the disciplines; teaching political science is not like teaching poetry or mathematics (Huber and Morreale 2002; Gurung, Chick, and Haynie 2009). And yet, a certain core remains constant across fields. None of us can adequately teach all the content in our field; there will always be historical events, or poems, or chemical processes that get pushed out of our crowded curricula. Thus, rather than teaching *all* the possible content, our primary goal must be to teach students the means by which *they* can explore content in the field (grounding these processes with multiple examples). Thus, a professor of Victorian literature teaches certain novels to her class for the benefits of teaching that particular novel, but also as a means of showing students how they can approach a piece of literature. Our goal cannot be to cover all the material but rather should be to teach students how to approach a disciplinary question as an expert would—in other words, how to think like a political scientist, or a chemist, or a literary scholar.

How do we put the ideas expressed by Pace and Bain into practice to improve our students' learning? One common source of strategies is so-called expert-novice methodologies, in which people with differing levels of skill and experience in a particular area are carefully observed attempting similar tasks. A goal in this body of literature is to understand the differences between how experts and novices approach a task; once we have done this, we are well positioned to help novices improve their performance.[2] In so doing, we "complete the circle," using scholarly investigations of teaching and learning to inform our practice. These studies have been performed in a variety of areas, ranging from chess (Chase and Simon 1973) to medicine (Patel, Groen, and Frederiksen 1986) to judicial decision making (Voss and Post 1988) to history (Wineburg 1991; Wineburg 2001). A similar type of study appears in the Bennett and Dewar chapter in this volume.[3]

Sam Wineburg (2001) offers a valuable example of this work when he studies how novice and expert historians deal with one particular question: who fired the first shot at Lexington and Concord in the American Revolutionary War? Wineburg compares how a group of high-achieving high school students and a group of history professors read through a series of documents intended to shed light on this question. In objective tests of factual knowledge given before the documents were provided, the students performed as well as the faculty members.[4] However, the groups worked differently with the documents. The history professors began by putting the documents in chronological order, carefully looking at the citation for each document before reading it. Some sources were weighted more heavily in their analysis than others. The professors also positioned the texts to "argue" with one another, pitting documents against each other in an attempt to give voice to competing viewpoints. Students, on the other hand, read the documents in the order in which they were given, paying no special attention to the source of the document; they also did not use the sources to argue with each other in the way the professors had. Each document was seemingly treated as an equally authoritative word on the subject.

The behaviors in which the professors engaged are almost certainly second nature; most might not even be able to articulate what they were doing if asked. These behaviors, however, appear in sharper relief when compared with extremely capable students' performance of the task. And, what is more, these behaviors are teachable. In short, expert-novice studies provide a useful way in which we can unpack how people perform the cognitive tasks associated with learning in a discipline and how we can teach others how to perform similar tasks.

Bottlenecks

In this chapter, I use the concept of bottlenecks to gain leverage on the question of how students learn politics. I borrow the definition from Arlene Díaz, Joan Middendorf, David Pace, and Leah Shopkow (2008), who define bottlenecks as "places where significant numbers of students are unable to grasp basic concepts or successfully complete important tasks" (1211). The concept is similar to Jan Meyer and Ray Land's work (2003; 2005) on "threshold concepts." Working through bottlenecks, or understanding threshold concepts, opens doors to deeper understanding of the subject matter at hand; as Meyer and Land suggest, threshold concepts are like portals through which one must pass in order to master a subject. Students stuck at a bottleneck, or at one of Meyer and Land's portals, cannot advance in disciplinary learning.

One example of this, again drawn from history, concerns *presentism,* the tendency of novice historians to view past events through the lens of today's world. Wineburg (2001, chapter 4) explores how two prospective public school teachers struggled through questions of whether Abraham Lincoln was actually a white supremacist. Applying present-day values to Lincoln's speeches might suggest that "The Great Emancipator" held racist views. When read in the context of when they were spoken, however, these views suggest a different interpretation—for his day, Lincoln was quite progressive on racial issues. Wineburg (2001) notes the importance of being able to view events in their natural context, arguing, "Judging past actions by present standards wrests them from their own context and subjects them to ways of thinking that we, not they, have developed. Presentism, the act of viewing the past through the lens of the present, is a psychological default state that must be overcome before one achieves mature historical understanding" (90). In spirit if not in word, Wineburg invokes the notion of a bottleneck here. Failure to get past this bottleneck will not allow a student to acquire "mature historical understanding."

This paper explores two potential bottlenecks in understanding of political science. The first concerns the essentially conflictual nature of politics. In their influential studies of public opinion toward political institutions and toward the political system, John Hibbing and Elizabeth Theiss-Morse (1995; 2002) note a fascinating paradox: while people support the idea of a democratic political system and are happy with the constitutional design of American government, they express a great deal of antipathy toward the actual political processes and the by-products of democracy that the system creates. Features of democracy such as debate, arguing, partisan conflict, and compromise are viewed in a negative light. Experienced political observers note that what the voters want is impossible; debate and conflict are inherent in a democratic political system. Hibbing and Theiss-Morse (2002) ultimately suggest that what the voters really want is "stealth democracy," the kind of democracy that exists but flies below the radar of most voters; voters, in short, want to be isolated from politics (for an alternative view on this question, which argues that voters are more willing than we think to be involved in deliberation, see Neblo et al. 2010).

This macro-level finding about American politics may apply at the classroom level as well. Anecdotally, it has been my experience that my students did not view conflict as part of the operation of a healthy political system. To them, conflict represented a failure of the system. Choosing to eschew conflict in their own political discussions ("let's just agree to disagree"), many students expected political officials to do the same thing. Hibbing and Theiss-Morse (1996) suggest that many students have been taught civics rather than "barbarics" and expect to see more civility and compromise than is possible in the real world. They may not understand that some problems are *that* intractable, and of such a serious nature, that happily papering over differences on the way to compromise may not be possible.

A second bottleneck explored in this paper is the tension between majority rules and minority rights. For most novice government students, democracy means majority rules. Thus, the notion that a set of procedural rules disadvantages majorities, allowing determined minorities to win, is problematic. Experienced political scientists, however, have a richer conception of the need to balance rule of the majority with protecting the rights of the minority; as Madison argued in Federalist Paper No. 10, just because a group comprised a majority did not rule out the possibility that it would act against the common good, or against the rights of others. There are no easy answers to the question of balancing the rule of the majority with the rights of the minority; the bottleneck occurs when students fail to move beyond a simplistic assumption that "might equals right" and that the system should ensure that majorities win.

This bottleneck is closely linked to the previous one. Were majorities to always be benevolent, and always protect the rights of minorities, there would be little reason to spend time worrying about this second bottleneck. But, as the first bottleneck concept reminds us, when the issue is important enough, majorities are likely to do whatever they can, even resorting to forms of tyranny, to defeat the minority. Thus, when students can move past the first bottleneck (understanding how majorities may tyrannize minorities), they gain a richer appreciation for the second bottleneck (understanding how important it is for a political system to concern itself with the protection of minority rights).

The Issue

To gain leverage on the bottlenecks described above, I focus in this chapter on how students come to understand one critical aspect of American government—the filibuster. The filibuster remains an important legislative tool in the U.S. Senate, forcing the majority party to achieve sixty votes to achieve its legislative goals.[5] This was an especially important consideration for the Obama administration as it attempted to move its health care plan through Congress—the struggle for the administration was not to secure 51 votes (a simple majority) but rather to secure a filibuster-proof majority of 60 votes.[6]

Aside from its practical importance, the filibuster also matters because it highlights a major theoretical issue in the study of governmental systems: the tensions between majority rule and minority rights. The House of Representatives, in contrast to the Senate, is a majoritarian institution; a simple majority of 218 members (out of 435) is able to pass virtually whatever it wants. The Senate is, and was intended to be, counter-majoritarian. Through its longer terms and indirect elections (senators were originally elected by state legislatures, not by the people), as well as by the fact that the Senate's design gives disproportionate power to less populous states, the Senate was designed to be insulated from the shifting tenors of popular opinion and to temper the passions of the House. It was intended to move more slowly and to give each individual senator a full voice on any issue on which they wish to be heard.

Rather than have the participants in the study explore the filibuster completely in a vacuum, I introduced a second political issue, the Employee Free Choice Act (EFCA), to study alongside the filibuster. Passage of the EFCA had long been a priority for organized labor when this study was done.[7] A key provision of the bill concerns its card-check provision. Currently, when a group of employees wishes to be represented by a union, they initiate a process by which employees fill out cards indicating that they wish to be represented by the union. When a majority of employees have turned in signed cards, the company is required to either recognize the union, or to call for a secret ballot election, supervised by the National Labor Relations Board. If the union wins the secret ballot election, it is designated as the representative of the employees. If the union loses the election, there will be no union representation. If the EFCA were to pass, the secret ballot requirement would be eliminated; whenever a majority of employees turned in their signed cards, the union would be immediately designated as the representative of the employees.[8]

Supporters of the EFCA contended that eliminating the secret ballot requirement was necessary to ensure that management could not intimidate workers into opposing the bill after the card-check process had begun. They pointed to stories about how employers forced workers to watch videos about the damage a union could do or distributed printed material discussing how many jobs would be lost if unionization succeeded. For their part, management suggested that many employees might sign the cards even if they did not want a union for fear that not doing so would rankle their fellow workers. Only the secret ballot would protect the workers by allowing them to cast their sincere vote in privacy rather than having to fill out a card (or not fill out a card), at which point everyone would know their decision about unionizing.

I pair the EFCA with the filibuster for three reasons. First, I hope students will see issues concerning a union and management as a zero-sum game, in which a gain for one side is a loss for the other.[9] This might help address the bottleneck where students minimize conflict and assume a willingness to compromise that might not be present nor warranted. This issue gives students experience with an issue when the battle is intense, with real stakes. Second, the EFCA got 51 votes in the Senate in 2007 but was defeated by a filibuster (the majority failed to muster the 60 votes necessary to invoke cloture). Students are able to see real-world consequences of the filibuster, when a majority is defeated by the minority.[10] Finally, by linking the filibuster to an actual issue, I hope to surface the possibility that students will form attitudes about the filibuster that are linked to the issue—students might decide they favor the filibuster because it was used to defeat a bill they hated (or that they oppose the filibuster because it was used against a bill they liked). In debriefing, I raise this possibility in an attempt to move students away from this position; ideally, our beliefs about whether filibusters should or should not be available as a legislative tool should be "issue-neutral" and not tied to any particular issue.

Methodology

This study uses two related data sources to build evidence regarding expert and novice thought patterns on these bottlenecks. First, the paper is based around twelve "think-alouds" done with six upper-class high school students and six first- or second-year university students. Think-alouds are a common method used in expert-novice studies, and more generally in education research (for a description of this method, see Ericsson and Simon 1984 and Perkins 1981; for some provocative think-aloud studies drawn from chemistry, mathematics, and history, respectively, see Bowen 1994; Sandefur 2007; Wineburg 1991). In a think-aloud, the participant is given a series of texts and asked to read them aloud, sharing their thoughts verbally (as the thoughts are being formed) as they go through the texts. The researcher's role is simply to encourage the participant to share their thoughts out loud—in my case, I would typically intervene by asking "What are you thinking now?" if the student went silent for too long (about ten to fifteen seconds). The goal is *not* to collect completed, fully formed thoughts, but rather to understand the thought process as it is unfolding. Gathering data through a think-aloud is the equivalent of being a fly on the wall as students are doing their work. Professors usually only see the finished product of a student's work; the think-aloud allows professors to view the process by which students reach their final product or their final judgment on a particular issue.

The students were recruited by word of mouth through people the author knew in the greater Ann Arbor, Michigan, community (for the high school students) and from the author's former students and through departmental colleagues at Eastern Michigan University (to reach the college students). These individuals were asked to participate in a study on how people form their political views on current issues; they were told that their participation in the study would take about sixty minutes and were paid $15 for their participation. The meetings were typically conducted in a faculty study office in the library on the Eastern Michigan University campus. The think-aloud sessions were audio taped and transcribed in order to permit further analysis. All of these sessions took place during October and November 2008.

The documents provided to the think-aloud participants began with a "cheat sheet" on the U.S. Congress, giving participants an overview of how Congress works, followed by a summary of the Senate filibuster and a discussion of the pros and cons of the filibuster. The material that followed focused on the Employee Free Choice Act. It included a summary of the EFCA, discussions of some pros and cons of the EFCA (including quotes from prominent supporters such as Barack Obama and opponents such as John McCain), one television commercial on each side of the issue, a letter from the United States Chamber of Commerce opposing the bill and a testimonial from a union worker supporting it. The packet concluded with a news story reporting on the failure of the bill to get enough votes to stop the filibuster and end debate.

The second data source consists of interviews with seven political science professors at Eastern Michigan University concerning how they view the filibuster, and how they treat it in their teaching. These brief interviews, which lasted an average of ten minutes, were meant to shed light on how experts view the filibuster, how they teach about it in class, and how/if they connect the filibuster to larger themes in their class. Most do not do very much on the filibuster in their classes, claiming not to spend more than ten to fifteen minutes a semester talking about the filibuster. But, drawing on a point made earlier, all connect the filibuster to many of the larger issues about which they teach, including quite prominently the rights of minorities and the challenges of rounding up enough votes in the Senate to overcome filibusters. All said they spice up their treatment of the filibuster, some with stories of famous filibusters by Huey Long or Strom Thurmond, or by referencing the filibuster scene in *Mr. Smith Goes to Washington*.

Results

In discussing the results of this inquiry, I focus primarily on the differences between how the experts (professors) and novices (students) approach the filibuster, considering the different extent to which the political science–

specific bottlenecks appear in their thought processes. Before this, however, some comments are in order concerning more general differences in how students interrogated the think-aloud materials; these differences are not necessarily linked to the study of political science but instead might be considered cross-disciplinary and therefore applicable to faculty teaching outside of political science. These results do not touch specifically on expert-novice distinctions because the faculty members in this study did not do the think-aloud tasks that the students did. Thus, any distinctions that I identify are differences found within the student group.

The most significant differences I observed concerned how students dealt with the information presented to them, broadly fitting under the rubric of information literacy (Association of College and Research Libraries 2000; Thornton 2010). Students differ (usually in predictable ways based upon political interest and engagement) in terms of the degree to which they consider the sources of material, argue with the sources, and explore connections between the different sources. This work closely parallels what Wineburg (2001) has observed in his studies of history students; it also parallels my previous work (Bernstein 2010) on expert-novice understandings of the capital punishment debate. These results are important for faculty to consider, no matter what they are teaching, because they reflect critical aspects of how students learn (and offer opportunities to help students enhance their learning while in college).

Moving from these more general issues to more discipline-specific ones, a first issue to consider is the nature of conflict in a political system. Recall that understanding the necessary role of conflict in a political system is a critical bottleneck to a deeper understanding of issues such as the filibuster; someone who does not understand that the issues being discussed represent real conflicts, about which each side is "playing for keeps," is unable to view the filibuster as anything more than a silly waste of time. Only when an observer views political conflict as real, as representative of the conflicting views of interested actors, and not as a failure of the system, can they understand aspects of the political system meant to channel conflict in a richer context. Thus, one critical piece of this analysis concerns how students view conflict in the political system.

To tap into this, I relied upon students' comments in their think-alouds about the Employee Free Choice Act. As noted above, union-management issues should have been easy ones through which students could identify meaningful and intractable conflict. Yet, as the following three quotations reveal, many students see the conflict on this issue as something that easily could, and should, be resolved.

> I don't see why this company needs to react as it did. How much trouble would having a union really cause? Is it really worth all of this effort to stop the unions from forming?

> The union folks are pushing this too far. I'm sure the description [contained in one of the texts] of what management has done is exaggerated. If the union would reach out to management and cooperate, management will return the favor.

> Why does it have to happen this way? Why can't the companies realize that when their workers are happy, they will do better work? It seems a lot of effort is being wasted with management battling the unions.

As these quotes reveal, significant numbers of students believe that conflicts between labor and management are either (1) low-stakes conflict, in which neither side stands to gain or lose a great deal from the outcome; and/or (2) easily resolved, in which simply reaching out and cooperating would solve the problem. The optimism, and idealism, is somewhat appealing; it is also, I would submit, a significant bottleneck to being able to understand a great deal of what happens in the political system.

Not all students, of course, had a view of the conflict that was quite this naïve. Most made no comments in their think-alouds that could be classified in one way or another on this dimension. But two students, both of whom identified themselves as being close followers of public affairs, had very different views on this dimension, both of which are worth quoting.

> There is just no way to resolve this situation. The workers will want higher pay, the company wants lower pay, and both sides are going to stick to what they want. I think that's why the question of whether a union is there becomes important. There's a lot at stake, so it's not surprising that both sides are concentrating this hard on the EFCA.

> I come from a union family; my dad was in the union, my brother is now, and my grandparents were, I think. So I want to make it easier for the unions. But I can see why companies want to shaft[11] the union—they lose a lot of money when they have to deal with the unions. I guess I don't blame them for trying to fire workers who try to organize.

These comments are certainly more negative than those above. They also are, in my judgment, far more realistic. A student who understands that political conflict is real and that both sides have a lot to gain or lose has moved past a critical bottleneck; he or she is well positioned to understand other political issues, including, but not limited to, the filibuster. Students who cannot get past this bottleneck will have a hard time understanding the filibuster and understanding other aspects of politics.

Next, we can look at how students dealt with issues of majority rules and minority rights. As noted above, a deep understanding of the challenges associated with how majority rule gets balanced with minority rights is critical for gaining a strong understanding of how legislatures, and political systems more generally, will work. The following two quotations show students who have a fairly elementary view of the nature of majority rule in a democratic political system.

> When the filibuster is used, the views of the minority can defeat the majority. I don't think that's right—this is a democracy, and the majority should be able to get what it wants.

> I know that the majority is not always right, but it still seems that putting these things in the way of the majority is a problem. It seems really unfair to me that the side that favored the EFCA had more votes than the side that did not, and yet they lost. The filibuster is just a bad idea.

These two students have an underdeveloped, and limited, sense of the tensions between majority rule and minority rights. They argue that what majorities want should become law and that any steps in the legislative process that inhibit this are problematic.

Some students, a distinct minority, did grasp some of the larger implications of the majority rule/minority rights tension. For example, one student noted the following:

> The filibuster really can look ridiculous. But, sometimes a minority feels it has no other choice, and the filibuster is one of the few tools it has available to it. I don't know if I like it in all cases—and I hate what it did to the EFCA in that last article—but I think there probably is a role for it here.

This student demonstrates an understanding of the tensions involved in the debate about the filibuster. His ability to grasp the competing and compelling arguments on both sides of the majority rules/minority rights debate allows him to develop a sophisticated argument about the filibuster. Another student, after describing the results engendered here by the filibuster, also offers a somewhat sophisticated viewpoint:

> The filibuster ended the legislation for the EFCA. It helped the minority like filibusters are supposed to. It helped the minority but

it hurt the majority, and the majority wanted the union. It hurt the Democrats and the labor unions but it helped the Republicans and businesses. Overall, I think the minority usually deserves more say in how things run. I think overall the filibuster is usually a good thing, but there are cases that show filibusters can be used and abused for the wrong reasons. It's a tough call—there's a lot to consider . . . [long pause] . . . but I think I favor it.

For this student, similar to the previous student, a judgment about the filibuster is reached, but it is a more tentative and uncertain judgment. Rather than reflecting poorly on students, I find this particular struggle to be impressive; these students have grasped the significant challenges inherent in dealing with this controversial legislative procedure.

What is left is to bring the experts into the equation. All faculty members interviewed immediately put the filibuster under the broader theme of majority rules and minority rights. The first three quotations from faculty interviews speak to this point in a straightforward way.

- We talk about minority viewpoints and the idea that in a healthy democracy you've got to have outlets for those viewpoints.
- The time it is most often to come up [in class discussion] is under majority rule and minority rights, because that's really what it's about.
- . . . protection of minorities, making sure that you don't have oppression of the minority by the majority.

The next two quotes go a little bit more into depth, beginning from the perspective of protecting the minority and then moving into other issues, such as the desire to slow the legislative body down (in the first quote) and to foster consensus building (second quote).

[I teach] it to explain how Congress works sometimes in an antidemocratic way, that there are counter-majoritarian measures that Congress uses to slow itself down, and that these things were created over time, and that these were mechanisms by which the body sort of protects itself from making rash and quick choices.

It makes the game a little more important for the minority party; it usually leads to a discussion of the importance of having ability to say no . . . and how that tends to lead to consensus building, which is what I think our system is designed to do.

The collection of quotes from the faculty interviews indicate that all of the faculty members are coming from a stronger, and a more integrated, understanding of the filibuster than are the students. Not surprisingly, faculty members are not caught in the same bottlenecks that ensnare students. Importantly, however, we can see the conceptual leaps that are possible once this bottleneck is overcome.

Discussion

One critique that is leveled with increasing frequency against the scholarship of teaching and learning is its failure to connect research on teaching and learning with improved teaching practice. In her well-received keynote address at the 2008 International Society for the Scholarship of Teaching and Learning Conference, Sue Clegg noted, "If the question is about improving teaching . . . the answer cannot solely be with scholarship." More pungently, Maryellen Weimer (2002) has suggested that literature in the scholarship of teaching and learning is "more likely to cure insomnia than to improve practice." Given this concern, it is well worth some time to directly connect this work to concrete ways in which we can improve practice (see McKinney 2007, chapter 9, for more work on application and SOTL).

What have we learned here that speaks to these points? First, bottlenecks matter. Bottlenecks (or threshold concepts) exist in all disciplines, and in all courses. If faculty can invest time in investigating student learning as a means of identifying where these bottlenecks are, the benefits will be significant. It will enable us to meet students where they are, which learning theories (Svinicki 2004) and brain research (Zull 2002) argue is important. The examples in this chapter show that the experts (along with the strongest novices) were far ahead of the novices in their understanding because they had moved past the critical bottlenecks. Thus, bottlenecks should become important focal points for faculty teaching in their discipline.

Moreover, those of us teaching about politics must explore with students the *necessary* conflict inherent in the political system. More than simply lecturing our students that this is the case, we would be on even stronger ground if we are able to *show* these lessons to students. Simulations, for example, can help show students that some political issues are zero-sum; when one side wins, another loses. Internships, service learning, or other activities that bring students into the actual political world, can be critical for helping students to see that some issues matter a great deal to many people, and are worth fighting for wholeheartedly.

When students internalize these lessons (that some conflict is inevitable and worth having), they are on their way to overcoming these bottlenecks. They will be realistic citizens, aware that conflict does not represent a failure of the system but rather represents the necessary task that government has of reconciling competing interests and demands of its citizenry. When the stakes are high enough, and the differences irreducible, conflict will occur. Understanding this will enable students to understand that political actors do not necessarily "play nice"—hence, they will more richly understand many political actions, including the use of the filibuster.

Additionally, we need to emphasize the important tensions between majority rules and minority rights whenever we teach government classes. This tension is important for understanding the filibuster—and for understanding the legislative process, checks and balances, public opinion, and countless other topics in political science. This concept can become a recurring theme; evidence presented in this paper suggests that perhaps it should be. Once again, those who understand this tension make significant strides in their political science thinking.

Bottlenecks matter—and studying how experts and novices work their way through bottlenecks helps us to understand their importance. This chapter has demonstrated that students who are able to get past critical bottlenecks in their disciplines are able to do things related to thinking in the disciplines that those who do not understand bottlenecks are unable to do. It would behoove people teaching across the disciplines to carefully explore what the bottlenecks might be in their disciplines and courses, and to teach with an aim toward addressing them (much as Shopkow et al. suggest in this volume). Time spent doing that will be time well spent.

NOTES

This work was funded by research grants from the Spencer Foundation and from the Dirksen Congressional Research Center. Earlier versions of this chapter were presented at the Annual Meeting of the Southern Political Science Association (January 2009) and in a talk at the Congress in the Classroom Workshop at the Dirksen Congressional Research Center (July 2009). I am grateful to participants in each of these sessions for their comments and challenging questions that helped improve this paper.

1. Hutchings (2000) offers a useful perspective on the role of these "What is?" or "What does it look like?" questions within the scholarship of teaching and learning.

2. This is not to say, of course, that novices must completely copy expert behavior; there may be multiple ways to approach a task, and different experts (and novices) may have their own preferences for how the task should be done. But learning from

a *range* of expert behaviors is likely to help novices in the quest to improve their performance on disciplinary tasks.

3. On expertise in general, see Chi, Glaser, and Farr (1988).

4. This may not be surprising, since only a small number of the experts in Wineburg's study were scholars of American history; there is little reason to expect a historian of Japan, or a historian of the medieval period, to know specific details of the American Revolution. What is telling about Wineburg's work, however, is how the lack of topic-specific knowledge proved no impediment to these historians' abilities to "think like historians" about the puzzle Wineburg posed to them.

5. On a typical measure in the Senate, a simple majority of 51 votes (out of 100 senators) would be enough to pass legislation. However, under Senate procedure, a senator or group of senators may stage a filibuster, in which the opposition holds the floor and prevents the Senate from proceeding to a vote on the legislation in question. Filibusters can be cut off by passing a *cloture* resolution, which would end the filibuster and permit the Senate to continue the process of considering the bill. A vote of cloture requires 60 votes. Thus, a minority of 41 individuals can effectively hold the Senate hostage, since the majority could not get the 60 votes required to invoke cloture and end the filibuster. On the filibuster, its historical development, and contemporary efforts to reform it, see Koger (2010) and Wawro and Schickler (2007).

6. As evidence of this, we can witness the banner headlines and extensive coverage of the January 19, 2010 special Senate election in Massachusetts, in which Scott Brown (R) defeated Martha Coakley (D) to fill the remainder of the late Edward Kennedy's senate term. The election, which normally would have merited little media attention, was of paramount importance, since losing this seat left the Democrats one vote shy of a filibuster-proof majority of 60 votes. Ultimately, the Obama administration was able to push its health reform bill through the Senate using the somewhat obscure legislative procedure of reconciliation, under which filibusters are not permitted.

7. In view of the assault on collective bargaining rights for public employees in early 2011, the priorities of organized labor certainly are changing to respond to new political circumstances.

8. The full bill is, of course, much more complicated, and multifaceted, than this description suggests. Additionally, existing labor law is quite complex. This description, however, is similar to what was presented to the students and provides a reasonable summary of one of the critical issues at stake in the battle for passage of the law. This piece of the bill, for example, is the one most likely to be reported in news accounts of the bill and its struggle for passage, and in television commercials regarding the bill.

9. Obviously, this need not always be the case. Both sides could come together and realize they have ways of working together, and that a smooth resolution of a contract could yield positive benefits for both sides. No doubt this happens, most likely far more often than we think. However, most of the time when union-management issues generate any publicity, it is because both sides are acting in a zero-sum manner rather than in a mutually cooperative manner.

10. To be fair, even had filibuster not existed and the bill been passed by the Senate, it was headed for an almost certain veto from President Bush.

11. Expletive edited.

REFERENCES

Association of College and Research Libraries. 2000. *Information Literacy Competency Standards for Higher Education.* Chicago: American Library Association.

Bain, Robert B. 2000. "Into the Breach: Using Research and Theory to Shape History Instruction." In *Knowing, Teaching, and Learning History: National and International Perspectives,* ed. Peter N. Stearns, Peter Seixas, and Sam Wineburg, 331–52. New York: New York University Press.

Bernstein, Jeffrey L. 2008. "Cultivating Civic Competence: Simulations and Skill-Building in an Introductory Government Class." *Journal of Political Science Education* 4, no. 1: 1–20.

———. 2010. "Using Think-Alouds to Understand Variations in Political Thinking." *Journal of Political Science Education* 6, no. 1: 1–21.

Bowen, Craig W. 1994. "Think-Aloud Methods in Chemistry Education: Understanding Student Thinking." *Journal of Chemical Education* 71, no. 3: 184–90.

Boyer, Ernest L. 1990. *Scholarship Reconsidered: Priorities of the Professoriate.* Princeton: Carnegie Foundation for the Advancement of Teaching.

Chase, W. G., and Herbert A. Simon. 1973. "Perception in Chess." *Cognitive Psychology* 4, no. 1: 55–81.

Chi, Michelene T. H., Robert Glaser, and Marshall J. Farr, eds. 1988. *The Nature of Expertise.* Hillsdale, NJ: Lawrence Erlbaum.

Clegg, Sue. 2008. "The Struggle for Connections." International Society for the Scholarship of Teaching and Learning Conference. Edmonton, Alberta, Canada.

Díaz, Arlene, Joan Middendorf, David Pace, and Leah Shopkow. 2008. "The History Learning Project: A Department 'Decodes' Its Students." *Journal of American History* 94, no. 4: 1211–24.

Ericsson, K. Anders, and Herbert A. Simon. 1984. *Protocol Analysis: Verbal Reports as Data.* Cambridge, MA: MIT Press.

Gurung, Regan A. R., Nancy L. Chick, and Aeron Haynie. 2009. *Exploring Signature Pedagogies: Approaches to Teaching Disciplinary Habits of Mind.* Sterling, VA: Stylus.

Hibbing, John R., and Elizabeth Theiss-Morse. 1995. *Congress as Public Enemy: Public Attitudes Toward American Political Institutions.* New York: Cambridge University Press.

———. 1996. "Civics Is Not Enough: Teaching Barbarics in K–12." *PS: Political Science and Politics* 29, no. 1: 57–62.

———. 2002. *Stealth Democracy: Americans' Beliefs about How Government Should Work.* New York: Cambridge University Press.

Huber, Mary Taylor, and Pat Hutchings. 2005. *The Advancement of Learning: Building the Teaching Commons.* San Francisco: Jossey-Bass.

Huber, Mary Taylor, and Sherwyn Morreale, eds. 2002. *Disciplinary Styles in the Scholarship of Teaching and Learning: Exploring Common Ground.* Washington, DC: American Association for Higher Education and the Carnegie Foundation for the Advancement of Teaching

Hutchings, Pat. 2000. "Introduction: Approaching the Scholarship of Teaching and Learning." In *Opening Lines: Approaches to the Scholarship of Teaching and Learning,* ed. Pat Hutchings. Menlo Park, CA: Carnegie Publications.

Koger, Gregory. 2010. *Filibustering: A Political History of Obstruction in the House and Senate.* Chicago: University of Chicago Press.

McKinney, Kathleen. 2007. *Enhancing Learning through the Scholarship of Teaching and Learning: The Challenges and Joys of Juggling.* San Francisco: Jossey-Bass.

Meyer, Jan H. F., and Ray Land. 2003. "Threshold Concepts and Troublesome Knowledge (1): Linkages to Ways of Thinking and Practising within the Disciplines." In *Improving Student Learning—Ten Years On,* ed. Chris Rust. Oxford: Oxford Center for Staff and Learning Development.

———. 2005. "Threshold Concepts and Troublesome Knowledge (2): Epistemological Considerations and a Conceptual Framework for Teaching and Learning." *Higher Education* 49: 373–88.

Neblo, Michael A., Kevin M. Esterling, Ryan P. Kennedy, David M. J. Lazer, and Anand E. Sokhey. 2010. "Who Wants to Deliberate—and Why?" *American Political Science Review* 104, no. 3: 566–83.

Niemi, Richard, and Jane Junn. 1998. *Civic Education: What Makes Students Learn.* New Haven: Yale University Press.

Pace, David. 2004. "The Amateur in the Operating Room: History and the Scholarship of Teaching and Learning." *American Historical Review* 109, no. 4: 1171–92.

Patel, Vimla L., Guy J. Groen, and C. H. Frederiksen. 1986. "Differences between Students and Physicians in Memory for Clinical Cases." *Medical Education* 20, no. 1: 3–9.

Perkins, D. N. 1981. *The Mind's Best Work.* Cambridge: Cambridge University Press.

Sandefur, James. 2007. "Problem Solving: What I Have Learned from My Students." In *Enhancing University Mathematics: Proceedings of the First KAIST International Symposium on Teaching,* ed. Ki Hyoung Ko and Deane Arganbright. Providence, RI: American Mathematical Society.

Svinicki, Marilla D. 2004. *Learning and Motivation in the Postsecondary Classroom.* Boston: Anker Publishing.

Thornton, Stephen. 2010. "From 'Scuba-Diving' to 'Jet-Skiing': Information Behavior, Political Science, and the Google Generation." *Journal of Political Science Education* 6, no. 4: 353–68.

Voss, James F., and Timothy A. Post. 1988. "On the Solving of Ill-Structured Problems." In *The Nature of Expertise,* ed. Micheline T. H. Chi, Robert Glaser and Marshall J. Farr. Hillsdale, NJ: Lawrence Erlbaum.

Wawro, Gregory J., and Eric Schickler. 2007. *Filibuster: Obstruction and Lawmaking in the U.S. Senate.* Princeton, NJ: Princeton University Press.

Weimer, Maryellen. 2002. *Learner-Centered Teaching: Five Key Changes to Practice.* San Francisco: Jossey-Bass.

Wineburg, Samuel S. 1991. "Historical Problem Solving: A Study of the Cognitive Processes Used in the Evaluation of Documentary and Pictorial Evidence." *Journal of Educational Psychology* 83, no. 1: 73–87.

Wineburg, Sam. 2001. *Historical Thinking and Other Unnatural Acts: Charting the Future of Teaching the Past.* Philadelphia: Temple University Press.

Zull, James E. 2002. *The Art of Changing the Brain: Enriching Teaching by Exploring the Biology of Learning.* Sterling, VA: Stylus.

CHAPTER 5

The History Learning Project "Decodes" a Discipline: The Union of Teaching and Epistemology

LEAH SHOPKOW, ARLENE DÍAZ, JOAN MIDDENDORF, AND DAVID PACE

Thirty years of the scholarship of teaching and learning have provided a plethora of books about teaching, containing potential assessments, advice about course design, teaching tips, and prescriptions. Much of this work, which arises from practical classroom experience, useful as it may be, treats symptoms—specific student difficulties—rather than diagnosing the underlying illness, so that there is no framework for applying solutions. The "Decoding the Disciplines" ("Decoding") methodology provides such a framework; it has led us first to identify and then classify student difficulties or "bottlenecks" in history. These turned out to be closely related to the epistemology of the discipline. While we do not expect that most of our students will become historians, our charge as college teachers is to teach students to think historically, whatever they go on to do, and this means that they must understand the ways of knowing of our discipline. Our teaching has been radically altered by this insight. We have found that the disconnect between epistemology and teaching is standard in many other disciplines. If we are to change student learning through our efforts, we will need to delve into the heart of this darkness.

"Decoding the Disciplines," a methodology developed by Joan Middendorf and David Pace as part of the Freshman Learning Project (Pace and Middendorf 2004), arose from the realization that there is a disciplinary unconscious, automatic moves learned tacitly by experts.[1] Teachers expect, however, that students will be able to make these moves equally automatically, without being told to do so, much less how or why they should. Pace and Middendorf developed an interviewing process that helps faculty see moves that are so deeply ingrained that they are invisible, and render these moves explicit. The methodology is a series of steps, beginning with the identification of the "bottleneck" the teacher is concerned with and ending with sharing the results, which we are doing here (see table 5.1).

The History Learning Project (HLP) has focused the decoding methodology on a single discipline. We began by interviewing twenty-seven faculty members in history about their students' difficulties. The faculty discussed an impressive list of bottlenecks (Díaz et al. 2008). What we did not realize at the time is that these bottlenecks all arise from the failure of the students to understand the epistemology of the discipline and of faculty to teach it explicitly.

The discipline of history does not proceed by laws and theories that are refined and updated (Mink 1966) and are widely accepted, nor does it seem to have essential "threshold concepts" (Meyer and Land 2006). Philosophers of history are not fully agreed on the nature of history, but they concur that history is narrative in form (Carr 2008) and that historical practice is held together by common features such as colligation, the linking of evidence from many sources into webs of meaning (McCullough 1989). Because interpretation plays such a powerful role in creating historical knowledge, history (and the other social scientific and humanist disciplines) can produce mutually incompatible truths, or explanatory pluralism (Van Bouwel and Weber 2008).

Students (and most laypeople), in contrast to historians, tend to assume that history is about facts (Wineburg 2001). They have mostly experienced historical facts as "display knowledge" and fixed narratives, rather than as objects for historical analysis (Barton and Levstik 2004). Consequently, they see history as uncontested and unintellectual. If historians disagree, one of them is "wrong" or "biased." The students do not understand that their job is interpreting the "facts," nor do they see that just like other interpreters, they themselves have a vantage point (often referred to as positionality in the pedagogical literature). In the absence of awareness of their own positionality, they cannot contextualize either contemporary historical writing or the actions of people in the past (Seixas 1994; VanSledwright 1997–98). So when we ask students to analyze, they tell us what happened.

This is not surprising. In most history classes, students are shown the end products of historical thinking, such as scholarly books, and are expected to be able to execute similar historical thinking untaught. They are tacitly expected to derive sophisticated meanings, perhaps from a single source, that historians themselves have arrived at only after long study and reading many sources. Students can learn to do these things, but they will be able to do so only if their instructors can ground the instruction in well-articulated, epistemologically justified moves and provide effective modeling, a lot of scaffolding, frequent practice, and regular feedback. While not all students will fully master disciplinary moves, the goal is for all students to make progress toward this.

TABLE 5.1. The Steps of the "Decoding the Disciplines" Methodology

Step 1	What is a bottleneck to learning in this class, a place where many students consistently fail to master crucial material?
Step 2	What do specialists do to get past this bottleneck?
Step 3	How can I explicitly model these operations for students?
Step 4	How can I give my students an opportunity to practice and get feedback on each of these operations?
Step 5	How can I motivate students and address the affective side of learning?
Step 6	How can I tell whether students have mastered these operations by the end of the process?
Step 7	How can I share what I have learned with others?

Each of us has taken a different method to resolving these student difficulties in our classes, but we share a common approach. The methodology is not prescriptive about what is most important, so each of us has focused on a bottleneck from our list that is crucial to learning in our individual classes. While we continue to teach essential historical skills—to "play the whole game" (Perkins 2008)—we decode the bottleneck we have chosen for our students all semester long, assessing their work both in progress and at the end.[2]

Our assessments have presented a methodological issue; social science research has traditionally relied on multiple coders independent of the instructor to turn qualitative data into quantitative data for analysis. In history, content knowledge and interpretative skill are powerfully interdependent (Leinhardt and Young 1996). Students need to know the content of an historical field in order to interpret within it competently, so a single instrument is not practical. Furthermore, historians generally only know the literature and sources of their own historical fields. An independent coder would not only need to know a given field well but also what specific materials the students in the course have been exposed to. Thus, to date, each of us has coded his or her own students' work. We began this way in order to make it very clear to ourselves what the criteria ought to be. We are now developing coding rubrics and testing them for inter-coder reliability. It is in this light that readers should take the evidence from the individual studies that follow.

David Pace: Assumptions and Values

Is there any common classroom experience more frustrating to both student and instructor than the effort to explain what it would take to transform a B+ paper into an A? A B+ student has done the work, understood the material, and written clearly. There is something missing—usually an analysis that transforms the repetition of the ideas encountered in the course into a personal interpretation of the phenomenon in question. But if the student understood how to create such an analysis or that such an analysis was required in history, he or she would probably already have done so.

The "Decoding the Disciplines" process allowed me to escape from this pedagogical catch-22. In an upper-level seminar on the history of Western ideas about conflict and competition since the Middle Ages, a central bottleneck to learning had been the fact that many students did not know how to move beyond a simple summary of ideas of the authors we read to create an analysis of different perspectives on conflict and competition, a crucial part of the way history creates knowledge about the past. With some guidance, most of my students were able to master the complex mental operations required to understand the often archaic words of these authors. But they often had great difficulty identifying the deeper patterns of reasoning that marked each thinker and distinguishing each system from those that preceded or followed it. They could provide the historical equivalent of a plot summary, but real analysis escaped them.

I could not help my students surmount this obstacle until I had defined for myself at least some of the operations that I, as a professional in the field, automatically perform to move from summary to analysis. The list of ways to make this transition is potentially quite extensive, but in this course I chose to place particular emphasis on two: the identification of the assumptions and of the values that are implicit in a text. As many of our interviews indicated, beneath these two skills there lurked a more fundamental capacity—the ability to recognize that choices must be made in the production of any historical object and that these choices reflect the concerns, values, and assumptions of the period in question.

Now I needed to find strategies for modeling these processes for my students. To help prepare students to recognize the constructed nature of historical sources, I first showed them a series of classic gestalt images, and we briefly discussed how the decision to foreground particular elements can completely alter the viewer's comprehension of the object. Then each learning team was asked to retell a classic story (Cinderella, the three little pigs, and so forth) from an entirely different point of view. Finally, I asked the teams to come up with a list of issues of concern to either the medieval theologian Thomas Aquinas or the early eighteenth-century writer Bernard Mandeville. Using the new Prezi presentation software, I entered the items they had produced (the afterlife, economic productivity, and so forth) around the names of both Aquinas and Mandeville. I then asked the class how important each quality was first to Aquinas and then to Mandeville, making the term expand or contract on the screen in response to the students' instructions. As the contrasts grew between the two representations, the students saw how differently the two writers organized their universe.

Over the remainder of the semester, I used class discussions to model the processes involved in identifying the assumptions and values built into particular passages, frequently asking them to contrast the values or assumptions behind specific passages from writers with very different world views. But as the decoding model suggests, it is rarely sufficient simply to demonstrate a complex disciplinary operation. Therefore, I gave students opportunities to practice and get feedback on these skills through in-class collaborative activities and online weekly assignments.[3] In the fourth week, for example, an online assignment began by requiring students to answer several questions about Thomas Hobbes's views on particular topics and then asked them to describe one assumption he made about human nature. They had to provide a passage in which this assumption could be detected and explain what about this passage convinced them that Hobbes was making this assumption. Then they were given the second sentence of the American Declaration of Independence ("We hold these truths . . .") and were asked to describe briefly one assumption of Hobbes that would have made him think that this passage was nonsense. Similar tasks were repeated across the semester, since multiple exposures to new ways of thinking are almost always required to fix them in students' minds.

Now that I had defined a bottleneck and the operations required to surmount it, modeled those operations for my students, and given them opportunities to practice and receive feedback, there remained the task of assessing the extent to which they had successfully mastered these skills. The earlier steps of the process made this easier because I was judging student mastery of two specific, well-defined abilities, rather than a vague and global concept like critical thinking. Moreover, the normal activities of the course itself provided a good deal of information about the extent that students had internalized these skills. For example, at the end of the course, I asked the students to write a letter to an imaginary friend giving advice about how to succeed in the course. Without any prompting and knowing that I would not see their "letters" until after the grades had been turned in, almost half of the students spontaneously referred (directly or indirectly) to the process of identifying assumptions and values as a crucial element. One student wrote, "The readings will challenge your understanding of history and deal mostly with ideas instead of facts. Look at the values and assumptions of the authors." Another suggested that "Professor Pace likes us to look at the assumptions and values underlying thought, at least in part because it gives us some degree of empathy for others. This is not trivial, and it is a valuable skill even in our daily lives."

I could also look at students' work across the semester to see if their mastery of these operations increased. While such comparisons can never provide absolute proof of learning, because the materials that students were working on at different points in the semester were not the same, they are highly suggestive. Therefore, I compared students' success in moving beyond literal descriptions in the questions concerning Hobbes's assumptions in the online assignment from the fourth week with their work on a parallel assignment from the end of the course. The comparisons showed significant improvement over this eleven-week period. I ranked their responses on a five-point scale (1 = repetition of literal meaning; 5 = polished presentation of the assumptions implicit in the text; n=20). The average score moved from 2.3 to 3.5, an increase of 34 percent. While I did not have a parallel assignment from early in the semester that focused on values, an analysis of a question from the fifteenth week using a similar scale produced an average value of 3.4 in their identification of writers' values.

These results, buttressed by other student work, suggest that the decoding process is giving me new tools to offer my students ways of thinking that produce successful history papers and that can be extremely useful throughout life. They also make it clear that there remains a minority of students who are still not fully mastering these skills. For their sake, I need to reexamine my model of historical thinking to see whether there are steps that I have left out and to add further in-class and online exercises that give them more practice. But I now have tools that are effective and I can answer with a much greater level of precision what is needed to transform a B+ paper into an A.

Joan Middendorf: Navigating Affective Bottlenecks

The literature on emotions and learning indicates that "human emotion is completely intertwined with behavior, memory, and decision making" (Dragon et al. 2008). Although historians talk about this only infrequently, and generally in the context of controversial topics (see Percoco 2001; Pace 2003), nearly all of the twenty-seven faculty members we interviewed mentioned emotional issues in learning. While these faculty members related this issue to different subject matters, this passage from an interview captured one of the important issues.

> When I talk about the rise of Anglo-Saxonism in 1870s and 1880s and manifest destiny, some students will say, "Hey! You're attacking my heritage," or "You're attacking this part of me," or "This is part of who I am and stop beating up on us." Other students will say, "Oh, that is so remote; I'm glad we don't have to worry about that anymore." . . . To the extent that [students] identify personally with the negative stuff, they are turned off. To the extent to which they can identify with a kind of the notion of a dominant culture or white culture, without feeling targeted or without feeling some kind of moral guilt or anything, then they do engage. [Professor G., Indiana University, interview by Middendorf and Pace, August 4, 2006]

Students like the ones described here bear no responsibility for the actions of nineteenth-century people, and therefore shouldn't feel guilty, but their sense of implication can lead them to respond on an emotional level rather than in the ways demanded by history's epistemology. The decoding process gave me a way to separate out these intertwined cognitive bottlenecks from emotional ones. Our experiments showed us that students cognitively frame ideas in different ways, some of which have a strong emotional charge (for instance, ideas routinely set in a patriotic framework). When the content of history approaches this material and appears to threaten its validity, students become distressed and may reject history's approach or "program of truth" (Veyne 1988).

A careful analysis of the faculty interviews revealed two kinds of preconceptions that we call disciplinary preconceptions and narrative preconceptions. Disciplinary preconceptions, misunderstandings about the nature and function of a discipline, shape how students practice the discipline and apply the "methods" of the field. These are the "ritual interactions" referred to by Robert Bain (2006), which have been inculcated over years of schooling, which for the most part do not derive from history's epistemology. When faculty members do not accept "ritual" products, students get frustrated. But due to limitations of space, I will focus here on the narrative preconceptions that students carry around in their heads about the content of the discipline. Consciously or unconsciously, students have powerful emotional attachments to these narratives, which relate to their self-identity, their religion,

their patriotic feelings, and their racial ideas, and these are frequently reinforced by what they hear in the media. When these narratives are threat-
ened, students may conclude that the teacher is "biased" or that the course is
"worthless" or simply "wrong."

To investigate student emotions in history, I formed the Affective
Learning Project with the assistance of the History Learning Project (HLP)
Graduate Research and Faculty Fellows. The experiments were carried out
in José Najar's class, Introduction to Latino History, a freshman course with
twenty to thirty students that provides an overview of the historical and cultural experiences of Latinos in the United States. Najar was actively involved
as we designed lessons, created opportunities for student practice and feedback, and assessed changes in the students' skills across successive semesters
for over two years.

We began by reviewing the literature on student misconceptions[4] such as
that of Michelene Chi (2008). She shows that to bring about a conceptual shift
in science requires the instructor to understand the categories students are
applying erroneously in their thinking and explicitly to teach them the characteristics of the applicable category side-by-side with their preconception. So
our first task was to identify what students were bringing into the classroom.

To assess the students' preconceptions prior to a lesson about Mexican
cyclical migration, we constructed a pre-test where students were given a
blank map of the Americas and were asked to draw a model of how Mexican
immigration has looked historically. Visual assessments are especially useful
to get at narrative preconceptions. (See Leah Shopkow's section in this chapter and Trustees 2011.) In Fall 2010 and Spring 2011, 57 percent and 66 percent of the students respectively drew maps that indicated a unidirectional
model of immigration from Mexico to the United States. We began referring
to this as the "invasion model." (These students' drawings often showed a
hail of arrows moving from Mexico and converging on the United States.)
Relatively few students (7 percent in Spring 2011) showed a sophisticated
understanding of Mexican migration, including *change* over time, while the
rest of the students demonstrated a somewhat complex view of Mexican
migration, which incorporated multidirectional immigration or included
vague references to historical context. Students were shown the results of
this pre-test. Barney Glaser and Anselm Strauss's (1967) constant comparative method was used for naturalistic data analysis.

Next, to show the teacher's narrative—a complex, multidirectional migration that changed over time—we designed a concept lesson. Presenting the
new way of thinking first through a familiar metaphor or vivid analogy outside the discipline works with memory principles (Savion and Middendorf

1994) and helps students retain the way historians approach historical problems by cognitively moving them away from a purely emotional understanding of the discipline. Najar's concept lesson described the cyclical migration of monarch butterflies to help students understand the pattern of Mexican cyclical migration. The underlying concept that students should have grasped from this concept lesson was that established life patterns take precedence over changing political borders. For the practice part of the concept lesson, students discussed examples of cyclical migration they had noticed in their own lives in small groups.

After the concept lesson, Najar gave his students the same map exercise that he gave for the pre-test to see if their concepts of cyclical migration had changed. In Fall 2010, 24 percent of the students reproduced a linear model and 76 percent drew a cyclical model. In Spring 2011, 3 percent of the students reproduced a linear model and 97 percent drew a cyclical model. This shows that the concept lesson improved comprehension of cyclical migration. By assessing student preconceptions, we were able to understand what they brought to the lesson and redirect them to a more complex, more historical way of thinking.

Knowledge of student preconceptions allowed Najar to provide students with an historical cognitive framework so that they did not default to a purely emotional one. While students may still be upset that their narratives are not featured in a course, careful attention to their preconceptions reassures them that their ideas are taken seriously. They need help to understand that the purpose of the class is not to indoctrinate or accuse them or their families, but to provide them with the skills of historical analysis so that they can explore and evaluate the range of perspectives and explanations over a single historical issue.

The simplified, emotionally charged narratives students bring into the classroom often disrupt the learning process before it even begins and prevent students from engaging in historical thinking. With such a drastically different understanding of the past, students struggle in a class that emphasizes complexity and ambiguity rather than simple identification. To their ears, the terms and ideas of such an approach sound like a foreign language. Knowing how students conceive of the subject matter before they enter the classroom makes the teacher better able to teach charged material. It also makes the students more aware of how they think about the material so that they are better able to distinguish between historical and nonhistorical ways of creating knowledge. This is our working prescription for helping students move through the bottleneck. It is toward this end that we will continue to refine our understanding of affect in the history classroom.

Arlene Díaz: Motivation and Accountability

Successfully introducing students to the ways of thinking in a discipline often requires careful consideration of teaching techniques that foster student motivation (step 5), because learning new ways of thinking requires hard intellectual work. In my Colonial Latin American history survey course, I identified the places where my students got "stuck." I carefully modeled how students should analyze historical sources and put the sources in conversation with other course materials in order to build a thesis statement. And I provided many opportunities for practice during the semester. Yet students were not using that knowledge to their advantage in their final essays. Just showing them the critical skills they needed did not capture their minds and hearts. Therefore, I adopted the Team-Based Learning (TBL) format to motivate the students to embrace new mental moves. TBL shifts content study outside of the classroom. Students come to class prepared to take individual and team quizzes, spending the majority of class time in team application projects (Michaelson, Knight, and Fink 2004).

In that first TBL course experiment, multiple-choice quizzes focused student attention on the arguments of the readings and the supporting evidence for them. To make it clear to the students that history is not simply remembering facts, I let students bring two pages of notes to the quizzes. The application projects built on the students' prior consideration of the arguments of others but targeted the skills I wanted my students to master: the analysis of different sources to solve a historical problem and the deployment of evidence to support a thesis statement. In the process of building this class, I realized that this TBL format was close to the way historians create meaning. Instead of listening to top-down lectures (which historians do relatively rarely), students in a TBL class work in teams to understand sources and analyze them, paying attention to their multiple perspectives, and then come up with the best answer they can based on their available evidence. All of these steps replicate activities historians routinely carry out, except for working in teams. Most of the class time was spent in a similar execution of the disciplinary skills that I wanted to see from them in their individual essay exams. In this sense, TBL provided a form for my history class that followed its function.

While the class could create a culture of teamwork, which is much desired in the workplace and for the citizens we are educating, students in the humanities have little exposure to teamwork and tend be skeptical about it. This meant that I had to invite the students to buy into putting their individual grades, as some interpreted it, at risk from others. The peer evaluation feature of TBL, which holds students accountable for teamwork, also proved to be a challenge. While this issue requires an article of its own, it is clear that students in the traditional college-age group at Indiana University do not like to evaluate their classmates, and one rarely sees a negative mark on a peer evaluation. The next version of this class will model basic tenets of good teamwork and productive interactions.

Was this "radical experiment" effective? Did the new class format address the motivation issue and get the students to put the required historical skills to work in their essays? To get at these core questions, I used three different assessments. The first analyzed students' essay exams by coding the level of thinking involved in their essays' thesis statement. When the thesis statement demonstrated a high-quality interpretation and synthesis of the course materials, I coded the thesis as a 4. If the thesis answered the question and offered a good interpretation, but had some inaccuracies, I gave it a 3. A broad, vague thesis that showed some understanding but included many inaccuracies would earn a 2, and a vague, inaccurate thesis would get a 1. I did this coding to a sample of the essays from my previous non-TBL 2008 course as well as to the whole class for my 2009 TBL course for comparative purposes. With just a glance at table 5.2, one can see that the TBL class showed progress in the level of thinking demonstrated in their essays' thesis statements throughout the semester, from an average 2.03 argument level to a 2.93 in the final exam. In the non-TBL class, there was a clear regression by the final exam and the improvement in numbers was not as significant as in the TBL class. While there is room for improvement, these results are encouraging.

The second assessment consisted of thirty-minute interviews with five students conducted by the History Learning Project' Graduate Research Fellows and Project Assistant during finals week.[5] Four of the interviewees talked about how the new TBL format encouraged students to devote time and effort to the course, a positive result regarding motivation. Surprisingly, they also described the effects of the course on student learning at the meta-cognitive level. Each student mentioned their concern with not letting their team down, which pushed them to complete most of the readings ahead of time. In addition, these students indicated awareness of the positive effects that team discussion had upon their ability to understand how much they had to read into something, to be specific on their use of evidence, or to further develop their ideas on a project, all of which they agreed helped them to better understand historical concepts. The one student who expressed unhappiness with TBL seemed "stuck" in her expectation that the professor be the sole source of knowledge and the one who should tell students what was important on the exams. Clearly, she did not understand the dynamics of TBL nor the interpretive nature of the discipline that I was fostering in this class.

TABLE 5.2. Comparison of Students' Level of Thinking in Their Essay Exam's Argument in a Non-TBL Class (Fall 2008) and a TBL Class (Fall 2009)

Course	Exam 1	Exam 2	Exam 3	Exam 4	N
Fall 2008 Non-TBL Class	2.12	2.25	1	Only 3 exams in this class	10 (Sample)
Fall 2009 TBL Class	2.03	2.89	2.73	2.93	47

Source: Indiana University, Department of History, H211/L210 "Latin American Culture and Civilization I," Exams, Fall 2008 and Fall 2009. Level of argument goes in a sliding scale from 1 (low level) to 4 (high thinking level).

Course evaluations provided a third assessment of the "radical" TBL experiment. Of the forty-four students who completed the course evaluation, 61 percent responded in a way that strongly indicated some aspect of the course, such as the teamwork, led to an increase in their learning and understanding of the subject matter, while 18 percent said that some aspect of the course—such as the difficulty of the assigned reading or the time allowed for the projects—hindered their ability to comprehend the course materials and to learn. The rest of the respondents did not address the question of learning, comprehension, or skills acquisition in their evaluations. Yet those students who did have a positive learning experience echoed many of the ideas of the interviewees, such as, "I learned the value of getting all sides of the story, to think objectively vs. subjectively when learning about history." The application projects, one student wrote, "were effective in helping me critically think about topics," while another added that "having multiple perspectives on subjects usually made me think of something I wouldn't have before, and as a result I think about things differently." Clearly, the format of the class did have some effect in helping many students open their minds to history's disciplinary way of thinking.

This experiment and students' responses to it convinced me that the structure of a course affects not only student motivation but also conveys the epistemology of the discipline along with the content of the course. I learned that to capture students' minds and hearts, one has to structure the class in a way that becomes meaningful and fun yet holds students accountable. In addition, the course format simulated the way historians operate, reiterating the targeted skills throughout the semester to the point that metacognition was achieved by some students. And while some aspects of this experience will surely need to be modified to reach even more hearts and minds, it provided me with the empirical evidence to get the students to come to their own solutions to historical problems rather than passively accepting those of other people

Leah Shopkow: Grasping the Concept of Historical Audience

Philosophers of history have argued that narrative is deeply engrained as a human way of creating meaning for readers—an audience—and that history explains primarily through narrative (Carr 1986; White 1980). This is why narrative preconceptions are so problematic. Audience is a concept historians use all the time, often informally, to understand primary sources. Even sources that do not seem to have an audience, such as contracts, served social purposes and had conventions that were understood by contemporaries when they read them. When students think about documents like contracts, they can grasp the purpose at the most obvious level but often do not grasp what the conventions meant to the audience. Narratives present even more difficulties for students. They may seem to have no purpose except to tell a particular story and have such a strong "reality effect" (Barthes 1989) that students simply accept them as givens. For many students, narratives do not "mean"; they simply are.

In a class I regularly teach, Medieval Heroes, a lower-level "topics" course of mostly first- and second-year students, my goal has been to get students to understand what narratives about heroes "meant" to the people who were the audiences for their stories. I use both "fictional" and "historical" narratives. But I constantly stumbled over the student tendency to read these works either as simple factual documents or as "just stories." They were unable to see these narratives as I do, as suspended in a web from which they draw their meaning. And yet for true civic engagement, students need to understand this about everything they read.

In the first year of my three-year project, I asked my students to draw the figure of Beowulf from the poem of the same name as the audience would see him. The students were to include citations for each of the traits they chose to illustrate so that I could see how they were reading the text. I was, in other words, examining their conceptions (see figures 5.1, 5.2).

I selected a random sample of twenty-two of the approximately eighty drawings done by students who gave permission to analyze their work (out of 100 students), and counted the overall number of traits the students

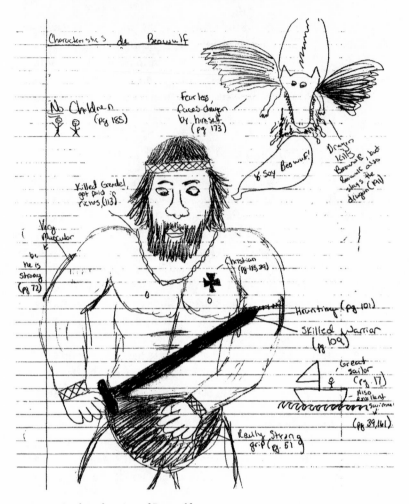

FIGURE 5.1. Student drawing of Beowulf.

illustrated (determined by the number of citations) and classified each trait. The average number of traits in each drawing was twelve. Of these, many qualities were generic, such as courage or strength, qualities possessed by many heroes in many cultures. What makes a hero "mean" something powerful to people of a society, however, are more specific traits, such as the fulfillment of social expectations. These emerge most clearly in character traits and social interactions. On average, however, only three of the twelve traits identified by the students were social or character traits. Since my students were focusing largely on generic qualities, plot points, and objects, rather

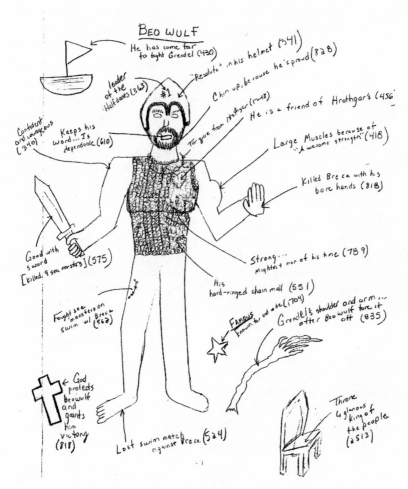

FIGURE 5.2. Student drawing of Beowulf.

than on social relationships or character, they didn't arrive at a portrait *specific to* Anglo-Saxon notions of heroism and thus to Anglo-Saxons. This was reflected in the final essays of the students, few of which demonstrated deep understanding of the concept of audience. To think about audience the way I do, the students would need a deep factual knowledge about the time and place a narrative came from and identify its intended or potential audience. They would have to hypothesize connections between these to arrive at the text's "social logic," the cultural work it was meant to do (Spiegel 1990). And they would need to test their hypotheses rigorously.

I was not providing the depth of content knowledge the students needed to make these moves, so I abandoned the survey approach I had previously taken and divided the course into five units, four from selected time periods and featuring a single hero or type of hero, while the fifth featured a single hero—King Arthur—across the Middle Ages. I hoped the students would, in this last unit, be able to see how changing the audience changed the details of Arthur's story. The students practiced individually in homework assignments but worked in teams to produce a series of posters discussing the audiences of particular texts. Students got feedback after each poster and were guided in the stages of making their posters by teaching assistants in their tutorials. The "final exam" was a juried poster session with a prize awarded by jury of outside judges to encourage the students to be engaged by making their work public.

Of the final sixteen posters, none failed to address the concept of audience in some way. Four posters referred to the concept but only partially grasped it, five connected the texts and their audience (albeit without making the connection entirely clear), four made a good connection and provided a plausible argument for it, while three provided a deep and convincing analysis and a clear presentation. A few posters were quite weak in their grasp both of the concept of audience and of the course content.[6] The poster that won the jury prize had a clear and powerful presentation but had some historical inaccuracies (not caught by the judges who were not medieval specialists) that flawed the argument.

In the third iteration, I simplified the course. The students did only three posters in their teams, but after the second poster we had a mini poster session in which the students were asked to review another team's poster and to critique it, and then afterward to critique their own poster and reflect on how they might improve their performance. In other words, I added a metacognitive element, which I hoped would help students do better on their third posters. As table 5.3 shows, every team improved at least a little across the semester, with a big jump occurring between the second and third posters. In the third posters, one-third of the class demonstrated excellent mastery of the concept of audience.

It was clear that the self-critique was very useful to the students. One student commented that the team needed "more effort on everyone's part, finding more evidence, finding a detailed and thorough hypothesis that is clearly backed by evidence." All five members of this team mentioned the need for more evidence, for the evidence to be more clearly presented, and for the evidence to be more carefully weighed. Their comments could not have been more to the point or more motivational. All five members of this team

TABLE 5.3. Student Mastery of the Concept of Audience in "Medieval Heroes"

Level of Mastery	First Poster	Revised First Poster	Second Poster (including revisions)	Final Poster
Little or None (0)	4	1	0	0
Beginning (1)	7	6	3	1
Partial (2)	1	4	7	5
Good (3)	0	1	2	2
Excellent (4)	0	0	0	4

had arrived at the same conclusions as I had about how to better master the concept of audience. They had grasped the underlying principles by which historical context is created, even if they could not fully execute the moves, and all of the teams had made progress in that direction by the end of the course.

Conclusions

While all four authors of this essay were taking different approaches to nominally different problems, we came to see connections between the discipline and the work we were doing in our classes in the process. As we struggled to help our students understand disciplinary moves, our classrooms became less and less traditional, as did our assignments and assessments. We imported historical practice into our classes or at least a "junior version" of it (Perkins 2008) but also explained why we were doing so. In other words, we drew on the discipline's understanding of itself, its epistemological underpinnings, to structure our classrooms, and we asked our students to play our epistemic games (Collins and Ferguson 1993). In the process, we strove to disrupt the "ritual interactions" of the traditional history classroom (Bain 2006) and to replace them with full-fledged historical analysis.

As Bain points out, students come to us after many years of "ritual interactions" in history classes (Bain 2006). Some of them have done no more than look at a primary source or be told to read it in high school (Barton and Levstik 2004). Instead, they have read the textbook, taken multiple-choice texts, listened to lectures, and been encouraged to memorize facts. If we want to disrupt these rituals, as Bain advocates, we have to be conscious of the signals we send the students. If we seem to replicate the familiar rituals, students will respond as they are accustomed to responding.[7] Instead, in our classrooms, we have over and over again stressed the way historians create knowledge and given students repeated opportunities to solve historical problems for themselves.

The alternative is to make classrooms exclusive clubs, where teachers determine which students are "smart" enough to intuit the processes of the discipline on their own and thus remain. We are disinclined to become educational bouncers. Instead, we are committed to helping students assimilate a mode of thought through explicit discussion of some characteristic of disciplinary thinking and explicit practice in it in each of our classes. Through this union of epistemology and teaching, we hope to create an environment in which to train our students intellectually to use history to think with.

Ernest Boyer (1997) distinguished the scholarship of discovery, where the epistemologies of the disciplines are developed, from the scholarship of teaching. But we would argue that they are inseparable. Effective teaching is deeply rooted in disciplinary understanding. Developing the scholarship of teaching requires systematic inquiry into both disciplinary ways of knowing and student ways of learning. Disciplinary research depends on disciplinary epistemologies to produce knowledge; teaching within the discipline must as well. This realization provides a way to define "signature pedagogies," as described by Lee Shulman (2005); a signature pedagogy must be a form of teaching that most clearly enhances a student's understanding about how a discipline produces knowledge and develops the student's ability to develop this kind of thinking.

We invite those in other disciplines to join us in exploring the relationship between the deep understandings deployed in their disciplinary research and what they teach in their classrooms. Naturally, the disciplines create knowledge in different ways, but our students need to have a basic grasp of all of these ways. Individuals who cannot understand the way history creates knowledge may fall into conspiracy theories. People who cannot understand how scientific theories function may not vaccinate their children. Men and women who do not understand notions of value may make foolish economic choices. Someone outside of the disciplines may well be able to see where students get stuck, but only those with great familiarity with the forms of knowledge of a given discipline can fully articulate why and lead students out of the epistemological bottleneck.

NOTES

The History Learning Project would like to acknowledge the support of grants from the Teagle Foundation, the Spencer Foundation, and the Office of the Vice-Provost for Undergraduate Affairs, College of Arts and Sciences, and the History Department of Indiana University; we are deeply grateful to all of them. We would also like to thank our project participants over the past three years: Keith Eberly, Michael Grossberg, Mayumi Hoshino, Padraic Kenney, Nicole McGrath, Jolanta Mickute, Lauren Miller, Marissa Moorman, José Najar, John Nieto-Phillips, Eric Sandweiss, and Tara Saunders. Finally and not least, we give our thanks to our project assistant, Catherine Brennan, to whom nothing is impossible.

1. Indiana University-Bloomington is a research-extensive, public, "selective" university, with around 40,000 students, most of whom are "traditional" eighteen- to twenty-two-year-old residential students.

2. Our study has been approved by our IRB as #11-11350, approved March 11, 2009. All students are required to consent or refuse to participate in the study. Consents are administered by third parties, who do not inform the instructors until final grades are submitted who has consented. No special work is required from participants.

3. Examples of these questions and other materials discussed in this section may be found on the History Learning Project web site at http://www.iub.edu/~hlp/j300exercises.

4. Because the term "misconception" has the connotation of "wrong" ideas, we use the term "preconception" to designate a preformed idea or opinion that is not shared by scholars or derived by scholarly methods.

5. All students in the class were invited to participate in the interviews and the instructor was neither involved in the invitation process nor in the interview, except as its subject.

6. Readers are welcome to contact me at shopkowl@indiana.edu for the criteria.

7. There has not been enough research on this point, but Russell (2008) found in a very small study that lecturing, even when primary sources were assigned, did not significantly enhance most university students' historical understanding.

REFERENCES

Bain, Robert B. 2006. "Rounding Up Unusual Suspects: Facing the Authority Hidden in the History Classroom." *Teachers College Record* 108, no. 10: 2080–2114.

Barthes, Roland. 1989. "The Reality Effect." In *The Rustle of Language,* trans. Richard Howard, 141–48. Berkeley: University of California Press.

Barton, Keith, and Linda Levstik. 2004. *Teaching History for the Common Good.* Mahwah, NJ: Lawrence Erlbaum.

Boyer, Ernest L. 1997. *Scholarship Reconsidered: Priorities of the Professoriate.* San Francisco: Jossey-Bass.

Carr, David. 1986. "Narrative and the Real World: An Argument for Continuity." *History and Theory* 25: 117–31.

————. 2008. "Narrative Explanation and Its Malcontents." *History and Theory* 47: 19–30.

Chi, Michelene T. H. 2008. "Three Types of Conceptual Change: Belief Revision, Mental Model Transformation, and Categorical Shift." In *The Handbook of Research on Conceptual Change,* ed. Stella Vosniadou, 61–82. Hillsdale, NJ: Lawrence Erlbaum.

Collins, Allan, and William Ferguson. 1993. "Epistemic Forms and Epistemic Games: Structures and Strategies to Guide Inquiry." *Educational Psychologist* 28, no. 1: 25–42.

Díaz, Arlene, Joan Middendorf, David Pace, and Leah Shopkow. 2008. "The History Learning Project: A Department Decodes Its Students." *Journal of American History* 94, no. 4: 1211–24.

Dragon, Toby, Ivon Arroyo, Beverly P. Woolf, Winslow Burleson, Rana el Kaliouby, and Hoda Eydgahi. 2008. "Viewing Student Affect and Learning through Classroom Observation and Physical Sensors." Center for Knowledge Communication, University of Massachusetts–Amherst, http://center forknowledgecommunication.com/publications/recentPubsandAwards /2008/DragonAffectITS08Final.pdf.

Glaser, Barney G., and Anselm L. Strauss. 1967. *The Discovery of Grounded Theory: Strategies for Qualitative Research.* Chicago: Aldine.

Leinhardt, Gaia, and Kathleen McCarthy Young. 1996. "Two Texts, Three Readers: Distance and Expertise in Reading History." *Cognition and Instruction* 14, no. 4: 441–86.

McCullough, C. Behan. 1989. "Unifying Themes of Historical Narratives." *Philosophy of the Social Sciences/Philosophie des sciences sociales* 19, no. 1: 55–74.

Meyer, Jan H. F., and Ray Land. 2006. "Threshold Concepts and Troublesome Knowledge: An Introduction." In *Overcoming Barriers to Student Understanding: Threshold Concepts and Troublesome Knowledge,* ed. Jan H. F. Meyer and Ray Land, 3–18. London: Routledge.

Michaelson, Larry, Arletta Bauman Knight, and L. Dee Fink. 2004. *Team-Based Learning: A Transformative Use of Small Groups in College Teaching.* Miami: Stylus.

Mink, Louis. 1966. "The Autonomy of Historical Understanding." *History and Theory* 15, no. 1: 24–47.

Pace, David. 2003. "Controlled Fission: Teaching Supercharged Subjects." *College Teaching* 51, no. 2: 42–45.

Pace, David, and Joan Middendorf, eds. 2004. *Decoding the Disciplines: Helping Students Learn Disciplinary Ways of Thinking.* Vol. 98, *New Directions for Teaching and Learning.* San Francisco: Jossey-Bass.

Percoco, James A. 2001. *Divided We Stand: Teaching about Conflict in U.S. History.* Portsmouth, NH: Heinemann.

Perkins, David. N. 2008. *Making Learning Whole: How Seven Principles of Teaching Can Transform Education.* San Francisco: Jossey-Bass.

Russell, William Benedict III. 2008. "Constructing Meaning from Historical Content: A Research Study." *Journal of Social Studies Research* 32, no. 2: 1–15.

Savion, Leah, and Joan Middendorf. 1994. "Enhancing Concept Comprehension and Retention." *National Teaching and Learning Forum* 3, no. 4: 6–8.

Seixas, Peter. 1994. "Confronting the Moral Frames of Popular Film: Young People Respond to Historical Revisionism." *American Journal of Education* 102, no. 3: 261–85.

Shulman, Lee S. 2005. "Signature Pedagogies in the Professions." *Daedalus* 134, no. 3: 52–59.

Spiegel, Gabrielle. 1990. "History, Historicism, and the Social Logic of the Text in the Middle Ages." *Speculum* 65: 59–86.

Trustees of Indiana University. 2011. "Indiana University's History Learning Project." Last modified 2011. http://www.iub.edu/~hlp/.

Van Bouwel, Jeroen, and Erik Weber. 2008. "A Pragmatist Defense of Non-relativistic Explanatory Pluralism in History and Social Science." *History and Theory* 47: 168–82.

VanSledwright, Bruce. 1997–98. "On the Importance of Historical Positionality to Thinking About and Teaching History." *International Journal of Social Education* 12, no. 2: 1–18.

Veyne, Paul. 1988. *Did the Greeks Believe in Their Myths? An Essay on the Constitutive Imagination,* trans. Paula Wissing. Chicago: University of Chicago.

White, Hayden. 1980. "The Value of Narrativity in the Representation of Reality." *Critical Inquiry* 7, no. 1: 5–27.

Wineburg, Sam. 2001. *Historical Thinking and Other Unnatural Acts.* Philadelphia: Temple University Press.

CHAPTER 6

Assessing Strategies for Teaching Key Sociological Understandings

CAROLINE HODGES PERSELL
AND ANTONIO E. MATEIRO

Teaching and learning in all disciplines requires decisions about ways of thinking and practicing, and judgments about threshold concepts needed in a discipline, followed by decisions about strategies for teaching and assessing learning. Ways of thinking refer to subject-specific skills and knowledge, including familiarity with the values and conventions governing scholarly endeavors in a disciplinary and professional community (Hounsell and Anderson 2009; McCune and Hounsell 2005). "A threshold concept . . . represents a transformed way of understanding, or interpreting, or viewing something without which the learner cannot progress" (Meyer and Land 2003, 2005, 2006). A final stage is ascertaining whether the methods used were effective in teaching them.

This chapter has two goals: (1) to assess the strategies used for teaching four key understandings in sociology and (2) to reflect on the methods used to assess those strategies. We ask several questions. What understandings did students construct? What aspects of the teaching approach helped or hindered their learning? And why? What can be learned about the strengths and limitations of the assessment strategies used? While clearly the understandings being taught vary from discipline to discipline, key educational goals may overlap and teaching and assessment strategies may transfer between disciplines. Bennett and Dewar (in this volume), for example, stress the importance of having students think within the conceptual framework of mathematics. Although disciplines differ, learning to think within each one is important. Thus, although this chapter is a case study in one discipline, hopefully it will also illuminate SOTL issues relevant for other disciplines.

Efforts to articulate key understandings occur in many disciplines. Some disciplines convene panels or task forces in an effort to articulate what understandings practitioners think are important for novices to gain. For example, in 2001 the American Sociological Association (ASA) appointed a task force to develop a sample curriculum for a college-level introductory sociology course that could be used in colleges or in high schools as an advanced course.[1] The task force articulated learning goals and drafted a possible curriculum.[2] It also collected pedagogical resources (for example, data explorations, films, in-class exercises, simulations, illustrations, and readings) considered effective for teaching those understandings.

Subsequently, the learning goals articulated by the task force were validated by conducting open-ended interviews with peer-recognized leaders (discussed in Persell, Pfeiffer, and Syed 2007) and through a fixed-choice electronic survey asking leaders to rank the learning goals articulated by the task force (Persell 2010). Leaders were also asked in the interviews how they taught those learning goals (reported in Persell, Pfeiffer, and Syed 2008).

The leaders identified were active and acknowledged producers of knowledge in the field. As such, they provided a way for the wider population of people teaching introductory sociology to compare what they stressed in their courses to what a sample of peer-recognized contributors and leaders in the field saw as important. Even if the leaders were not currently teaching introductory sociology, they often taught upper-level undergraduate and graduate courses. Thus, they had a sense of what they would like students to understand after having completed an introductory course. To define a sample of leaders in the field of sociology, we drew on Randal Collins' (1998) view of the socially validated nature of knowledge and professional standing. From this perspective, we, in consultation with the late Carla Howery, then deputy director of the ASA, defined a population of leaders in terms of various forms of peer recognition. We included all presidents of the ASA from 1997 to 2005; the presidents of regional sociological associations as of October 2005; national award recipients, including ASA dissertation award recipients from 1995 to 2005; recipients of the ASA Distinguished Contributions to Teaching Award from 1995 to 2005;[3] scholars who received Fund for the Advancement of the Discipline (FAD) awards[4] from the ASA between 2002 and 2004; and scholars receiving research funding in sociology from the National Science Foundation (NSF) as of November 2005. The final sample size was 103, and 48 percent responded.

Building on the learning goals and teaching strategies identified by the task force and by peer-selected leaders, we chose to examine several active teaching strategies designed to convey an understanding of parts of four of the nine themes[5] sociological leaders deemed important for students to understand after taking an Introduction to Sociology course. Some of the themes are clearly relevant for other sociology courses as well. The specific teaching strategies were ones that could be used and assessed within a two-hour framework. The strategies aimed to teach some understanding of the "social" part of sociology (or learning to think sociologically), the scientific nature of sociology, the centrality of inequality, and the social construction of ideas.

Two learning theories underlie this extended project, namely the theoretical idea of "communities of practice" and constructivism. The interdisciplinary concept of "communities of practice" (well-articulated by John Seely Brown and Paul Duguid [2000], a scientist and educational researcher, respectively) emphasizes that there is much tacit knowledge and understanding that practitioners (whether Xerox repair technicians, doctors, lawyers, scientific researchers, or literary scholars) bring to their work that goes beyond the explicit knowledge that is formally taught. It is important to investigate these understandings. Constructivism as an interdisciplinary learning theory assumes that students retain more of what they learn when they construct their own understandings of the social world, and that it would be best if they could use the tools of practitioners in the field whenever possible. Constructivism influenced the selection of experiences and activities that engage students in developing their own understandings. The teaching strategies all required students to be actively involved in doing something, whether discussion before and after viewing a film or examining data, writing responses to questions before and after viewing data, exploring published abstracts in the field, playing a modified board game, or classifying circles with varied patterns of shading. We believe these active strategies might be used successfully in many disciplines because students "must talk about what they are learning, write about it, relate it to past experiences and apply it to their daily lives. They must make what they learn part of themselves" (Chickering and Gamson 1987).

Research Methods

We used multiple methods to assess the teaching strategies, including small undergraduate student focus groups and qualitative analysis of student responses before, during, and after discussions, writing, exercises, and games. Many instructors rely on class discussion to gauge what students understand, and even more use some kind of writing to evaluate student learning (Baker 1976; Grauerholz and Gibson 2006; Werder and Otis 2010). We used those assessment methods in the context of focus groups, allowing close observation of student reactions, in addition to direct questions about the teaching approach being used after students experience it. Because they were not students in the principal investigator's (PI) class[6] and had never seen the PI before, they may have felt freer to discuss what did not work for them in a particular teaching module and why, as well as say what they thought was helpful. Focus groups are less costly of time and money than individual interviews but offer comparably rich data (Morgan 1988, 20). They yield similar results to surveys while often providing more detail (Ward, Bertrand, and Brown 1991, 266). One limitation of using focus groups is that the number of students is much smaller than the number in most undergraduate classes, so the issue remains whether the method can be "scaled up" to a college class. Concerns over the generalizability of results in SOTL to contexts different from those in which the research was conducted are also cause for caution (Grauerholz and Main, this volume), and which results are context dependent and which are generalizable can be controversial (Scharff, this volume). The flexibility and openness of focus groups can also result in digressions from the research goal (Henderschott and Wright 1993, 158). However, several studies reveal the value of focus groups for learning about the perspectives and thoughts of students (Hendershott and Wright 1993; Pippert and Moore 1999; Robinson and Schaible 1993).

The research reported here was conducted at a large, selective, private, multiethnic urban research university in 2006. After clearing the project and the recruitment methods through the University Human Subjects Review Committee, we recruited participants through advertisements on the university's electronic classified ads and by distributing flyers in introductory sociology, anthropology, and psychology classes. In total, these methods attracted several dozen inquiries and yielded twelve participants. To preserve confidentiality, all participants were assigned a pseudonym consisting of a generic, although gender specific, first and last name, which was used throughout. All participants were paid a token sum of $20.

We conducted four focus groups over a two-month period. Each was devoted to one of the key understandings and used one or more teaching strategies that could be completed in less than two hours. All focus groups were based on scripts prepared in advance by the PI. Focus groups were conducted with between five and eight participants and attended by the three-person research team (consisting of PI, graduate research assistant, and undergraduate research assistant). The PI described the purpose of the study and the focus groups, collected responses to written pre-test questions, taught the theme, and posed the discussion questions.

After the discussion, either a video or an exercise was employed, followed by a discussion based on the film or exercise, and by written or discussion questions. The focus group ended with a series of moderator questions (after the PI left). It was run by the graduate research assistant and sought to obtain students' responses to the teaching strategies used, including their strengths and limitations. The undergraduate research assistant collected consent and student information forms, gave students their pseudonyms, and prepared materials such as handouts and question sheets in advance. Everyone took notes whenever they were not doing something else, and the sessions were tape recorded and transcribed by the undergraduate assistant.

Results

Understanding the Social

The most frequently mentioned teaching goal of sociology leaders was having students understand the "social" part of the field. This refers to the importance of being able to understand and explain behavior in terms of social factors that go beyond an individual's psychological attributes. For a thoughtful discussion of one strategy for teaching this understanding, see Chad Hanson's (2002) work on using depression-era photographs to illustrate the intersection of biography and history.

After a brief introduction, students wrote responses to the question, "Why do you think people commit suicide?" Following this, state-by-state suicide data were distributed, and students were asked to write a response to a second question, "Why do you think suicide rates vary by states?" followed by discussion of their responses. This teaching strategy is very usefully discussed in greater detail by David S. Adams (1993).

Then the film *Quiet Rage: The Stanford Prison Experiment,*[7] was introduced and the following questions were discussed: "How do you think the participants playing the role of prisoner will act?" "Why do you think they will act that way?" "How do you think the participants playing the role of guard will act?" and "Why do you think they will act that way?" The film was then shown, followed by a discussion of the questions "Why do you think the prisoners and guards behaved the way they did in the Zimbardo simulated prison experiment?" "What is the most important idea you got from the film?" "Suppose all the people who were randomly assigned to be guards had instead been assigned to be prisoners, and vice versa. How do you think that would have affected the behavior of the people? Do you think they would have behaved differently? Why or why not?" Returning to the suicide data, students were again asked, "Why do you think the rates vary by states?" These questions were designed to illuminate how students were constructing their ideas about human behavior, and whether their understandings changed as a result of the film, data, and discussion. The session ended with a series of moderator questions regarding participant responses to the materials and exercises.

Comparing student answers written before and after seeing the film suggests that the film was effective in teaching students to see the importance of social as well as psychological factors. When initially asked to give possible reasons for people committing suicide, responses emphasized psychological factors: "I think people commit suicide because of a combination of overwhelming pressures and sadness possibly coupled with some sort of emotional/psychological issue that leads them to this sort of drastic decision, generally after some sort of tragic experience in their lives" (Maria). The answers changed when presented with state-level suicide data, but more opinions changed after seeing the film: "I think it goes back to feeling isolated, trapped in rural areas. People can get around easily in a city and do things on their own, with public transportation, etc. This is less true in rural areas" (Patricia). Her response indicates how she had begun to consider contextual factors that might be related to suicides.

This change is also evident when comparing students' expectations before the video and their responses after seeing what actually happened. Those who had not previously read about the Zimbardo experiment did not believe that the participants would act differently in their roles as prisoners and guards: "There should be no difference between prisoners and guards. Since the assignments [of prisoner/guard roles] were arbitrary, why should there be a difference?" (Jeff). Afterwards, all of the students' responses noted how real the experiment seemed, and how real the situation became: "People can become dehumanizing just to maintain their status as a guard. It's pretty astounding how people can change like that" (Jeff). The reality of the prison experiment captured on the film dramatically affected how students constructed their understanding of behavior.

In the focus group, several students noted the advantage of seeing a video of the Zimbardo experiment over just reading an article about it. Several noted how it made the experiment much more believable: "I've read the article before. When I read it, it was less believable. Actually seeing it was much more effective" (Maria). Another said, "I liked the video 'cause you hear about the experiment. It means a lot to actually see it" (Patricia). These responses suggest the greater power of appropriately chosen visual media compared to textual descriptions of the same experiment. It seems reasonable to infer that well-chosen videos could enhance understandings in history, other social and behavioral sciences, and perhaps even literature, consistent with James Zull's (2002) stress on the importance of using the visual sense in teaching.

The film clearly helped convey to students how powerfully social situations can affect the behavior of individuals. The variations in suicide rates by states also enabled them to go beyond thinking only of individual explanations for suicide and consider possible variations in social contexts. This film and suicide data by states are strategies that could be used in classes of almost any size. In mass classes, students could break into pairs or small groups to discuss some of the questions raised in the focus group. Such discussion is important for helping students construct their own understandings of how social contexts can affect behavior (as underscored by Chickering and Gamson 1987).

Understanding the Scientific Basis of Sociology

The second most frequently mentioned learning goal by sociological leaders was having students understand the scientific basis of sociology, something central to all the social and natural sciences. For particularly useful discussions of this understanding, see Edward Kain (1999) and the January 2006 special issue of *Teaching Sociology* devoted to cultivating quantitative literacy. This focus group occurred in a computer lab with Internet access. Students were asked to give written responses to the questions "Do you think sociology is scientific?" and "Why or why not?" These questions were discussed, and students wrote answers to the questions "What does a field need to have to be a science?" and "What keeps a field from being a science?" which were also discussed. The discussion was followed by a brief PowerPoint presentation by the PI regarding what makes a field scientific.[8] Students were then asked to find and print four sociological abstracts based upon original research studies from the CSA Sociological Abstracts database, on a topic of interest to them. Students discussed the abstracts they found and indicated whether they thought the papers contained primary research or not, and why. This was followed by discussion of the questions "Do you think sociology is scientific?" and "Why or why not?" and the moderator questions about the exercises.

Initially, most wrote that they thought sociology was scientific. Several qualified this by saying that it was not as scientific as hard sciences like physics or biology: "I think it's somewhat scientific, but not quite on the same level as biology, chemistry, physics, and other sciences. Sociology does involve research, theories, and experiments as sciences should. However, it's still somewhat subjective, and mathematical formulas and the like rarely apply to it or aid it in figuring out exact answers" (Mary). Most students mentioned the importance of research, theory, and observation in their answers, and in response to the second written question, "What does a field need to have to be a science?" they identified these as criteria for deciding if a field is scientific. Perhaps because students were largely recruited from introductory social science classes, they were predisposed toward thinking sociology is scientific. Only one felt that sociology is not a science: "No. While sociology uses facts as a springboard for thought and research, it is concerned with human practices which cannot really be predicted. . . . To be able to prove and/or disprove its theories and get the same result every time [is what makes a field scientific]" (Ronald). Even this student, however, who felt sociology was not a science, thought that sociology was fact- and research-oriented.

Because of most students' preexisting beliefs in sociology as a science and because of the relative lack of discussion after the exercise, it is difficult to determine what students learned. Many students did not respond during the post-exercise discussion, and the one student who was skeptical of sociology as a science responded after the exercise by saying "I don't know. There is definitely scientific method, but it's being used to . . . but that's still . . . I still have my doubts" (Ronald). Interestingly, while some students were unable to determine whether an article was research-based or not, at least one was analyzing the articles based on their abstracts and suggesting some flaws in a given study: "Well, one thing I noticed was that a lot of my data was from surveys, and like, the thing is, once I read that this many teens smoke pot, but to get that information they would have to . . . ask 'do you smoke pot,' but then there might have been kids who don't admit or kids who almost tried it and feel that counts and it's not exact" (Patricia). In this example, the student was thinking critically about the research studies she had found, a learning goal many would affirm in higher education.

Reactions to this exercise were not particularly positive in the moderator questions. Although they enjoyed being able to choose the topics they explored in the abstracts database, at least two students were unclear as to the point of the exercise: "Maybe I missed something, but today we . . . discussed whether or not sociology was a science and we discussed whether or not something is research or not, and that just seems very trivial . . ." (Jeff). This reaction is consistent with the relative lack of discussion following the exercise, where several students did not respond. One also stated that trying to determine whether an article was research or not was confusing because they were looking only at the abstracts: "The whole abstract thing. Everything I got I was pretty sure it was research, but not totally. Without the full article I was not able to tell for sure" (Mary). Based on these responses, it seems that for students who are relatively unfamiliar with sociology or the idea of sociology as a science, it may be beneficial to thoroughly explain what indicators in abstracts suggest the paper is based on research and to explain beforehand the reasons why the question of whether sociology is scientific is an important one.

The focus group brought out how the teaching strategy might benefit from presenting more stage-setting and background knowledge. Variously called contextualizing or providing "scaffolding" for learning, many disciplines need ways to identify when and where such background is needed for students to develop useful understandings. Focus groups may be one way to identify such lacunae.

Clearly all social and natural science fields face the issue of helping students to understand what makes something scientific or not, how scientific thinking differs from other kinds of thinking, and what is considered sufficient evidence for inferring causality. Although their methods differ, disciplines in the humanities also have standards of evidence and reasoning. Analysis of literary works, for example, requires students to learn how to provide reasonable and sufficient evidence to support arguments they want to advance. While different disciplinary communities of practice may differ in how they do this, virtually all have ways of doing it. The process called "Decoding the Disciplines" focuses on specifying the kinds of thinking and acting required for success in a discipline and identifying where students are having trouble understanding (Pace and Middendorf 2004; Shopkow 2010).

Understanding the Centrality of Inequality

Understanding social inequality was the third most common goal identified by sociological leaders. Specifically, in the words of one leader, this refers to "The way in which opportunities are enhanced or constrained by previous life experiences—in families, schools, neighborhoods, based on race, gender, social class, where you grew up." The third focus group attempted to assess two ways of teaching the importance of social class inequality by discussing family income data and using a modified version of the game *Monopoly*.

Students were given a handout of 2005 Household Earnings from the U.S. Census Bureau and asked to give a written response to the question, "Why do you think different households receive different amounts of income?" They discussed the question and wrote a response to a second question: "What affects what people in different occupations, or with different amounts of education, skill, and years of experience, are paid?" The participants were then randomly placed into one of four teams, representing four social classes.

Prior to the session, the undergraduate RA prepared money piles and printed the modified rules for a version of the game *Monopoly* called *Sociopoly* (developed by Jessup 2001). These rules changed the game several ways. First, players were organized into four teams, the first of which started the game with $1,500 and collected $200 and two houses each time they passed Go. The second team started with $1,030 and received $150 and one house each time they passed Go. The third team began with $960 and received $125 and one house each time they passed Go. The fourth team started with $505 and received $100 for passing Go. Second, unlike *Monopoly*, *Sociopoly* does not require ownership of all properties of the same color before players can buy houses and hotels. Third, the game began with $1,000 dollars in Free Parking, and all fines (that is, Jail fines, Community Chest and Chance fines, and so forth) went into Free Parking. In order to win the Free Parking pot, however, each player had to pay a $20 "Parking Fee" each time they passed Go. Fourth, if a Team 1 player landed in Jail, they paid $200 and continued playing. Upon leaving jail, they advanced to their nearest owned property. If a Team 2 player went to jail, they needed to wait three turns, roll doubles or pay $50. If Teams 3 or 4 rolled doubles, they went to jail and had either to wait three turns or pay $100 to get out. Fifth, a team that went bankrupt had to stand in the corner until the game ended. Finally, each team had to keep a record of assets and liabilities and the number of times they went around the board. Given everyone's lack of familiarity with the new rules, they were not always enforced in the early part of the game. For example, Teams 3 and 4 rolled doubles several times without going to jail.

Students played for forty-five minutes and then discussed the game. Referring to the census earnings tables, they discussed several questions: "Why do you think some household incomes differ from others? Is there anything besides the hypothesized reasons suggested earlier? What affects what people in different occupations, or with different amounts of education, skill, and years of experience are paid? Do you think that starting points, i.e., how much wealth people are born into and the rules of the game, might influence their social class? How?" The session ended with the moderator questions.

Student learning was assessed based on a comparison of responses to pre- and post-questions. Written responses before the game emphasized various social factors that might influence a household's social class, including education, age of members, and number of working family members: "Single parent families would earn less income because only one person is working; families with a stay-at-home parent would earn less income. Families with two or more people contributing to income would earn more money" (Patricia). One student also emphasized the importance of luck and personal connections. In many ways, despite being asked to add to or alter their responses to the initial questions, oral responses did not always directly address the question. They did, however, suggest that by playing the game students had gained some understanding of the importance of "the rules of the game" and who makes them. One student mentioned that the sales tax has a greater effect on the poor than the rich: "Sales tax—poor people spend a larger share of their income on household goods, so they're actually paying relatively more in taxes than the rich. We learned this in my economics class" (Jordan). Others addressed the issue of who determines these rules: "They can afford to make their voices heard. Money buys everything. It buys advertising, policy, power. It buys people, it pays people off. Nobody at this table would say that our government is not corrupt to the point where you can buy people off. So, if you have enough money you can make things happen" (Madison).

Students stated in response to the moderator questions that the exercise helped them better understand the importance of social structure in relation to income and social class: "You cannot get away from the structure. You cannot get away from 'Well the rules say you don't get $200 for passing Go, you get $125 and a house.' You can't get away from what the rules dictate. So it gets you thinking and you have all these preconceptions but then acting it out like, the rules are the rules and you can't get away from it" (Madison). Students also reported that the game allowed them to relate better to more abstract issues of class inequality:

> The simulation was starting out with unequal resources and money and unequal distribution even when you do get paid. It's very similar to real society and it helps to like . . . we were just playing a game, but we were all getting emotional and sensitive because it's money and it's our houses and lives and it's good to see it on a small scale. I feel that it helps you apply it to a bigger scale more easily if you can act it out, and then, we can't really act any of this out for another fifty years of our lives to like actually buy houses and acquire money but to act it out right here helps your understanding of how life is. (Madison)

They also found the discussion helpful, saying, "I thought talking about it afterwards to kind of make the connection between real life, like, yeah 'it sucks,' we always had to go to jail, but then we made the connection that like, poorer people and people that don't make as much money end up in jail a lot more because they can't buy themselves out" (Patricia).

The focus group comments illustrated the power of the game, specifically how acting "it out right here" drove home the understanding that some people have more difficulty getting ahead than others, and the importance of preexisting wealth and structured rules for such unequal outcomes. There was only one person on each social class "team," and it is difficult to imagine the game working with more than two or three people on each team. Using this strategy in a large class would require a number of sets of *Monopoly* and considerable advance work preparing the packets of money for each social "class." It also might be difficult to play long enough in a single fifty-minute class session for the simulation to have its full effect. In the forty-five minutes students in this session played, no team went bankrupt and had to stand in a corner, but bankruptcy was looming for Class 4 when they stopped playing. Simulations such as this may help students to understand an abstract idea like socially structured inequality. Finding or developing effective and practical simulations that can help students gain a deeper understanding of important ideas should be useful in all disciplines. The natural sciences, especially physics and chemistry, use simulations frequently,[9] but it is our impression that they are used less in the humanities and social sciences.

Social Construction of Ideas

A fourth key understanding was the social construction of ideas. This refers to the idea that concepts like race and gender are the product of social rather than natural factors. For a related study of the social construction of ideologies used to explain inequalities, see Pat Antonio Goldsmith's (2006) work. The aim of the teaching session was to assess the degree to which a particular video and discussion contributed to student understanding of the social construction of the concept of race.

Students wrote answers to the question, "Do you think different racial groups exist in the world?" and three follow-up questions: "If yes, please list the racial groups you see as existing in the world," "If yes, please list the characteristics used to distinguish racial groups," and "Have you ever discussed the nature of race in a college class before?" The students then did an exercise developed by Brian Obach (1999), in which they were presented with six circles with varied shading patterns and asked to place these circles into two different groups.[10] This was followed by discussion and showing the thirty-seven-minute version of part 1 of the film *Race: The Power of an Illusion*. Students then discussed the following questions: "Do you think racial categories are based on scientific criteria?" "Why or why not?" "Where do you think racial categories come from?" "Why?" The session ended with the moderator questions.

Student understandings were assessed by comparing responses to the pre- and post-movie questions. This comparison offers two possible interpretations. It can be said that students did learn from the exercise because answers to the initial questions tended to emphasize physical features. A typical response listed "facial features/skin color." After the exercise, however, most respondents emphasized the social and subjective nature of race: "Yeah, well, we don't interact with people based on tint but on perceived cultural difference" (Jason). In the discussion following the film, one respondent also said that, "I thought it was interesting that the video said we created race. I never really thought of it that way" (Elizabeth). At the same time, however, many participants also listed things like "heritage" or "nationality" as distinguishing characteristics, indicating that they already had the social in mind. This is also suggested by responses in discussion, such as, "I've seen things like this before in other classes and wasn't really under the impression of biology being the real basis of race" (Mary).

This interpretive ambiguity could result from differences in the wording of the before and after questions, which make it difficult to assess what students thought before the exercise and to compare it with their responses following the video. Clearly, to make inferences regarding the effectiveness of an exercise from student responses, the same questions must be asked before and after the teaching process. Based on student comments in the focus group, we learned that asking for written responses before doing the Obach exercise shaped participants' responses to the exercise, making them assume that the exercise related to race.

This observation suggests that a better teaching strategy might be to begin with the circle classification exercise before asking questions about racial groups. Perhaps because the film took up such a large portion of instructional time, student comments tended to respond to it rather than to the Obach exercise. In addition, some students felt that the video was too long and "overdramatic" (Patricia), with one referring to it as "pretty after-school special" (Mary). Some videos, like this one, consist primarily of talking heads, while others, like Zimbardo's film of the actual experiment, use the power of drama to demonstrate rather than simply say something.

Conclusions

Teaching and learning in every discipline involve a series of complex decisions and practices, including ascertaining what understandings are important for students to obtain from the courses they take and finding and/ or developing strategies for teaching those understandings. These strategies are subject to a number of constraints, including the length of class periods, class size, and the advance preparation required. There are also questions of how to assess whether students' understandings of complex and abstract ideas benefit from the strategies used to teach them, how and why. Finally, there is the question of analyzing how the methods chosen to assess understandings are related to what students learn.

This chapter shows the value of using multiple methods for assessing student learning and particular teaching strategies, including before-and-after essays, discussion questions, and open-ended discussion in focus groups run by someone other than the students' instructor. All too frequently today, assessment is based on large-scale testing (frequently multiple-choice) of student learning. Testing can show whether students know more or less of what was covered by the test before and after a given educational "exposure." However, it tells us nothing about what understandings they have constructed, *how* they learned what they know, what worked and didn't work, what else they may have learned, or *why* an educational exposure did or did not work. In contrast, focus groups can provide insights into students' thinking and reveal more about how students perceive a given teaching strategy such as an exercise, game, or film.

Several insights were obtained from the focus groups. In the case of understanding the scientific basis of sociology, students already had the understanding we were hoping they would construct, so a pre- and post-test revealed no change. However, we did learn that if we were to use the location and analysis of sociological abstracts exercise again, for example to prepare students for doing a research review, we would need to provide more background information on how students could determine whether an article is research-based and how practitioners assess different sources such as refereed journal articles, unpublished papers, and dissertation abstracts. More discussion of the rationale for doing such an exercise was needed. We also saw that students learned other things besides the understandings we were seeking, for example, in the critical questions a student asked about a research study.

We noticed that the conditions of learning are important from a student who wrote, "I liked talking about race in a serious way. Usually, whenever anyone talks about race they try to make it humorous" (Jason). We did not realize that students might appreciate having the chance to talk seriously and openly about race. This comment represents an unexpected insight gained from the student's perceptions.

The focus groups showed the importance of engaging students' emotions as well as their cognitive reasoning. For example, despite the poor technical quality of the film *Quiet Rage,* students responded more positively to it than to *Race: The Power of an Illusion.* Why? *Quiet Rage* is a film of the actual social experiment Zimbardo did at Stanford University and students saw how the guards behaved rather than reading or being told about it. One student even noted how the poor quality of the film made it seem more authentic. In contrast, the very professionally produced *Race: The Power of an Illusion,* with "talking heads," was less engaging for the students. The *Sociopoly* simulation also engaged students' emotions. They became very excited as the game progressed. Research suggests that learning that is accompanied by high states of emotional excitement tends to last longer than learning unaccompanied by emotions (Zull 2002).

There are ethical and practical limitations to conducting this type of SOTL research on our own classes, however. Ethically, we cannot ask students to participate in our research outside of class because they may feel coerced into doing so. Practically, students may be understandably less willing to express negative views about teaching strategies or materials when their own professor is conducting the research. It might be possible for faculty members to "exchange" classes with a colleague, with each one conducting research on the other's class, but stringent efforts to protect the identities of participating students would be required. Such an endeavor would demand considerable time and effort, and it seems unlikely on any large-scale basis without some form of supplemental funding.

As we better understand how and why various teaching strategies do or do not work to help students understand ways of thinking identified by communities of practice, we can refine our teaching methods and improve student learning experiences and understandings. We also need to know whether various strategies work differently for different types of students and why. As a method of assessment, focus groups can yield important insights into both student learning and the strengths and limitations of various teaching strategies that go beyond what can be learned from before-and-after essays or oral discussion. It seems likely that focus groups could be relevant in all disciplines. The chapter also shows how disciplinary leaders and communities of practice can help identify threshold concepts and ways of thinking important for students to understand a discipline.

NOTES

The project was supported by the National Science Foundation's Course, Curriculum, and Laboratory Improvement division Collaborative Research grant DUE-0442836. We thank project officer Myles G. Boylan for his encouragement. The information and ideas presented in this chapter are the authors' alone and do not necessarily reflect the views of the NSF.

1. See http://www.nyu.edu/classes/persell/aIntroNSF/Documents/Task%20Force%20Members%20and%20Years031708.htm for a list of task force members and affiliations.

2. The goals, outline, and curriculum narrative are available at http://www.nyu.edu/classes/persell/aIntroNSF/Documents/CurriculumIntroSoc032709.html#thecourse.

3. Eleven years were included because one recipient was deemed ineligible.

4. These awards are grants that fund "small, groundbreaking research initiatives and other important scientific research activities" (http://www.asanet.org/research/FAD.cfm).

5. The nine themes were (1) understanding the "social" part of sociology, or learning to think sociologically; (2) the scientific nature of sociology; (3) complex and critical thinking; (4) the centrality of inequality; (5) a sense of sociology as a field; (6) the social construction of ideas; (7) the difference between sociology and other social sciences; (8) the importance of trying to improve the world; and (9) understanding the important social institutions in society.

6. Asking students in a professor's course to participate in research about their learning outside of class raises ethical and research-related questions such as, will students feel coerced into participating, will they feel free to voice negative opinions, how can their identities be protected, will participating students gain an advantage in the course, and others.

7. The Stanford Prison Experiment was conducted in 1971 by Philip G. Zimbardo, who planned a two-week simulation of prison life. As he says, they "ended the experiment prematurely after only six days because of what the situation was doing to the college students who participated. In only a few days, the guards became sadistic and the prisoners became depressed and showed signs of extreme stress" (http://www .prisonexp.org/).

8. A field was understood as being scientific if it included theories that helped explain phenomena that were tested empirically with research. The main features of scientific research were systematically collected observations (data); efforts to reduce bias; and attention to sampling, validity, and reliability issues.

9. See, for example, the web site of the National Science Teachers Association (http://www.nsta.org/store/?gclid=CJiZ6P6UtacCFQY65QodNBW1BA), Natural Sciences Simulations (http://natsim.net/), or EduMedia (http://www.edumedia-sciences.com/en/).

10. For a copy of the visual used in this exercise, see http://www.nyu.edu/classes /persell/aIntroNSF/Documents/TSObach1999.pdf.

REFERENCES

Adams, David S. 1993. "Technique 58: Sociological and Individualistic (or Non-sociological) Explanations for Human Behavior." In *Innovative Techniques for Teaching Sociological Concepts,* ed. Edward L. Kain and Robin Neas, 100–101. Washington, DC: American Sociological Association.

Baker, Paul J. 1976. "Mass Instruction in Sociology: On the Domestication of a Pedagogical Monster." *Teaching Sociology* 4: 5–28.

Brown, John Seely, and Paul Duguid. 2000. *The Social Life of Information.* Boston: Harvard Business School Press.

Chickering, Arthur W., and Zelda F. Gamson. 1987. "Seven Principles for Good Practice in Undergraduate Education." *American Association for Higher Education Bulletin* 39, no. 7. http://honolulu.hawaii.edu/intranet/committees /FacDevCom/guidebk/teachtip/7princip.htm.

Collins, Randall. 1998. *The Sociology of Philosophies: A Global Theory of Intellectual Change.* Cambridge, MA: Harvard University Press.

Goldsmith, Pat Antonio. 2006. "Learning to Understand Inequality and Diversity: Getting Students Past Ideologies." *Teaching Sociology* 34, no. 3: 263–77.

Grauerholz, Liz, and Greg Gibson. 2006. "Articulation of Goals and Means in Sociology Courses: What Can We Learn from Syllabi." *Teaching Sociology* 34, no. 1: 5–22.

Hanson, Chad M. 2002. "A Stop Sign at the Intersection of History and Biography: Illustrating Mills's Imagination with Depression-Era Photographs." *Teaching Sociology* 30, no. 2: 235–42.

Henderschott, Anne, and Sheila Wright. 1993. "Student Focus Groups and Curricular Review." *Teaching Sociology* 21, no. 2: 154–59.

Hounsell, Dai, and Charles Anderson. 2009. "Ways of Thinking and Practicing in Biology and History: Disciplinary Aspects of Teaching and Learning Environments." In *The University and Its Disciplines,* ed. Caroline Kreber, 71–83. London: Routledge.

Jessup, Michael M. 2001. "Sociopoly: Life on the Boardwalk." *Teaching Sociology* 29, no. 1: 102–9.

Kain, Edward L. 1999. "Building the Sociological Imagination through a Cumulative Curriculum: Professional Socialization in Sociology." *Teaching Sociology* 27: 1–16.

McCune, Velda, and Dai Hounsell. 2005. "The Development of Students' Ways of Thinking and Practicing in the Final-Year Biology Courses." *Higher Education* 49, no. 3: 255–89.

Meyer, Jan H. F., and Ray Land. 2003. "Threshold Concepts and Troublesome Knowledge: Linkages to Ways of Thinking and Practicing." In *Improving Student Learning—Theory and Practice Ten Years On,* ed. Chris Rust, 412–24. Oxford: Oxford Centre for Staff and Learning Development (OCSLD).

———. 2005. "Threshold Concepts and Troublesome Knowledge (2): Epistemological Considerations and a Conceptual Framework for Teaching and Learning." *Higher Education* 49, no. 3: 373–88.

Meyer, Jan H. F., and Ray Land, eds. 2006. *Overcoming Barriers to Student Understanding: Threshold Concepts and Troublesome Knowledge.* London: Routledge.

Morgan, David L. 1988. *Focus Groups as Qualitative Research.* Newbury Park, CA: Sage.

Obach, Brian K. 1999. "Demonstrating the Social Construction of Race." *Teaching Sociology* 27, no. 3: 252–57.

Pace, David, and Joan Middendorf, eds. 2004. "Decoding the Disciplines: Helping Students Learn Disciplinary Ways of Thinking." Special issue, *New Directions for Teaching and Learning* 98.

Persell, Caroline Hodges. 2010. "How Sociological Leaders Rank Learning Goals for Introductory Sociology." *Teaching Sociology* 38, no. 4: 330–39.

Persell, Caroline Hodges, Kathryn May Pfeiffer, and Ali Syed. 2007. "What Should Students Understand after Taking Introduction to Sociology?" *Teaching Sociology* 35, no. 4: 300–314.

———. "How Sociological Leaders Teach Some Key Principles." 2008. *Teaching Sociology* 36, no. 2: 108–24.

Pippert, Timothy D., and Helen A. Moore. 1999. "Multiple Perspectives on Multimedia in the Large Lecture." *Teaching Sociology* 27, no. 2: 92–109.

Race: The Power of an Illusion. 2003. DVD. Directed by Christine Herbes-Sommers. San Francisco: California Newsreel.

Robinson, Betty D., and Robert Schaible. 1993. "Women and Men Teaching 'Men, Women, and Work.'" *Teaching Sociology* 21, no. 3: 363–70.

Shopkow, Leah. 2010. "What 'Decoding the Disciplines' Has to Offer 'Threshold Concepts.'" In *Threshold Concepts and Transformational Learning,* ed. Jan H. F. Meyer, Ray Land, and Caroline Baillie, 317–32. Rotterdam: Sense Publishing.

U.S. Census Bureau. 2006. "Income in the Past 12 Months." Washington, DC: U.S. Census Bureau, American FactFinder.

Ward, Victoria, Janet Bertrand, and Lisanne F. Brown. 1991. "The Comparability of Focus Group and Survey Results." *Evaluation Review* 15, no. 2: 266–83.

Werder, Carmen, and Megan M. Otis, eds. 2010. *Engaging Student Voices in the Study of Teaching and Learning.* Sterling, VA: Stylus.

Zimbardo, Philip. 1991. *Quiet Rage: The Stanford Prison Study.* Videocassette. Directed by Ken Musen. Palo Alto, CA: Stanford University.

Zull, James E. 2002. *The Art of Changing the Brain: Enriching the Practice of Teaching by Exploring the Biology of Learning.* Sterling, VA: Stylus.

PART 2 • SOTL Across the Disciplines

CHAPTER 7

Square One: What Is Research?

GARY POOLE

A team at a large research-intensive university is working to enhance the value of the SOTL research on their campus. After a series of meetings and surveys, they become aware of significant amounts of SOTL activity on campus, but it is being carried out in isolated pockets. The team has aspirations for their university to not only be a learning organization but a learning laboratory, bringing SOTL researchers together to learn from each other and help create a coherent picture of learning in all its forms.

The meetings among SOTL researchers from a wide range of departments are lively and revealing, especially in terms of the differences that are uncovered. Two of the team members are talking about these differences as they walk across campus following one of the meetings. One colleague, a specialist in art education, asks the other, "Why are some people so hung up on cause and effect?" The other colleague replies, "I doubt that our friends in medicine would call a focus on cause and effect a hang-up."

From this conversation, and from the work of this team more generally, we can learn that the "differences" their meetings revealed run deep. If their university is to become a "learning laboratory," the participants need to develop more than a common language. They will have to come to some agreements regarding the very nature of research. This challenge is well illustrated at another institution that has established a Teaching Scholars program to support SOTL research.

A cohort of ten faculty members, most of them new to SOTL, meets regularly to learn about various SOTL methods, provide updates on the progress of their own work, and discuss ways to disseminate that work as it comes to fruition. In an early meeting, one participant described her research as follows: "I have a mature student in my class who is the first in her family to pursue higher education. She is a mother of two and she must hold down a part-time job as well as maintain her schoolwork. She and I are studying her progress through her first year."

Upon hearing this description, another participant asked, "This is interesting, but what is the research project?"

"As I just described it. We are researching her progress through first year."

"But this is an 'n' of one. You have no hypotheses and no objectivity. This might be an interesting activity, but it isn't research."

"Objectivity in research is a myth. All researchers bring biases that affect outcomes. The key is to be honest and forthcoming about those biases. And one story, well told, is most certainly research."

And so it goes. When academics from a range of disciplines collaborate to look at issues, opportunities and problems, they face the challenge of translating disciplinary research languages and of understanding research cultures. More fundamental still is the challenge of coming to an agreement on the definition of "research" itself. This is a significant challenge for research in the scholarship of teaching and learning. If it cannot be met, the scholarship of teaching and learning, as a movement for constructive change in higher education, could stall.

In this essay, I will attempt to help us meet this challenge by looking at the ways conceptions of research differ in terms of beliefs about the purpose of research and the nature of knowledge. The essay concludes with an exploration of how much consensus is required regarding the definition of research in order for us to work together and learn from SOTL research.

At the outset, it must be acknowledged that research activity is one of a number of defining activities for SOTL. As Carolin Kreber and Patricia A. Cranton (2000) point out, engaging in SOTL involves reflection on both research-based and experience-based knowledge. It also involves a dialectic between research and practice. In these and other SOTL-related activities, research is often at the core.

When we try to understand discipline-based differences in beliefs about research, we might start by acknowledging differences in the valuing of quantitative versus qualitative methods. However, many researchers, and not just those pursuing SOTL, have moved well beyond an "either/or" debate regarding qualitative and quantitative methods such that mixed approaches are common (Butler 2006; Denzin 1978). As Norman K. Denzin and Yvonne S. Lincoln (2005) observe, "No longer is it possible to categorize practitioners of various perspectives, interpretive practices, or paradigms in a singular or simplistic way" (1115). Given the complexities of disciplinary perspectives on research, disciplinary differences are more fundamental than whether one values words or numbers as data. They touch upon the very purpose of research and the relationship between the studier and the studied.

Why Does SOTL Feature Multiple Beliefs about the Nature of Research?

As a field, or "movement" as some might call it (for example, Atkinson 2001; Dewar, Dailey-Hebert and Moore 2010), the scholarship of teaching and learning has ambitiously invited in all those with a curiosity for the nature of teaching and learning. Its conceptual and organizational connections with teaching enhancement initiatives have dictated that SOTL be inclusive of all disciplines. This noble embrace of the many has resulted in a salad of perspectives and backgrounds.

The multiplicity of SOTL is not simply a result of many invitations to the party, however. It is also a response to a need for multi-method approaches to understand the phenomena under study. Multiple methods, paradigms, and definitions of research are not simply the result of disciplines "colliding" in SOTL. They are a necessary strategy to meet the challenge of studying complex educational topics (Husén 1988). In this regard, the scholarship of teaching and learning is not unique as a field with diverse participants, beliefs, and methods. Indeed, as Kreber (2008) points out, "There is now a growing awareness that, in a world characterized by rapid change, complexity and uncertainty, problems do not present themselves as distinct subjects but increasingly within trans-disciplinary contexts" (xvii).

Thus, multiple methods don't just complicate things. They can also be used to increase our confidence in research designed to understand a complex world. It has long been believed that if we can come to the same conclusions using multiple methods—if we can triangulate our findings—then those conclusions are more likely to be valid (Webb et al. 1966).

Understanding the Ways in Which Disciplines Work Together

In order to understand how beliefs about the nature of research differ among the wide range of people conducting SOTL research, we must begin with a clear understanding of the ways in which diverse disciplines attempt to work together in the first place. There are a number of models to describe these attempts, some of which are well presented in the nursing education literature (see, for example, Dyer 2003; MacRae and Dyer 2005). These models help us understand how diverse paths do and should cross in the pursuit of SOTL, and each has different implications for the extent to which we must come to an agreement on the fundamental nature of research.

Multidisciplinarity

According to Howard Garner (1995), multidisciplinary work features one discipline as a "gatekeeper." From that discipline, other disciplines are called upon to provide their discipline-specific knowledge. The intention is to achieve the goal of the gatekeeper; thus, through the work, each discipline remains essentially unchanged. Based on this conceptualization, multidisciplinary approaches have the advantage of considering multiple methods, perspectives, and knowledge while retaining a manageable, conceptually straightforward focus on the work at hand. Psychologists call upon anthropologists when psychological research requires an understanding of cultural differences. Biologists ask educationalists for ways to assess learning in a self-directed laboratory assignment.

This sort of multidisciplinary approach, in which other disciplines are called up like reference books, does not require an enduring consensus regarding the definition of research. This is because the research agenda remains under the control of one discipline. If the biologists go looking for a survey tool, they do not expect to be asked why they are conducting survey research or why they are not using "think-aloud" procedures in which students verbalize their thoughts while they solve problems. Yet these might be the questions that need to be asked in order to get at what is learned in that self-directed laboratory setting. For example, survey research in these settings has discovered that students develop more effective self-regulation strategies when conducting biology labs of their own design (Butler et al. 2008). In other words, they become more skilled at accessing the appropriate skills for a give academic task. A finding of this nature might not surface in typical end-of-the-course surveys.

Interdisciplinarity

On the other hand, if such questions about the suitability of approaches do get asked and, moreover, get seriously considered by our biologists, the work may move beyond the realm of multidisciplinarity, as Garner (1995) construes the term. In this case, the researchers may adopt an interdisciplinary approach (see for example, Hoeman 1996). According to Shirley Hoeman, an interdisciplinary approach features more paths of communication among the participants. In other words, it is not simply a matter of the gatekeeper reaching out as necessary to communicate with others in a pursuit of his or her goals. Interdisciplinary teams feature a greater sharing of responsibility for the goals of the work and related outcomes. They engage in mutual problem solving and move "beyond the confines of their disciplines" (Dyer 2003, 186).

The sharing of goals and responsibility for outcomes requires a greater consensus around research viability and purpose, and of acceptable roles for the researchers. If the biologists are going to enter into an interdisciplinary working relationship with their colleagues from the faculty of education, the biologists should be prepared to consider the value of interview transcripts, think-aloud procedures, and discourse analysis related to student reflections on their learning because these methods may be very helpful in shedding light on the nature of students' strategies for self-regulation. Conversely, the educationalists need to value the biologists' use of pre-test/post-test designs and careful categorizations when appropriate for their SOTL research questions.

Transdisciplinarity

At this point, the research team still consists of members who define themselves by their individual disciplines. They are an interdisciplinary team because they are coming to understand and value the contributions of the other and share responsibility for the research outcome. For this team to become transdisciplinary, the boundaries between biology and education as disciplines must begin to blur. With a transdisciplinary team, an outsider sitting in on a research meeting would be hard pressed to distinguish the biologists from the educationalists. There will have been so much "cross-training" that it is hard to locate each participant's "turf."

True transdisciplinarity, then, as Jean Dyer (2003) describes it, does not come quickly and easily to a field. The notion of a university as a "learning laboratory," as introduced in this chapter's opening vignette, would feature transdisciplinary work. The team developing that idea had a vision of a center on campus where researchers gathered to engage in transdisciplinary research in which it would be difficult to ascertain the disciplines of the team members. The cross-training that is required can be deliberate and lengthy—like becoming multilingual such that one can *think* in multiple languages. As I have said elsewhere (Poole 2008), as an aspiration, transdisciplinarity is an *identity,* not an *identity crisis.*

If a field adopts this approach, research methods proposed by diverse team members are not contested as being "strange." Rather, they are assimilated into a larger whole that comes to constitute the field's research arsenal. Given that many SOTL researchers also maintain non-SOTL research programs within their disciplines, it is asking a lot to expect them to engage in the learning required to become transdisiciplinary in their SOTL team endeavors. As historian David Pace (2004) puts it, "Developing knowledge about our students and their learning might take us into areas that seem

distant from our professional training. If it is necessary to abandon completely our approaches to scholarship and to begin from scratch to master a
new discipline, few historians are apt to contribute to this effort" (1184).

Of course, if SOTL efforts were pursued solely within one discipline,
researchers might never have to concern themselves with crossing bridges
into other disciplines. However, they may never enjoy the benefits of studying learning and teaching from diverse research and theoretical perspectives,
either.

Others have written in SOTL literature about the relative merits and
pitfalls of SOTL's multiple disciplinary nature (see for example Huber 2006).
This multiplicity appears to be both a strength and weakness of SOTL—on
the one hand, bringing richness and multiple perspectives to our understanding of teaching and learning processes; on the other, creating wide chasms
between those immersed in SOTL and those who feel like "amateurs" dab-
bling in entirely unfamiliar research contexts (Pace 2004).

Of the three models presented here and elsewhere, I would argue that
what Hoeman (1996) calls interdisciplinarity is a reasonable and useful goal
for SOTL. It does not put to rest concerns about amateurism. It does, however,
place in context our need to address differences in the way we think about
and define research. Interdisciplinarity features a useful sharing of responsibility for research outcomes. The model invites a greater sharing of perspectives than that of multidisciplinarity. At the same time, it does not require
that researchers become entirely versed in the methods and beliefs of other
disciplines, a requirement that would be unmanageable for many.

Differing Beliefs about the Purpose of Research

This chapter began with the lament that some colleagues adopt a narrow
view of the purpose of research—solely in terms of a search for links between
cause and effect. In this section, we will take a closer look at some of the different purposes people perceive for research. Some research is intended to
prove "what works." Other research attempts to discover characteristics of
learners. Still other research is designed to build and refine theory. Another
purpose of research is to inform change agendas. Finally, the purpose of some
SOTL research is to preserve this form of scholarship as a field. In the following section, we will look at each of these purposes to further understand
differences in views about research and why these differences are problematic
for SOTL.

Research to Prove "What Works"

In a paper entitled "It Isn't Rocket Science: Rethinking Our Metaphors for Research in Health Professions Education," Glenn Regehr (2009) contrasts a range of beliefs about the purpose of theory. While Regehr is talking about theory rather than research per se, his observations apply to the current discussion. He invokes the phrase "It isn't rocket science" to make the point that the purposes of theory in aeronautical engineering will differ from those in education.

Specifically, theory (and in our case, research) is designed to describe, explain, predict, or control phenomena. Some people might arrange these purposes hierarchically, as my order might imply, with research leading to control of a phenomenon being more valuable than that which aims to describe that phenomenon. Others might see this order as indicative of a progression; before something can be explained, it must be described, and so on.

Regehr challenges the notion that these purposes are hierarchical or deserving of differing value. Writing for an audience of health education researchers, he points out that the dominant view of health education research has been shaped by the physical sciences. The result has been an acceptance of an "imperative of proof" (32) and an "imperative of generalizable simplicity" (31). The former is linked closely to the question "Does it work?" and the demand "Prove to me that this method works and I will use it." This is a manifestation of the cause-effect purpose of research. The latter imperative—generalizable simplicity—speaks to the perceived utility of scientific theory; it should be accessible, robust, and broadly applicable.

Both of these imperatives, or purposes, can be problematic for SOTL research. First of all, a considerable amount of good educational research is descriptive in purpose. It is not designed to *prove* something. Rather, it does a good job of describing what is going on in a learning environment. This task, of course, can be challenging, given the complexity of those environments. This leads to a problem with the imperative of generalizable simplicity. Many learning environments are neither generalizable nor simple.

In the context of the current chapter, Regehr's ideas help us further understand the conundrum of differing definitions of research in SOTL, namely, that some rigorous and insightful SOTL research is dismissed as non-research because it does not provide proof or generalizable simplicities. As a more useful alternative, Regehr recommends that the purpose of educational theory, and thus research, should shift from an imperative of proof to an imperative of understanding. It should also move from an imperative of generalizable simplicity to one of representing complexity well.

We will never escape the need to "show what works and what doesn't." This is a vital purpose for SOTL research, given that we have spent many decades in higher education employing teaching practices because they either felt good or were organizationally expedient. In fact, they didn't "work" when their effectiveness was measured in terms of student learning.

However, Regehr reminds us that, if we are going to acknowledge this imperative of proof, we cannot forsake the imperative of understanding, and certainly, we must not oversimplify the learning context or assume that such contexts do not matter by erroneously expecting broad generalizability of findings. Indeed, a clear description and understanding of context might be the best contribution SOTL research can make (Gibbs 2010).

Under the general question of "Did it work?" we have all the SOTL research that measures educational impact. The "it" in "Did it work?" can be enormously varied, from a ten-minute exercise in class to sector-wide strategies to widen participation in higher education. Not surprisingly, we encounter disciplinary differences when we look for evidence that something "worked." Some will be most comfortable with pre-test/post-test designs that measure "normalized learning gains." (See, for example, Hake 1998.) Others will be more interested in attitudinal outcomes. Still others require institution-level evidence, including data such as enrollment and graduation patterns. Regardless of where one looks for evidence, there is a unification of purpose here—pursuit of the "Did it work?" question.

Problems with Research Designed to Determine If Something "Worked"

The "did it work?" purpose for research is, in itself, potentially divisive within SOTL. There are those who contend that questions about "what works" are simply not answerable empirically (Barrow 2006). Robin Barrow argues that there are a number of good reasons why empirical research in education is not possible. For example, educational research attempts to investigate phenomena for which there are no adequate definitions. Barrow observes, "Empirical research is conducted into phenomena such as giftedness, creativity, or critical thinking without a clear and plausible definition of the notion in question" (293). Barrow contends that most of our attempts to define such phenomena are restricted to behavioral indicators, which are often inadequate. The problem is that such phenomena are not purely behavioral. They are also cognitive and affective in nature.

Barrow's claim challenges the work of George Kuh and colleagues using the National Survey of Student Engagement (NSSE) to measure relationships between processes associated with engagement and educational outcomes. For the most part, engagement is defined behaviorally in the NSSE, with examples such as the following: made a class presentation, worked with classmates outside of class, and discussed ideas with faculty outside of class (National Survey of Student Engagement, 2010). Moreover, NSSE researchers have identified what they call "high-impact practices" based on NSSE findings.

The views of Barrow on one side and Kuh and colleagues on the other illustrate the chasm that exists regarding views of research in SOTL. On the one hand, some authors say that no generalizable laws can be ascertained for relationships between teaching and learning. On the other, highly influential NSSE research defines concepts in behavioral terms and makes the claim that there are knowable and generalizable relationships between these behaviors and educational outcomes. Ultimately, if one does not accept a behavioral definition of engagement, one will not be convinced by the NSSE work.

Even if one accepts that it is possible and advised to define educational phenomena in other than behavioral ways, Barrow argues that we cannot adequately control these other factors such that convincing cause-effect research can be conducted. Nor can we randomly assign participants to conditions so that factors can be evenly distributed between groups or controlled for statistically (see also Grauerholz and Main in this volume).

Research to Identify Learner Characteristics

While some have argued that it makes sense to conduct educational impact studies, it is still inadequate to do so without becoming well acquainted with those upon whom the impact is meant—our learners. Are the "millennials" (Oblinger 2003) really unique? Do they have a greater preference for social construction of knowledge because of the prevalence of social software in their lives? Do they bring a greater sense of "entitlement" to the learning environment? (see, for example, Roosevelt 2009). People who find these questions most fascinating might say that the main purpose of SOTL research is to better know the learner.

Again, one's discipline will dictate where one looks for the answers to these questions. Psychologists may employ survey research or other forms of psychological testing such as personality inventories. Sociologists might rely on the tenets of symbolic interactionism to study learners. From this latter perspective, each event in the classroom carries a host of meanings beyond the words spoken and the actions observed. Survey methods are not likely to fit with this perspective; rather, interviews and observation might be employed.

At the heart of these social science approaches is the belief that people are, in fact, empirically *knowable*. Also, as different as these methods may appear, they are still united in purpose. There may be fewer misunderstandings about *what* they are trying to achieve even if there are differences in *how* to go about it.

Research to Develop Theory

Some disciplines view the principle purpose of research as being to help build and refine theory. However, there are differing views on the nature and purpose of theories. In SOTL, can we pursue the development of broadly applicable, overarching theories? Janet Parker (2009) thinks not. As Parker states, "The question of theory is contentious and difficult—what theory? Or, rather, whose theory? That of educational psychology, sociology or philosophy?" (146). Parker concludes that a field investigating pedagogy cannot and should not strive for one unifying theoretical foundation.

It might make no more sense to look for a unifying definition of research. This is problematic for the physical scientist who comes from a tradition that values the development of widely applicable and elegantly simple theory (Regehr 2009) and considers this development a central purpose of research.

Research to Inform Educational Change

An ultimate purpose of research investigating pedagogical impact, or the nature of the learner, or the development of theory, might be to inform and motivate educational change. Consider the illuminating research from Canada and the United States on academic integrity (see, for example, McCabe, Treviño and Butterfield 2001; Christensen Hughes and McCabe 2006). This research indicates that students cheat with disconcerting frequency. It also concludes that such behavior is more prevalent when students perceive their instructors to be uninterested in integrity or, worse, demonstrative of a lack of integrity. The purpose of this research has less to do with shedding light on "students these days" and more about convincing us in higher education to take a long, hard look at the environments we have created and think seriously about changing them.

Research to Further Legitimize the Field

Another purpose for SOTL research concerns the preservation of the field. Unlike disciplines such as physics or anthropology, the strain for credibility in SOTL research is so fundamental that we still must prove research in the field can actually be conducted (see, also, Grauerholz and Main in this volume). SOTL conferences are attended by people who believe they are presenting "real research." At the same time, presenters are often mindful of how this research is received in their local environments and what is required to enhance that reception. An important purpose is to convince others of the viability of the field.

This purpose becomes particularly hard to achieve with research paradigms that are outside the comfort zones of the intended audience. Conversely, research that uses repeated measures or random assignment to a "treatment" is "real research" in the eyes of some and, thus, can be used more easily to make the case that such research is doable and worth considering. Other eyes would view words like "treatment" to be antithetical to what education is all about.

These are but a few of the purposes of SOTL research. This list does not include other purposes of research such as that intended to define key concepts. What do we mean by "competency"? "Feedback"? "Collaboration"? Research intended to explore these issues could be seen as being further away still from the purposes accepted in disciplines outside the social sciences and humanities.

Beliefs about the Nature of Knowledge

At times in this chapter, I have alluded to assumptions that something is *knowable*. In some disciplines, this assumption is a given. In others, it is a central focus of contention. A positivist holds that knowledge—that which is knowable—is restricted to that which is observable and measurable. Phenomena that do not fit into these categories might be interesting to talk about, but they cannot constitute knowledge. Changes in physical reaction times, skill levels, and exam scores are comforting to the positivist because they represent that which can be observed and, thus, known.

Furthermore, that which can be known in the positivist sense can be predicted and controlled. The aforementioned research on "learning gains" fits well within a positivist's view. Pre-tests and post-tests make change in learning observable. Using these observations, we can implement methods to affect those observations. We can determine "what works."

One problem with the positivist approach in educational research is that a number of phenomena are, at best, on the edge of the observable. Some examples include cognitive functions, the intended meaning of survey responses, and the cause-effect relationship between learning environments and learning itself. Each discipline holds its own views about positivism and the way things come to be known and what, in fact, can be known. Some will recognize this as the stuff of epistemology, or the study of knowledge and what has been called "justified belief" (Steup 2005).

Some time ago, Anthony Biglan (1973) categorized disciplines along two dimensions: "hard-soft" and "pure-applied." "Hard" disciplines are those in which academics and students are more likely to ascribe to one or more unifying theories. If one agrees with Parker, then one would not consider SOTL to be a "hard" discipline, given her argument that unifying theories do not exist in the field. The "pure-applied" distinction harkens back to differences in beliefs about the purpose of research. One might expect much SOTL research to be applied in nature. Thus, if SOTL is a "soft-applied" discipline, how can those from "hard" or "pure" disciplinary traditions find a home in the field?

In the mid-twentieth century, psychology was positivist in its approach. Rats ran mazes and pigeons pecked disks to provide observable, overt manifestations of learning. At about the same time, the field of psychology was having a considerable influence on the development of educational research, which took a positivist approach to research on learning (Husén 1988). Researchers within and without the field of education have since challenged and rejected this positivist approach, though it still holds a place in research practice.

Closely related to a rejection of positivism is the notion of "scientism" (see Habermas 1978). In essence, scientism is a pejorative reference to the belief that all that can be known, or is worth knowing, must be discovered through the methods of natural science. Contrast this with Susan Haack's (2003) position that what has been called the scientific method is really no different from everyday thinking, but it has benefited from a great publicity campaign by science culture.

Again, we can see the applications of this debate to our understanding of how academics' views of research differ, especially as they apply to SOTL research. First, we have the debate about what is knowable. Then we have the debate about *how* things can be known.

Apply these perspectives to Carl Wieman's (2010) assertion: "The hypothesis that I and others have advanced is that [transforming science teaching for the better] is possible, but only if we approach the teaching of science like a science. That means applying to science teaching the practices that are essential components of scientific research and that explain why science has progressed at such a remarkable pace in the modern world" (176). This language and characterization of research is likely to resonate well with members of the science community. For those who make accusations of scientism, however, Wieman's appeal amounts to using scientism to propagate what they might call the myths of science. For Wieman, however, his focus *is* science, so he does not have to be particularly concerned about interpretations of his appeal from those outside his target disciplines.

In summary, a discipline's beliefs about the purpose of research and the nature of knowledge help define that discipline and the people who align with it. These beliefs tell us what a discipline *is* and what it *is not*. In so doing, they build "barricades" between themselves and other disciplines (Poole 2008, 50). While these barricades might help people know when they are in their disciplinary homes, they make interdisciplinary or transdisciplinary work difficult. Nowhere is this more clearly demonstrated than in the scholarship of teaching and learning. This is because SOTL is a field that requires the crossing of disciplinary boundaries. It must be about tearing down barricades as is the case when researchers work in truly interdisciplinary ways.

Toward a Universally Acceptable Definition of Research

Given this multitude of beliefs about the nature of knowledge, the discovery of knowledge, and the purposes of research, can we make any headway toward a definition of research that provides sufficient criteria for us to find widespread agreement and understanding? I believe that the future of SOTL may depend on our ability to do so. While it makes sense that SOTL work would originate within the disciplines, it cannot be imprisoned there. My own experience in helping develop SOTL capacity has made clear to me the richness and importance of bringing disciplines together to clearly understand phenomena related to teaching and learning.

As a starting point, consider the definition of research forwarded by Canada's Tri-Council, the body that governs the lion's share of research funding in that country. In an attempt to provide clarity for the Tri-Council Policy Statement on research ethics, a working committee of the Interagency Advisory Panel on Research Ethics (PRE) presented a paper exploring the definition of research. The paper began with a previously accepted definition of research: "an undertaking which involves a systematic investigation to establish facts, principles, or generalizable knowledge" (Abbott et al. 2008, 2).

The vast majority of definitions of research, whether provided by funding agencies, ethics review boards, or academic departments, use the phrase "systematic investigation." This Tri-Council definition also considers the notion of generalizability. In the Tri-Council paper, these terms are explored in some depth. The authors address the concern that the use of the term "systematic investigation" to define research limits unreasonably the number of endeavors that can be called research. The authors disagree with this concern, stating that all research benefits from some degree of planning or focus, and this is what they say is meant by "systematic." Researchers investigating educational phenomena will have their own view on the meaning of the word.

The Tri-Council considered more problematic the stipulation that the results of research be generalizable in order for the endeavor to be called research. In this, we are reminded of Regehr's recommendation that we move from "an imperative of generalizable simplicity" to "representing complexity well." Consistent with this recommendation, the authors of the Tri-Council paper contend that it is entirely possible that a research discovery could apply solely to the context in which the discovery was made. This discovery could still be gained via research even though it is not generalizable. The authors of the Tri-Council Policy Statement (TCPS) Report acknowledge this and present a revised definition of research: "Research is an undertaking intended to extend knowledge through a disciplined inquiry or systematic investigation" (Abbott et al. 2008, 3).

This definition is intended to sit well with many research traditions. It does not make stipulations regarding sample sizes, statistical procedures, forms of data, or the purpose of research. It can accommodate "n of one" research as well as research designed to represent complexity or correlate scores on behavioral surveys of engagement with institutionally generated learning outcomes. At the same time, there may still be clashes between the phrasing of the definition and the accepted epistemologies of some disciplines. For example, phrases like "extend knowledge" might assume positivist assumptions of a knowable world.

It is beyond the capabilities of SOTL, or perhaps any human creation, to resolve all interdisciplinary differences regarding the nature of research and how it should be conducted. What is proposed here, however, is that we explore the viability of using the Tri-Council definition as a starting point. The Tri-Council must acknowledge the legitimacy of research from all academic disciplines while at the same time engaging committees of academics to evaluate the worth of funding proposals. This might be an easier task for committees working within narrow disciplinary traditions. For SOTL research, we have seen that the challenge is more substantial. To meet that challenge, we must return to our "goodness of fit" approach.

If an endeavor satisfies the Tri-Council criteria of being a "systematic investigation," featuring planning and focus, and is intended to "extend knowledge," whatever form that knowledge might take, then it is research. It is viable research if its methods fit the purpose. We may debate the extent to which a proposed research program is systematic or the nature of what can be known within a particular domain, as Barrow (2006) does. However, these debates can be situated within a commonly accepted definition of what research *is*.

Researchers in engineering education attempting to learn about students' work in project teams should entertain ethnography as viable research to the extent that it fits their purpose (Aman et al. 2007). If they entertain other possible questions that ethnography can help answer, then they enter the realm of interdisciplinarity, as Hoeman (1996) defines it. The research is better in that it uses expanded methods to fit expanded purposes. Herein lies the excitement of SOTL.

In SOTL research, as in teaching, there can be a "plurality of good" (Pratt 2002, 5), in which we do not simply tolerate differences but we give them enough respect for serious consideration. As one colleague so aptly described the SOTL research process, "I need to suspend my views about what constitutes research in order to consider other possibilities, and I don't have to apologize for the views that I bring to the conversation" (Sandra Jarvis-Selinger, personal communication).

The focus of this chapter has been on differences in views about research as seen across disciplines. Another chapter (or more) can be written about differences based on culture (see, for example, Denzin and Lincoln 2005). Ultimately, this issue is about the legitimacy of voices. If we allow SOTL to fall into "methodological retrenchment" (Denzin and Lincoln 2005, 1116), in which each discipline protects its territory and identity by valuing exclusively its own methods and purposes, we will not only restrict the range of participants in SOTL, we will also restrict the voices of teachers and learners we might hear and who might hear us. Conversely, if we begin with a useful overarching agreement on the nature of research, as presented by the Tri-Council definition or one like it, SOTL has the potential to engage multiple voices in an exciting exploration of what it is to teach and to learn.

REFERENCES

Abbott, Judith, Michael Bergeron, Susan Hoddinott, Patrick O'Neill, Heather Sampson, Janice Singer, and Susan Sykes. 2008. "Proportionate Approach to Research Ethics Review in the TCPS: Towards a Revised Definition of Research in the TCPS." Interagency Advisory Panel and Secretariat on Research Ethics. Ottawa, Canada.

Aman, Cheryl, Gary Poole, Scott Dunbar, Daan Maijer, Rob Hall, Fariborz Taghipour, and Pierre Berube. 2007. "Student Learning Teams: Viewpoints of Team Members, Teachers, and an Observer." *Engineering Education Journal of the Higher Education Academy* 2, no. 1: 2–12.

Atkinson, Maxine P. 2001. "The Scholarship of Teaching and Learning: Reconceptualizing Scholarship and Transforming the Academy." *Social Forces* 79, no. 4: 1217–23.

Barrow, Robin. 2006. "Empirical Research into Teaching." *Interchange* 37, no. 4: 287–397.

Biglan, Anthony 1973. "The Characteristics of Subject Matter in Different Academic Areas." *Journal of Applied Psychology* 57, no. 3: 195–203.

Butler, Deborah. L. 2006. "Frames of Inquiry in Educational Psychology: Beyond the Quantitative-Qualitative Divide." In *Handbook of Educational Psychology,* 2nd ed., ed. Patricia A. Alexander and Philip H. Winne, 903–29. Washington, DC: American Psychological Association.

Butler, Deborah L., Carol Pollock, Kathy Nomme, and Joanne Nakonechny. 2008. "Promoting Authentic Inquiry in the Sciences: Challenges Faced in Redefining First-Year University Students' Scientific Epistemology." In *Inquiry in Education: Overcoming Barriers to Successful Implementation,* vol. 2, ed. Bruce M. Shore, Mark W. Aulls, and Marcia A. B. Delcourt, 301–24. Boca Raton, FL: Erlbaum-Routledge.

Christensen Hughes, Julia, and Donald L. McCabe. 2006. "Understanding Academic Misconduct." *Canadian Journal of Higher Education* 36, no. 1: 49–63.

Denzin, Norman K. 1978. *The Research Act: A Theoretical Introduction to Sociological Methods.* New York: Praeger.

Denzin, Norman K., and Yvonne S. Lincoln, eds. 2005. *The Sage Handbook of Qualitative Research.* 3rd ed. Thousand Oaks, CA: Sage.

Dewar, Jacqueline, Amber Dailey-Hebert, and Theresa Moore. 2010. "The Attraction, Value, and Future of SOTL: Carnegie Affiliates' Perspective." *Transformative Dialogues: Teaching and Learning Journal* 4, no. 1: 1–15.

Dyer, Jean. 2003. "Multidisciplinary, Interdisciplinary, and Transdisciplinary: Educational Models and Nursing Education." *Nursing Education Perspectives* 24, no. 4: 186–88.

Garner, Howard. 1995. *Teamwork Models and Experience in Education.* Boston: Allyn and Bacon and Prentice Hall.

Gibbs, Graham. 2010. "The Importance of Context in Understanding Teaching and Learning: Reflections on Thirty-Five Years of Pedagogic Research." Plenary address to the Seventh Annual Conference of the International Society for the Scholarship of Teaching and Learning, Liverpool, October 19, 2010.

Haack, Susan. 2003 *Defending Science—Within Reason: Between Scientism and Cynicism.* Amherst, NY: Prometheus.

Habermas, Jürgen. 1978. *Knowledge and Human Interests.* London: Heinemann Educational.

Hake, Richard. 1998. "Interactive-Engagement versus Traditional Methods: A Six-Thousand-Student Survey of Mechanics Test Data for Introductory Physics Courses." *American Journal of Physics* 66, no. 1: 64–74.

Hoeman, Shirley. 1996. *Rehabilitation Nursing: Process and Application*. St. Louis: W. B. Saunders.

Huber, Mary T. 2006. "Disciplines, Pedagogy, and Inquiry-Based Learning about Teaching." In *Exploring Research-Based Teaching*, special issue of *New Directions for Teaching and Learning* (107), ed. Carolin Kreber, 63–72. San Francisco: Jossey-Bass.

Husén, Torsten. 1988. "Research Paradigms in Education." *Interchange* 19, no. 1: 2–13.

Kreber, Carolin, ed. 2008. *The University and Its Disciplines: Teaching and Learning Within and Beyond Disciplinary Boundaries*. New York: Routledge.

Kreber, Carolin, and Patricia A. Cranton. 2000. "Exploring the Scholarship of Teaching." *Journal of Higher Education* 71: 476–96.

MacRae, Nancy, and Jean Dyer. 2005. "Collaborative Teaching Models for Health Professionals." *Occupational Therapy in Health Care* 19, no. 3: 93–102.

McCabe, Donald L., Linda K. Treviño, and Kenneth D. Butterfield. 2001. "Cheating in Academic Institutions: A Decade of Research." *Ethics and Behavior* 11, no. 3: 219–32.

National Survey of Student Engagement. 2010. *Major Differences: Examining Student Engagement by Field of Study—Annual Results 2010*. Bloomington: Indiana University Center for Postsecondary Research.

Oblinger, Diane. 2003. "Boomers, Gen-Xers and Millennials: Understanding the New Students." *Educause* (July/August), 37–47.

Pace, David. 2004. "The Amateur in the Operating Room: History and the Scholarship of Teaching and Learning." *American Historical Review* 109, no. 4: 1171–91.

Parker, Janet. 2009. "Is There a Theory for SOTL?" *PRIME* 3, no. 2: 145–51.

Poole, Gary. 2008. "Academic Disciplines: Homes or Barricades?" In *The University and Its Disciplines: Within and Beyond Disciplinary Boundaries*, ed. Carolin Kreber, 50–57. New York: Routledge.

Pratt, Daniel. 2002. "Good Teaching: One Size Fits All?" *New Directions for Adult and Continuing Education* 93: 5–15.

Regehr, Glenn. 2009. "It's Not Rocket Science: Rethinking Our Metaphors for Research in Health Professions Education." *Medical Education* 44: 31–39.

Roosevelt, Max. 2009. "Student Expectations Seen as Causing Grade Disputes." *New York Times*, February 17, 2009. http://www.nytimes.com/2009/02/18 /education/18college.html.

Steup, Matthias. 2005. "Epistemology." In *The Stanford Encyclopedia of Philosophy* (Spring 2010 ed.), ed. Edward N. Zalta. http://plato.stanford.edu/archives /spr2010/entries/epistemology/.

Webb, Eugene J., Donald T. Campbell, Richard D. Schwartz, and Lee Sechrest. 1966. *Unobtrusive Measures*. Chicago: Rand McNally.

Wieman, Carl. 2010. *Taking Stock*. Kingston, ON: Queens University Press.

CHAPTER 8

Fallacies of SOTL:
Rethinking How We Conduct Our Research

LIZ GRAUERHOLZ AND ERIC MAIN

We serve at a large metropolitan research university where scholarship of teaching and learning initiatives have been well supported by administration and where many faculty members across multiple disciplines have successfully published their SOTL research. Our institution offers substantial incentives for excellence in SOTL research, and the initiatives have greatly increased the visibility of teaching within our culture. We continue to advocate for the increased valuation of teaching, and we predict SOTL initiatives will continue to grow here. We recognize that we have been fortunate to work within an environment that supports SOTL. We also know many SOTL researchers have not been as lucky and have had to confront administrators' and colleagues' questions about the legitimacy of SOTL as "real research."

Indeed, as a new field of study, not grounded in any core disciplinary tradition, SOTL has struggled with legitimacy and acceptance in many academic circles (Huber and Hutchings 2005; McKinney 2007; Schroeder 2007). We are concerned that perhaps in an effort to counter these perceptions and establish SOTL as a legitimate field of academic inquiry, the SOTL movement may be moving in directions that are actually counterproductive to two primary goals of SOTL: to improve student learning and to encourage work within "trading zones" (see McKinney, this volume) or across disciplines that do not share similar methodologies or epistemologies. The risk, as Nancy Chick notes in chapter 1 of this volume, is that the SOTL movement will be shaped by (hegemonic) standards that privilege certain types of methodologies over others.

Our own work with SOTL research has led us to conclude that some of the basic tenets or assumptions upon which much SOTL is founded (and evaluated) are unattainable (here, we are speaking primarily of the types of SOTL that Chick claims is privileged above others). In particular, some SOTL researchers insist on rigorous methodology and are urged (or required if they hope to publish their studies) to apply the same methodological skills to researching teaching and learning as they do to any academic question within their disciplines, and insist that SOTL is no different from other scholarly pursuits and inquiries (Cross and Steadman 1996; Glassick, Huber, and Maeroff 1977; Moore 2001).

We examine four assumptions upon which much (currently privileged) SOTL is based—that SOTL research should employ control groups, that studies conducted at a particular institution can be generalized to other (often very diverse) settings, that current assessment measures adequately tap students' learning, and that certain pedagogical approaches championed by SOTL researchers are superior. Here, we argue—as Kathleen McKinney (2005) has—that SOTL cannot live up to, or be evaluated by, the same methodological standards applied to other types of research. Although the methodological concerns raised about SOTL research are not unique to SOTL, they have particular relevance to SOTL as its practitioners attempt to bring legitimacy to research in this area and build productive and rewarding interdisciplinary collaborations.

The observations and arguments we bring to this inquiry arise from our individual involvement with SOTL, from our collaborative work with our university's SOTL initiatives, and from sharing SOTL experiences with regional and national groups of SOTL researchers and faculty development centers. We bring to this discussion insights into the nature of social groups, institutional structures, and social development as well as insights from working with faculty across the disciplines on SOTL projects.

The Fallacy of Control Groups in Classroom Research

Control groups are one of the best methods for determining whether a pedagogical "treatment" significantly impacts students' behavior, attitudes, or values. As Liz Grauerholz and John Zipp (2008) note, "The use of control groups is a powerful means by which to establish the effects of a particular approach or method" (92). Typically, researchers use different sections of the same courses, taught either in the same semester/term or in subsequent periods, to ensure that students enrolled in the course match on basic demographic characteristics, academic level, and so on. More problematic, but not uncommon, are situations where the control and experimental groups are students enrolled in different sections of the same course taught by different instructors.

If the use of control groups in SOTL research is key to enhancing the methodological rigor of any study and helping to ensure publication of SOTL research (Maurer 2011), what is the problem? Even dismissing, for the moment, factors that can jeopardize internal validity such as "experimental mortality" (Campbell and Stanley 1963; for example, students in the experimental group may dislike the pedagogical intervention so much that they are frequently absent or withdraw from class), we argue that it is impossible to construct true control groups due to the nature of the classroom itself.

This realization became all too clear in 2008 when I (Grauerholz) began to implement a carefully designed pre-test/post-test control group research study of the effects of student-centered learning approaches on student engagement and attitudes. Given the movement towards student-centered learning (Barr and Tagg 1995; Blumberg 2009; Weimer 2002), I thought it important to empirically test whether the approach enhanced or inhibited learning outcomes. Specifically, my research sought to test empirically whether student-centered learning approaches worked as well as their advocates claim. Of particular interest was whether student engagement, measured directly through observation and attendance records and indirectly through self-reported engagement and interest in the course, was enhanced in the student-centered classroom.

The setup was ideal: I was scheduled to teach two sections of "Women in Contemporary Society." One section met for three hours on Tuesday evenings, the other for three hours on Thursday evenings. The courses and students enrolled were comparable in terms of number of students enrolled, gender ratio, and background. I structured Tuesday's class as a highly student-centered course in which students had significant input into topics covered and options to earn their grade. Specifically, students voted during the first class period on what topics they wished to pursue in depth and were allowed to select which assignments they would complete in order to earn their grade using the same rules developed by Weimer (2002). During the Thursday class, students were given no choice in topics—the topics covered were those determined by the first class, thereby keeping content consistent between the two sections. They were not given choices in determining grades; they were required to complete a set number of exams, projects, and writing assignments.

What I learned did not have as much to do about the effects of student-centered teaching but something more profound and obvious—that there is no such thing as a control group when it comes to research on the classroom. "The first day of class sets the tone for the rest of the term" (Davis 2009, 37), and without a doubt, these two classes were octaves apart on the classroom dynamic scale. The differences observed on the first day were immediate and unlikely to be due solely to different course structures (although such an immediate effect might occur, which makes establishing comparability challenging). During the first class in the learner-centered classroom (LCC), an intense argument broke out between three students during an ice-breaking exercise after two students (who were friends) told another student she was "misguided." These two students continually challenged my authority as the semester progressed, at one point insisting that the information I presented about women and the family (my particular area of expertise) was "wrong." In the Thursday class, the "teacher-centered classroom" (TCC), students displayed an entirely different attitude from day one. They were highly respectful towards the instructor and other students. In the first class session, during the ice-breaking exercise in which students in the LCC had engaged in heated arguments, students were careful to couch their disagreements with other students in polite terms (for example, "I can see where you're coming from"). Even though several students were dissatisfied with the grading over the course of the semester, they never openly confronted me. While some of these differences may have stemmed from the "experimental manipulation," the fact remains that the two classrooms became unique, and importantly, *noncomparable*.

These observations confirmed what many instructors anecdotally know to be true—no two classes are alike. Many of us have taught the same course back-to-back, to seemingly similar groups of students, only to find ourselves enthusiastic and inspired by one group and dreading the other. Yet, with a few notable exceptions, the idea that the classroom is first and foremost a *social* space with unique dynamics seems to be missing in much SOTL research (Atkinson, Buck, and Hunt 2009; Billson 1986; also see Gurung and Schwartz, this volume). That is, we often fail to recognize the classroom as a socially constructed environment, which (though largely predictable in terms of roles and expectations) gives rise to unique dynamics, power structures, and experiences.

The variables in any educational setting are too many to control or predict and make proving a hypothesized effect impossible (Walvoord 2004). Even employing control groups within a class or bridging classes is too problematic to be reliable. In such situations, instructors will typically try to assign students to the control and experimental groups randomly; however, randomization can never be absolute, it is only achieved in degrees (Becker 2004) because students are always "partners and collaborators in the pedagogical enterprise" (Shulman 2004, 20). They choose to what degree they will attend to the lessons, participate in the discussions, or collaborate with their peers, and they will make their choices based on their own pedagogical goals. Students in a classroom cannot "be treated as if they were randomly assigned rats in a laboratory experiment where descriptive statistics are sufficient for analysis" (Becker and Andrews 2004, 288). Students are coming to our classrooms with an increasing variability of readiness, backgrounds, interests, and commitment levels. For instance, in just one of the lower-division, general education classes that I (Main) teach every semester, only half of the student enrollment is typically made up of first- and second-year students. Consistently, about a quarter are juniors and another quarter are seniors. Some are transfer students from local community colleges, some are adult learners returning to education after many years in the workforce, some are retired, some are veterans of recent military service, some are disabled, many are medicated for various health conditions, and a few are too young to buy a beer. They are each a unique mixture of racial, ethnic, gender, and linguistic identities. They are falling in love, getting divorced, taking care of children or parents, and, according to one student recently, "getting called in to work the E.R. on Sunday night, the only free night in my schedule to do homework for this class." Additional threats outside of the instructor's control include the significant change in the roster between the first day of class and sometime during week two following the add/drop period and those students who officially withdraw or stop coming to class. How meaningful is the concept of "control group" under these conditions, especially given that classroom sizes are often too small to achieve true randomization of even the most basic demographics? While some classes may be more stable, these conditions are typical for our lower-division classes and confound the would-be SOTL scholar's efforts to study differences between individual classes.

Thus, even though the concept of a "'control group' is probably an anachronism" (Shulman 2004, 31), and even though the problems of experimental designs in classroom research are "major and made even more serious by the uncritical acceptance given this work" (Weimer 2006, 97), indeed, "almost useless in determining effective instructional procedures" (Sweller, Kirschner, and Clark 2007), many SOTL researchers continue to define SOTL as an extension of educational research, with methodologies consistent with those in traditional disciplines (Kanuka 2011). On the other hand, SOTL practitioners willing to work with less control over variables could, still, conduct a meaningful study of contrasting treatments if they were comparing total educational approaches rather than trying to isolate a single variable (Shulman 2004). The comparison of performances and experiences could then produce a case study that captured a range of responses, concrete examples, and narrative descriptions that could lead to the identification of indicators of relationships with potential value to innovative teachers; however, the two groups should remain unlinked as treatment one and treatment two. The SOTLer risks, here, that such case studies, observations, or classroom ethnographies might not be valued as educational research nor their results necessarily generalizable to other or larger settings.

The Fallacy of Generalizable Results

Just as the notion of "control group" is fundamental to the language of empirical research but inappropriate to SOTL literature, so too is the concept of the generalizability of results across settings. While classrooms and groups of students are too unique to meet the "randomizable" parameters required of a scientific study, institutions are even more different from each other in their vast assemblage of variables and so will confound any attempt to produce specific generalizable research findings. At almost every point of comparison, institutions present unique challenges to researchers hoping to adopt or transfer outcomes.

At the broadest level, we know (but often hesitate to acknowledge publicly) that there is tremendous variation in quality of universities and colleges in the United States that stem in large part from the radical expansion and transformation of American higher education, especially during the nineteenth and twentieth centuries (Calhoun 1999). There are undeniable differences in students' academic abilities across these institutions, as well as differences in teachers' expectations and attitudes (Boyer 1990). For example, students in two-year colleges have substantially lower test scores than students in four-year colleges (Calhoun 1999). This fact, Calhoun claims, is not necessarily problematic. The problem is assuming that the same teaching methods work equally well in these different settings:

> The same textbooks, techniques and styles of instruction, and assignments are unlikely to be appropriate for both sets of institutions.... Is it reasonable to expect students at schools where the majority of students enter in the bottom 40 percent of national achievement test takers to achieve at the same level as those at schools where the majority come from the top 20 percent of such test takers? (16)

And for SOTL researchers, the problem is assuming that the same teaching methods or student learning outcomes can be used in different types of institutions. Yet that is often the assumption upon which SOTL rests. Indeed, such replication or application is often considered a hallmark of scholarship (Shulman 1999).

Thus, some SOTL studies describe a technique or approach that was "tested" in one type of institution yet assumed to be externally generalizable, or replicable, to different settings. As a case in point, and assuming authors publish in part to generalize their work, an analysis of 331 articles published in *Teaching Sociology* from 2000 to 2009 found that only 14 described a method or approach that was used in sociology courses at different institutions, and only 5 described methods used in different disciplines in different institutions (Paino, Blankenship, Grauerholz, and Chin 2010).

Critical differences exist that make generalizability difficult, even to similar types of institutions. There is wide variation within institutional types in how students are recruited and supported, how instructors are supported and rewarded, what instructional methods are popular and assessment approaches encouraged. Differences in institutional traditions, departmental structures, culture, goals, resources, and students make each setting unique so no single method can guarantee successful learning (Booth and Hyland 2000). These differences may explain, in part, the failure "to show substantial changes in curriculum-level outcomes" across programs (Leiberman et al. 2010, 1239). And while many educators place faith in standardized tests and surveys, others more attuned to contextual factors remain unpersuaded: "there is no measure of learning that can be applied across institutions and states" (Kuh 2004, 163).

SOTL supporters at our university have been struggling with this question of generalizability for a few years, and recently, following explicit recommendations made by Shulman in 2004, our Institutional Review Board (IRB) changed its approach to SOTL research applications by holding that if the pedagogical intervention and associated assessment methods being studied are consistent with what instructors normally do in the course of their teaching, and if the students are placed at no greater risk in the study than they would be in a normal teaching situation, then the "study does not fit the federal definition of 'human subjects research.'" While such investigations might still be seen as "systematic," our IRB concludes the knowledge gained by such a study "is not generalizable." Although this change was welcome news for many of our SOTL practitioners in the arts and humanities fields where research projects are not typically judged according to the standards of empirical science, it was most unwelcome news for some faculty members in education research and social sciences because lacking the designation of human subjects research is perceived as significantly lowering the scholarly value of their work.

Our point here is that SOTL findings should not be *assumed* generalizable or transferable across settings, and teaching methods should not be viewed as isolated behaviors. They are social acts informed by cultural traditions that become most meaningful when described in terms of specific histories and larger social contexts. We encourage application and replication, but only with careful attention to context, and exploring the factors that make some approaches transferable to other settings.

The Fallacy of Meaningful Assessment

Arguably, there is an inverse relationship between methodological sophistication and meaningful outcome assessment. That is, the requirements needed to make a quantitative study methodologically rigorous such as large samples, control groups, standardized measures, and so on necessarily restrict what outcomes can be tested. In particular, as sample size increases, the necessity of using quantifiable outcome measures increase. In classroom research, this almost always means students' grades on tests or their final course grades. But who has faith in current grading practices? At our university and nationally, we consistently hear faculty members complain that students who transfer from community colleges or other universities arrive at their classes underprepared despite having received high grades in prerequisite coursework. Teachers of lower-division courses at community colleges and universities complain that many of their students should not have graduated high school. How is it, we so often hear, that seniors in their last semester of college cannot write an effective argument despite receiving As in most of their coursework, including college composition?

If some SOTL researchers do have blind faith in quantitative measures of student learning, perhaps they should not. Arguing against such faith, Chris Rust (2011) points out that numbers and percentages cannot stand in place of actual learning outcomes. Students with the same scores in a class, for instance, will possess very different capacities and understandings. Also, small mathematical differences in scores cannot capture actual differences in student learning. Does a one-percentage point difference in a score, for instance, equate to a one-one-hundredth difference in learning? The assumption is absurd. Thirdly, he notes that scores almost always represent aggregations of criteria, which explains why students can pass examinations and courses without necessarily achieving passable understanding in all criteria. Further, numerical scores are often distorted by instructor feedback on student behaviors such as attendance and participation.

Rust's stronger argument against quantitative assessment practices addresses the negative effect of their use on learning. Because educational culture puts so much value on grades and rankings, students have been trained to focus on summative assessment scores and strategies to improve them rather than internalizing formative feedback for the purpose of improving learning. We have many times experienced our own students coming to us to justify the final score on their papers while completely ignoring the many comments we have written on them. The students' experience of our classes is a kind of soft battle among values. They may hear us emphasize the importance of student learning outcomes, but they tend to see our feedback as our validation of the grade we assign. They will recognize, from some degree of engagement, the value of their time spent with lessons. But neither outcome statements nor time on task will, for students, outweigh the value of the letter grade that accompanies assessment. The grade functions, to employ an idea from Neil Postman (1995), as a "controlling metaphor" in the students' educational worldview, one that will war against other core values as it unfolds into other domains. The push to quantifying SOTL has, we believe, shifted the focus from the types of learning most educators hope to achieve ("holistic," "deep learning," "life-long learning," "critical thinking," and so forth) to largely decontextualized, less meaningful outcomes.

While some SOTL researchers seem intent on measuring minute changes on a socially constructed grading scale, others make broad, but largely unsubstantiated, claims about deep learning—an equally problematic error in measurement. Indeed, an often-stated goal for SOTL researchers is to produce evidence of critical thinking, deep-structure thinking, or critical problem solving. However, William Becker (Becker and Andrews 2004) analyzes and rejects most of the research that attempts to prove how particular teaching methods result in deep learning. He points out a "relative dearth of quantitative work aimed at measuring changes in student outcomes associated with one teaching method versus another . . . given the rhetoric surrounding CATs and the numerous methods that fit under the banner of active and group learning" (266).

Alyssa Wise and Kevin O'Neill (2009) claim that empirical methods of assessment are typically inappropriate for evaluating deep learning outcomes; however, here we come to a fundamental contradiction. "In order to assess learning, to find out at what level a student is currently thinking with respect to a particular topic, it is necessary to be able to describe what the learning will be like at any particular stage" (Lueng 2000, 153). If educators are to employ effective outcome statements, they need those statements to be relevant, attainable, measureable, and significant; yet, by definition, deep learning and problem-based learning vest agency for the meaning making and solution finding with the student, and so, are difficult or impossible to predict, which makes post hoc analysis a more appropriate research tool for SOTL practitioners. Unless or until effective ways to tap meaningful learning are better understood and developed, we may be wise to consider measuring behaviors associated with learning, as well as processes surrounding learning rather than learning outcomes per se.

The Fallacy of Aligning a Single Teaching Approach with Effective Learning

In the research on deep learning, the SOTL discourse community has often attempted to validate a constructivist approach that champions what many would call a student-centered curriculum. The most often-stated goal for adopters of constructivist methods and those SOTL researchers who study them is to produce evidence of critical thinking, deep-structure thinking, or critical problem solving. The methodologies of collaborative learning (Nicholson and Ellis 2000), cooperative learning (Millis 2010), and often problem-based learning (Curle et al. 2006) are promoted, while simultaneously methodologies are criticized that are construed as "traditional" or teacher-centered where lecture and recall are emphasized. The claim most often heard against "traditional" methods is that they only foster surface learning and encourage rote learning of facts and superficial understandings of relationships.

Most surveys of the research on deep versus surface learning begin with Ference Marton and Roger Säljö (1976) who found that some students approach reading assignments looking for personal meaning and understanding while others focus more on disconnected facts and memorization in order to just "get through" the task. The research also mentions the work of Paul Ramsden (1992) and Graham Gibbs (2006) who noted that deep learners do things with facts to make them meaningful while surface learners focus on reproducing facts and not trying to change them in any way. Deep approaches to learning include trying to relate evidence and argument (Barker, McLean, and Roseman 2000), vigorously interacting with the subject (Davis and Salmon 2000), focusing on skills and processes rather than on transmission of information (Peters, Peterkin, and Williams 2000), showing a concern for how meaning is constituted as opposed to a noninterpretive focus on arrangement (Hounsell 2000), and relating new ideas to previous knowledge and seeking personal understanding (Hyland 2000).

The developmental story of constructivist theory is well known (Bruner 1986; Dewey 1916; Piaget 1950/1970; Vygotsky 1986), as is the history of its implementation, especially regarding problem-based learning (PBL) in medical education beginning with the McMaster model in 1969. The effectiveness of PBL has been, and remains, a common topic of examination for SOTL, despite the lack of convincing research to validate its claims as a superior teaching method. John Biggs (1999) proclaims, "Problem-based learning is alignment itself. The objectives are to get students to solve problems they will meet in their professional career—the teaching method is to present them with problems to solve; the assessment is based on how well they solve them.

It seems so obvious" (71). Biggs's reasoning seems intuitive enough, but PBL research is complicated by the fact that problem solving, per se, can be found in a range of activities including, for instance, "worked examples," a common feature in "traditional" classroom lectures.

Constructivist assumptions have also been challenged by cognitive psychologists, as evidenced by the constructivist/instructivist debate launched at the 2007 annual convention of the American Educational Research Association and later captured in the collection by Sigmund Tobias and Thomas M. Duffy, *Constructivist Instruction: Success or Failure?* (2009). The occasion for the debate was the challenge put forward by Paul A. Kirschner, John Sweller, and Richard E. Clark (2006) who charge that constructivist, discovery, problem-based, experiential, and inquiry-based teaching all fail to live up to their claims as superior teaching methods. In particular, they attack one of the central tenets of problem-based approaches to teaching that advocates presenting students with ill-structured problems with which they must grapple in small groups while receiving little guidance from the teacher.

What began with Marton and Säljö as a simple description of different student approaches to learning or habits of studying has grown into a belief held by most constructivists that novices learn best by trying to do what experts do; however, Daniel T. Willingham (2009) contradicts this belief by pointing to research that concludes "cognition early in training is fundamentally different from cognition late in training" (97), that there is a qualitative difference in thinking between the ways that experts and novices approach problem solving. Further, John D. Bransford, Ann L. Brown, and Rodney R. Cocking (2000) conclude that experts see meaningful patterns across large sets of well-organized content knowledge. Experts are context-oriented when they go about solving problems. They have multiple perspectives on issues and can be flexible in their selections of strategies. Novices, because their facility with the target domain by definition is superficial, cannot be expected to demonstrate critical thinking within the domain, much less be expected to demonstrate transfer across similar domains. Clearly, educators must move novices toward expertise and the ability to function autonomously in real-world scenarios, and this debate between constructivists and cognitivists reveals a potentially richer field for SOTL research into mixed modalities than that of taking either side exclusively.

A similar but unheeded challenge to a dichotomist or reductive approach to deep versus surface learning was put forward by Biggs and David A. Watkins (1996) and Watkins and Biggs (2001) regarding the "paradox of the Chinese learner." They observed that Chinese students were often thought (by Western educators) to embody a surface approach to learning. They were considered passive before the authority of the teacher and text. They were thought to focus almost exclusively on rote memorization. Chinese teaching was considered an extreme case of a traditional, teacher-centered approach. Classes were often large and those responsible for assessment were often not those responsible for the curriculum. The "paradox" was that Chinese students consistently scored well on problem-solving exams despite the absence of a problem-based learning curriculum as understood in the West. What Biggs and Watkins discovered was that Chinese students were not learning passively, that while repetition and memorization were prominent, meaning and interpretation were also emphasized. They noted that, because American teachers typically encouraged their students to apply a single problem-solving method to multiple problems, moving on to new material quickly and often, the Chinese method encouraged students to stay with one problem for multiple iterations, incorporating small elaborations and focusing on subtle complexities of a problem as well as multiple pathways to the solution. So what appeared to be strictly a surface approach to learning according to American educators was really an approach that intertwined deep and surface approaches within the context of Chinese culture. The Chinese teachers sought to create synergies between didactic and constructivist approaches (Chan and Rao 2009), and we propose that this kind of synergetic approach inform more SOTL research. While there is strong logic for including constructivist methods in the higher education curriculum to promote student engagement and to simulate realistic scenarios, too often SOTL researchers base their studies on constructivist assumptions about learning in exclusion to behaviorist, cognitivist, and humanist approaches. Certainly, students can—and should—grapple with problems beyond their present ability, but grappling alone will not make them deep thinkers; they must also develop mastery of the domain, which requires sustained attention and commitment of new information and processes to memory. Teachers need to draw from a spectrum of learning activities appropriate to the readiness of the learner in each facet of desired understanding (Wiggins and McTighe 1998).

• • •

The actions of teaching and researching are not always mutually exclusive, and evidence gathered in good conscience for the primary purpose of student development can constructively be shared with secondary audiences for broader benefits. Institutions should clearly distinguish between SOTL activity and pure research (Shulman 2004), and they should clearly distinguish between teaching activity and SOTL. Scholarship is best conducted before and after the teaching act. When teaching, the teacher's focus should be student learning. The SOTL researcher, then, must be careful to maintain the primacy of the teaching environment for student learning and resist the potential, if not likely, promotion of a tertiary audience for assessment data—the future readers of SOTL articles—to primary importance. As Grant Wiggins (1993) observed, "Because the *student* is the primary client of all assessment, assessment should be designed to *improve* performance, not just monitor it. Any modern testing (including testing used for accountability) must ensure that the primary client for the information is well served" (6).

What we have tried to set forth here is not a repudiation of SOTL as systematic inquiry, nor a denial of the role of the instructor in the critical observation of classroom teaching, nor a call to abandon empirical methods in SOTL. We warn of the risks for SOTL researchers who adopt the assumptions of more established disciplines like educational, social, or psychological research to secure credibility. While qualitative research methods that might include such evidence as auto-ethnographies or personal reflective statements may never prove causal relations between variables in the learning environment and will likely never convince empiricists to innovate in their own teaching or to support a colleague's promotion or tenure based on SOTL research alone, we argue that they are appropriate to the practice of teaching and for our primary interest holders. Where the aim of SOTL is to increase the value of teaching in higher education, especially in relation to the value of research, we need to base that increase on the inherent characteristics of teaching and learning, not on the transformation of teaching into research or the transformation of students into subjects. We urge classroom teachers who wish to engage in SOTL to adopt methods that always align with their primary ethical responsibility to their students. The scholarship of teaching and learning remains a worthy initiative in search of itself.

REFERENCES

Atkinson, Maxine, Alison R. Buck, and Andrea N. Hunt. 2009. "Sociology of the College Classroom: Applying Sociological Theory at the Classroom Level." *Teaching Sociology* 37, no. 3: 233–44.

Barker, Hannah, Monica McLean, and Mark Roseman. 2000. "Re-thinking the History Curriculum: Enhancing Students' Communication and Group-Work Skills." In *The Practice of University History Teaching,* ed. Alan Booth and Paul Hyland, 60–69. Manchester: Manchester University Press.

Barr, Robert B., and John Tagg. 1995. "From Teaching to Learning: A New Paradigm for Undergraduate Education." *Change* (Nov/Dec): 13–25.

Becker, William E., and Moya L. Andrews, eds. 2004. *The Scholarship of Teaching and Learning in Higher Education: Contributions of Research Universities.* Bloomington: Indiana University Press.

Biggs, John. 1999. "Assessing for Quality in Learning: Abstract of Highlights of a Plenary Session at AAHE's 1999 Assessment Conference." In *Assessment to Promote Deep Learning: Insight from AAHE's 2000 and 1999 Assessment Conferences,* ed. Linda Suskie, 65–68. Washington, DC: American Association for Higher Education.

Biggs, John. 1999. "What the Student Does: Teaching for Enhanced Learning." *Higher Education Research and Development* 18, no. 1: 57–75.

Biggs, John B., and David A. Watkins, eds. 1996. *The Chinese Learner: Cultural, Psychological, and Contextual Influences.* Hong Kong: Comparative Education Research Centre.

Billson, Janet Mancini. 1986. "The College Classroom as a Small Group: Some Implications for Teaching and Learning." *Teaching Sociology* 14, no. 3: 143–51.

Blumberg, Phyllis. 2009. *Developing Learner-Centered Teaching: A Practical Guide for Faculty.* San Francisco: Jossey-Bass.

Booth, Alan, and Paul Hyland, eds. 2000. *The Practice of University History Teaching.* Manchester: Manchester University Press.

Boyer, Ernest L. 1990. *Scholarship Reconsidered: Priorities of the Professoriate.* Stanford, CA: Carnegie Foundation for the Advancement of Teaching.

Bransford, John D., Ann L. Brown, and Rodney R. Cocking, eds. 2000. *How People Learn: Brain, Mind, Experience, and School.* Washington, DC: National Academy Press.

Bruner, Jerome. 1986. *Actual Minds, Possible Worlds.* Cambridge: Harvard University Press.

Calhoun, Craig. 1999. "The Changing Character of College: Institutional Transformation in American Higher Education." In *The Social Worlds of Higher Education,* ed. Bernice A. Pedcosolido and Ronald Aminzade, 9–31. Thousand Oaks, CA: Pine Forge Press.

Campbell, Donald T., and Julian C. Stanley. 1963. *Experimental and Quasi-Experimental Designs for Research.* Chicago: Rand McNally.

Chan, Carol K. K., and Nirmala Rao, eds. 2009. *Revisiting the Chinese Learner: Changing Contexts, Changing Education.* Hong Kong: Comparative Education Research Centre.

Cross, K. P., and M. H. Steadman. 1996. *Classroom Research: Implementing the Scholarship of Teaching.* San Francisco: Jossey-Bass.

Curle, Christine, Jim Wood, Catherine Haslam, and Jacqui Stedmon. 2006. "Assessing Learning in a PBL Curriculum for Healthcare Training." In *Innovative Assessment in Higher Education,* ed. Cordelia Bryan and Karen Clegg, 180–90. New York: Routledge.

Davis, Barbara Gross. 2009. *Tools for Teaching,* 2nd ed. San Francisco: Jossey-Bass.

Davis, John R., and Patrick Salmon. 2000. "'Deep Learning' and the Large Seminar in History Teaching." In *The Practice of University History Teaching,* ed. Alan Booth and Paul Hyland, 125–36. Manchester: Manchester University Press.

Dewey, John. 1916. *Democracy and Education.* New York: Macmillan.

Gibbs, Graham. 2006. "Why Assessment Is Changing." In *Innovative Assessment in Higher Education,* ed. Cordelia Bryan and Karen Clegg, 11–22. New York: Routledge.

Glassick, Charles E., Mary Taylor Huber, and Gene I. Maeroff. 1997. *Scholarship Assessed: Evaluation of the Professoriate.* San Francisco: Jossey-Bass.

Grauerholz, Liz, and John Zipp. 2008. "How to Do the Scholarship of Teaching and Learning." *Teaching Sociology* 36, no. 1: 87–94.

Hounsell, Dai. 2000. "Reappraising and Recasting the History Essay." In *The Practice of University History Teaching,* ed. Alan Booth and Paul Hyland, 181–93. Manchester: Manchester University Press.

Huber, Mary Taylor, and Pat Hutchings. 2005. *The Advancement of Learning: Building the Teaching Commons.* Stanford, CA: Carnegie Foundation for the Advancement of Teaching and Jossey-Bass.

Hyland, Paul. 2000. "Learning from Feedback on Assessment." In *The Practice of University History Teaching,* ed. Alan Booth and Paul Hyland, 233–47. Manchester: Manchester University Press.

Kanuka, Heather. 2011 "Keeping the Scholarship in the Scholarship of Teaching and Learning." *International Journal for the Scholarship of Teaching and Learning* 5, no. 1. http://academics.georgiasouthern.edu/ijsotl.

Kirschner, Paul A., John Sweller, and Richard E. Clark. 2006. "Why Minimal Guidance during Instruction Does Not Work: An Analysis of the Failure of Constructivist, Discovery, Problem-Based, Experiential, and Inquiry-Based Teaching." *Educational Psychologist* 42, no. 2: 75–86.

Kuh, George. 2004. "The Contributions of the Research University to Assessment and Innovation in Undergraduate Education." In *The Scholarship of Teaching and Learning in Higher Education: Contributions of Research Universities,* ed. William E. Becker and Moya L. Andrews, 161–92. Bloomington: Indiana University Press.

Leiberman, Steven, Michael A. Ainsworth, Gregory K. Asimakis, Lauree Thomas, Lisa D. Cain, Melodee G. Mancuso, Jeffrey P. Rabek, Ni Zhang, and Ann W. Frye. 2010. "Effects of Comprehensive Educational Reforms on Academic Success in a Diverse Student Body." *Medical Education* 44: 1232–40.

Lueng, C. F. 2000. "Assessment for Learning: Using SOLO Taxonomy to Measure Design Performance of Design and Technology Students." *International Journal of Technology and Design Education* 10: 149–61.

Marton, Ference, and Roger Säljö. 1976. "On Qualitative Differences in Learning." *British Journal of Educational Psychology* 46: 115–27.

Maurer, Trent W. 2011. "On Publishing SOTL Articles." *International Journal for the Scholarship of Teaching and Learning* 5. http://academics.georgiasouthern.edu/ijsotl.

McKinney, Kathleen. 2005. "The Value of SOTL in Sociology. A Response to 'The Scholarship of Teaching and Learning—Done by Sociologists: Let's Make that the Sociology of Higher Education.'" *Teaching Sociology* 33, no. 4: 417–19.

———. 2007. *Enhancing Learning through the Scholarship of Teaching and Learning.* San Francisco: Jossey-Bass.

Millis, Barbara J. 2010. "Promoting Deep Learning." IDEA Paper No. 47. Manhattan, KS: IDEA Center. http://www.theideacenter.org/IDEAPaper47.

Moore, Helen. 2001. "Comment from the Editor: Publishing in Teaching Sociology." *Teaching Sociology* 29, no. 4: v.

Nicholson, Tony, and Graham Ellis. 2000. "Assessing Group Work to Develop Collaborative Learning." In *The Practice of University History Teaching,* ed. Alan Booth and Paul Hyland, 208–19. Manchester: Manchester University Press.

Paino, Maria, Chastity Blankenship, Liz Grauerholz, and Jeff Chin. 2010. "SOTL in *Teaching Sociology.*" Paper presented at the Centennial Symposium on Scholarship of Teaching and Learning, Banff, Alberta, Canada, November.

Peters, John, Christie Peterkin, and Chris Williams. 2000. "Progression within Modular History Degrees: Profiling for a Student-Centred Approach." In *The Practice of University Teaching,* ed. Alan Booth and Paul Hyland, 137–53. Manchester: Manchester University Press.

Piaget, Jean. 1950/1970. *Genetic Epistemology.* Trans. E. Duckworth. New York: Columbia University Press.

Postman, Neil. 1995. *The End of Education: Redefining the Value of School.* New York: Vintage.

Ramsden, Paul. 1992. *Learning to Teaching in Higher Education.* London: Routledge.

Rust, Chris. 2011. "The Unscholarly Use of Numbers in Our Assessment Practices: What Will Make Us Change?" *International Journal for the Scholarship of Teaching and Learning* 5, no. 1. http://www.georgiasouthern.edu/ijsotl.

Schroeder, Connie M. 2007. "Countering SOTL Marginalization: A Model for Integrating SOTL with Institutional Initiatives." *International Journal for the Scholarship of Teaching and Learning* 1, no. 1. http://www.georgiasouthern.edu /ijsotl.

Shulman, Lee S. 1999. "The Scholarship of Teaching." *Change* 31, no. 5: 11.

———. 2004. *The Wisdom of Practice: Essays on Teaching, Learning, and Learning to Teach.* San Francisco: Jossey-Bass.

Sweller, John, Paul A. Kirschner, and Richard E. Clark. 2007. "Why Minimally Guided Teaching Techniques Do Not Work: A Reply to Commentaries." *Educational Psychologist* 42, no. 2: 115–21.

Tobias, Sigmund, and Thomas M. Duffy. 2009. *Constructivist Instruction: Success or Failure?* New York: Routledge.

Vygotsky, Lev S. 1986. *Thought and Language.* Cambridge: MIT Press.

Walvoord, Barbara E. 2004. *Assessment Clear and Simple: A Practical Guide for Institutions, Departments, and General Education.* San Francisco: Jossey-Bass.

Watkins, David A., and John B. Biggs, eds. 2001. *Teaching the Chinese Learner: Psychological and Pedagogical Perspectives.* Hong Kong: Comparative Education Research Centre.

Weimer, Maryellen. 2002. *Learner-Centered Teaching.* San Francisco: Jossey-Bass.

———. 2006. *Enhancing Scholarly Work on Teaching and Learning: Professional Literature that Makes a Difference.* San Francisco: Jossey-Bass.

Wiggins, Grant. 1993. *Assessing Student Performance: Exploring the Purpose and Limits of Testing.* San Fransisco: Jossey-Bass.

Wiggins, Grant, and Jay McTighe. 1998. *Understanding by Design.* Alexandria, VA: Association for Supervision and Curriculum Development.

Willingham, Daniel T. 2009. *Why Don't Students Like School? A Cognitive Scientist Answers Questions about How the Mind Works and What It Means for the Classroom.* San Francisco: Jossey-Bass.

Wise, Alyssa F., and Kevin O'Neill. 2009. "Beyond More versus Less: A Reframing of the Debate on Instructional Guidance." In *Constructivist Instruction: Success or Failure,* ed. Sigmund Tobias and Thomas M. Duffy, 82–105. New York: Routledge.

CHAPTER 9

Exploring Student Learning in Unfamiliar Territory: A Humanist and a Scientist Compare Notes

DAVID A. REICHARD AND KATHY TAKAYAMA

This chapter is written in an unconventional form to underline our shared interest in exploring student learning through genres that are not conventional to our disciplines. Our work did not start out as a collaborative project between faculty from very different disciplines to investigate what happens when students engage the learning process in ways atypical of their disciplines, what we came to call working in "unfamiliar territory." In fact, it began as a conversation about the student learning in our respective classes and how we encouraged them to engage deeply with what they were learning. As teachers, we were both challenging our students to think "outside the box." For Reichard, this meant having students of history present their final research projects through an interactive poster session modeled on a format more typically used by scientists, a somewhat foreign genre for historians (Berry, Schmied, and Schrock 2008). For Takayama, this meant having microbiology students create what she called a "Bug Book" to supplement a traditional laboratory notebook; a place where students could create a narrative about their "bug" (the microbial subject of their research) in a creative format more typical of the humanities. Ongoing conversations about our practice led to an increasing interest in the implications for understanding what such "unfamiliar" moments mean for student learning and to our own more sustained investigation of the question. As we came to argue, engagement with the unfamiliar became a way for students to understand what it means to think in disciplinary ways, especially by moving beyond the expected disciplinary conventions in their learning process. We agree that students need to understand what Velda McCune and Dai Hounsell (2005) describe as the "ways of thinking and practising" in particular disciplines and that faculty serve students well in "decoding" their disciplines (Pace 2004b; Shopkow et al. in this volume). However, we also suggest that by working in unfamiliar territory, students can refine their understanding of what it means to think in disciplinary terms and gain a deep appreciation for how creativity can push disciplinary boundaries and create experiences that enhance the learning process for students and foster an appreciation of the excitement of "doing" science[1] or history.[2]

What became equally apparent, and the central purpose of this chapter, is how we reached such conclusions through cross-disciplinary collaboration. Such collaboration played a critical role in shaping our respective areas of inquiry and understanding what we were finding in those inquiries as researchers and as teachers. Having met as Carnegie scholars with the Carnegie Academy for the Scholarship of Teaching and Learning (CASTL) program, we are testament to the value of those interactions, amazed and delighted that a microbiologist and an historian could sit down and talk about these issues and continue to learn from each other's scholarship. As we contend in this chapter, the scholarship of teaching and learning (SOTL) provides a unique opportunity for researchers from a variety of disciplines to come together, share their work, and build enriched projects from that interaction, whether through the kinds of questions asked, the variety of research methods used, or approaches to analyzing data collected. As we suggest, these cross-disciplinary conversations are a defining feature of SOTL, a signature practice and methodology.[3]

To capture the spirit of our intent, what follows is not a typical presentation of our respective research project findings. Rather, it is organized to capture our ongoing, and arguably incomplete, conversation about what happens when students work in unfamiliar territory. Because that conversation emerged over the last few years in a nonlinear fashion, often taking the form of short snippets at an SOTL conference, over dinner with colleagues, via Skype or email, we wanted to reproduce the way our thinking has evolved and our collaboration has developed. Yet reproducing an ongoing conversation is a challenge. Thus, to do so, we recently sat down and synthesized what we have been discussing over the past few years. This time, we captured our dialogue through a digital recording, transcribed the conversation, and met after reviewing that transcript to discuss the conversation we recorded one more time, pinpointing essential issues and questions about our investigations of student work in unfamiliar territory as well as the value of cross-disciplinary collaboration in SOTL. What emerged from this process, perhaps not surprisingly, was more than a synthesis of what we had been discussing for several years. Rather, a host of new, and unexpected, questions emerged from the process itself, perhaps highlighting the value of such conversations in the first place.

While we have not reproduced our conversation verbatim, as it has been edited and organized thematically for greater clarity, we did want to capture our process by presenting the dialogue itself. This stylistic choice is deliberate as we wanted to capture the interactive nature of our collaboration. For clarification and elaboration, we have included a brief introduction to various sections of the text as markers for the reader. Our format is, admittedly, only a partial representation of what transpired in the actual recorded conversation as well as several years of unrecorded interactions. As such, it is an act of translation, a way to fit a rich and ever evolving conversation into a more traditional scholarly format—a written text. But we sort of like it that way, and invite you to join in as well.

Engaging Meanings of the Disciplines in Unfamiliar Territory

Perhaps one of the most important by-products of our ongoing conversation about what it means for students to work in "unfamiliar territory" has been how to help students think about the meaning of disciplinary conventions (Pace 2004b). Our conversation reveals a lot about how cross-disciplinary collaboration in SOTL helps explain why such questions emerged in the first place. In this section, note the movement back and forth from discussion of our own courses, process for collecting data in our respective research projects, and how SOTL inspired our understandings of what we wanted to accomplish in both our teaching and our research.

KT: One of the things I think we talked about earlier was that you don't recognize unfamiliar territory unless you deeply know what familiarity is and what that looks like in your discipline. My microbiology students certainly weren't experts, but they were science students, so they had a comfort zone that defined their familiar territory. If they're taking a science course, there are things they expect: they would expect that there would be a lab component associated with the lecture and that the labs would be very methodical. They think that they would be expected to have documentation in a structured way. That was the norm for the discipline. And, there's some sense, I guess, of linearity in their thinking with respect to how the concepts they are learning in the lectures apply in the lab, and how they document the manifestations of that application. So when I introduced the notion of the Bug Book, I thought I was freeing them from this rigidity, because I thought not all people can really appreciate the excitement of the ongoing investigation they were doing for the whole semester, trying to isolate a bug—a microbe—from the environment. And so I thought, why not make it more open-ended and unstructured, so they could just get newspaper clippings, or write thoughts down about their bug, or if they saw a movie about it, it would give them the opportunity to think more broadly and deeply about their organism. But, as we discussed earlier, some of them were really freaked out initially because they were stepping into unfamiliar territory. And some of them continued to use the standard lab notebook protocol because that was safe and that was the norm.

DR: *Do you mean they used the format of the lab book in the Bug Book?*

KT: Yes, they did. I have one here with me. It's blank and there are no lines, no table of contents. The first year I did this, it had grids. After that, I just went with completely blank books. At least the first year, when they had the grids, they still felt safe, because they had a structure. But later on, when there were no grids, you started to see the evolution of their sense of freedom from not having the structure.

DR: *I remember seeing one with drawings, multicolored sorts of notes, scribbles and pictures.*

KT: I guess even as the teacher, I thought, "Wow, this is pretty unconventional." For me, my familiar territory was even deeper and this was a leap. Once I made it blank, there were more illustrations. The grid lines were no longer there to give them that safety net.

DR: *Did the need for the blank page come from your desire for students to have a freer space than a lab book?*

KT: I realized that many of them were not doing things much differently from what they were doing in their laboratory notebooks. It seemed as if they were trying to maintain two lab notebooks at the same time. And I thought, "Well, this defeats the purpose." They thought this is what I wanted to see. So long as the grid lines were there, they felt beholden to adhere to this formal scientific structure, and of course, grid lines are very scientific—hence, there were a lot of graphs in their Bug Books. And so I realized, I, as a teacher didn't have a self-awareness of how much structure the grid lines provided because my perception was quite different from theirs.[4]

DR: *You mentioned the disciplinary familiarity piece. It's very similar in my history class. It was a gay and lesbian history class and the students are already in unfamiliar territory. But, the subject aside, in the human communication major, they write a lot of papers, they write a lot of reflections, they write text for presentations that they sometimes translate into PowerPoint.[5] So, in the major itself, there is an expectation that when they come into this class, they're going to write. Also, it's a history class and the disciplinary conventions for presenting your work tend to be research papers or written exams. And if you do an oral presentation, it tends to be very linear. Professional historians tend to present their work in public as a written paper you read for twenty minutes on a panel with several other presenters and a commentator pulls it all together. That's your typical history conference. So I wondered what would happen if the students presented their research like scientists? That was the motivation for the approach I wanted to try.*

The conversation turned to how our involvement in SOTL shifted our understanding of each other's disciplinary conventions, and how those cross-disciplinary interactions inspired the way we think about what "unfamiliar territory" might mean for our students.

DR: *Using posters grew directly out of my experience of working with folks like you, with scientists in CASTL, and going to SOTL conferences. My experience of learning from scientists included working with you, Heidi Elmendorf and others in our cohort, and then going to a SOTL conference and talking to scientists at a poster session—my first ever. I was blown away by that idea that you could present your research in this visually interesting way, which appealed to me, but also in a conversational way. It's developmental. You're not presenting necessarily the final version of this, learning from folks like you that science is an ongoing process. History does that too, but the presentation of historical research tends to look like an argument, a final argument.*

KT: So, the converse is true with me, where I learned to appreciate the weight and significance of the written word for historians. Previously I would naïvely think, "Why do historians stand there and read their papers verbatim [at conferences]? Why can't they just get up and speak, the way scientists do without any papers in front of them?" And I realized, from speaking to historians like yourself, that the structure of the argument and the choice of words are so critical that you must adhere to what you've created. The written document that you're reading from is equivalent to the data that I'm selecting to support my argument as a scientist; it's accurate and it's well considered in the way I've selected the samples to use for my experiment. Everything on that one PowerPoint slide counts. So, I'm curious to know, when you had to give your poster presentation at CASTL and were thrust into unfamiliar territory, what went through your mind?

DR: *That's a great question. I hadn't really considered how that specific experience influenced my decision to use posters in my history class. When I remember that experience, the first thing that leaps to mind is "How can I put all this information on a poster?" I learned through that process that you have to select your evidence carefully. I recall Lee Shulman's discussion about rich representation and how it makes a big difference in how the research results are presented to an audience, particularly in an interdisciplinary context, where the audience for the research or the presentation might not be of your discipline but you share an interest in that piece of student learning. I had to learn to choose carefully and think, visually, how it will be laid out in a single space.*

That process is very different than a linear paper where you build an argument from beginning to end with an introduction, a really good example, a research question, go into the story a bit, and then wrap it up with a conclusion in twenty minutes. In a poster you have to elaborate to some degree on your whole argument and place it in a flat plane. So it's not linear anymore, it's . . . I don't even know what the word is.

KT: It's representational, I think, but you're right, it's not linear. It's selective.

DR: *When I worked with my students on how to translate historical research into a visual format, this was the biggest lesson they learned. I interviewed students about doing their posters and the selection of evidence became one of their biggest observations, learning how to make choices about what's the best piece of evidence.[6] The other piece was the conversation, since that's why a piece of evidence is so critical. In a history context, you present your argument in a paper and the audience might ask a question later. In a poster session, there is a face-to-face dialogue, and the students talked about how the evidence they selected were simply prompts to engage in conversation where they could go deeper.*

Similarly, our cross-disciplinary conversations consistently presented opportunities for us to learn more about each other's disciplinary processes in general. The following exchange about whether the creation of open-ended Bug Books in Takayama's microbiology course helped prepare the "habits of mind" students need to do scientific inquiry and the way the exchange helped us find common ground in terms of student learning.

DR: *Do you think the Bug Book prepared students for the unfamiliarity they would encounter in the professional context? That's part of the scientific process, right? Would they record items in the Bug Book in a different way than in the lab book?*

KT: What do you mean by "they would encounter"?

DR: *In their experiments, the results are completely not what they expected to see, and perhaps it moves them in an unfamiliar direction.*

KT: Oh, that is science! You observe those unexpected results and you think, "Wow! What just happened?" It's part of the scientific process, whereby things do occasionally reveal themselves in ways that are totally unexpected. Sometimes they are just total flukes, anomalies, because of the way you set up the experiment; something's weird. So the first rule of thumb is, you repeat it. If it still happens, then you think, "I'm going to figure this out. What's going on?" That is part of the scientific process, where something unfamiliar leads to new questions. And really important discoveries were made because of that. Suddenly there is an unfamiliar thing that rears its head and you're so intrigued by it, you have to figure out what's going on. I think that's really inherent to the excitement of science. Science should never be predictable all the time. It's about the unknown. It's about constantly asking questions and asking more questions.

DR: *That's interesting to me. Because if you think about it, introducing the Bug Book is just like that, in the sense that students were faced with this unfamiliar thing that they have to do in this class and they have to really figure out what to do with this new piece of information, and how do I respond. It's not exactly the same but I wonder if it picks up on the same skill that they need to develop as scientists, that is, working with the unfamiliar, in an unfamiliar kind of context.*

KT: That's an interesting point, and I can see how that preparation of mind can be useful, but I think for these students, they would probably view the comparison as apples and oranges. They would say, "Well if you get an unexpected result in science, you're still doing science." But, in this case, they didn't think this was science, so they weren't thinking about this in the context of preparedness of mind. It was, "Here's science and here's 'not science.'"

DR: *But don't you think that, in terms of the general development of thinking skills, that they are similar in the sense. . . .*

KT: They are.

DR: *But they don't look the same . . .*

KT: Right.

DR: *. . . on the surface. For example, when my students assemble a poster, they are assembling an argument.*

KT: Right.

DR: *They're marshaling their evidence. They're presenting their sources, their bibliographies, they're engaging in doing history, but it doesn't look like what they normally do in a research paper.*

KT: That's right.

DR: *And they didn't see it in some ways as the same thing.*

KT: I totally agree.

Another important part of our conversation was a discussion of how students responded to working in unfamiliar territory in different ways. This part of the conversation highlights the importance of how the impact of such liberation from convention led to creative, sometimes unconventional, and sometimes jarring experiences. The following exchange illustrates:

KT: I was thinking about your students when you were speaking earlier about students choosing what images they were going to use for their poster, and those choices becoming points of dialogue for them. Similarly, how did your students feel when given the importance of the written word for their argument; they did not have that familiar format anymore?

DR: *There was a mixture of reactions. Some students, similar to yours, were freed from that convention. In interviews, some of them talked about it this way: "I could really represent this in a way that allowed me to explore the multidimensions of the topic that I researched. And I could represent it in a way that captured the fun." I'll give you a good example. A student who did a project on drag queen culture covered the whole poster with glitter. You'd never see that, I assume, in a scientific poster. When I asked her about the glitter, she said, "Well I needed to capture the fun of this drag scene and the only way I could do it was to describe it or I could use glitter. And the glitter allowed me to really capture the spirit of what I found out when I did my research." So there's a good example of a student who embraced the medium, the best of what the medium can offer for her topic.*

KT: That's fantastic. That's wonderful because this gave her something she wouldn't have had it been an essay, right?

DR: *Exactly.*

KT: But if it had been an essay how would she have captured that spirit? I mean, would she just write about it?

DR: *She might have described it using firsthand experience. She would have likely found a quote from a drag queen describing glitter, or the use of costume and fantasy and all these other things she read about, and she would have translated it into the written word probably through a piece of evidence.*

In Takayama's microbiology class, some students embraced the "Bug Book" format and its invitation to creativity. Reflecting on which students did so, she explains:

KT: Some students who enjoyed the Bug Book were more multidimensional. They were probably like me in that they appreciated having different ways of integrating and considering science. Some of them were inherently artistic. They were very talented—visually talented—students. I told you about one student who created a manga,[7] a version of the story of his bug. He also happened to be the class clown. He always sat front and center in every single lecture. I came to expect him to deliver his corny jokes during class. So I think people like that really latch on to the nonconventional because it's inherent in their own personalities. It probably is a combination of personality, and learning styles, and interests. They did have an interest in the humanities and arts. In the Australian system, students don't receive a liberal arts education. They enter a major as soon as they arrive in college, so I think it perhaps freed them from that strain, from that structure of being pigeonholed into a career path.[8]

Some students, while embracing the unconventional—and creative—formats, nevertheless saw its limitations for what they hoped to accomplish. One of Reichard's students, who created one of the most visually striking and successful posters, nevertheless revealed later that she would have preferred a traditional paper, and in fact, when describing her poster during an interview, demonstrated how she had organized the poster using a written text as her model, hinting that the poster was not as comprehensive or as rigorous as a paper. Takayama asked about this and Reichard replied:

DR: *I had some students who considered posters not as comprehensive a way to present your research as would be a paper. A good example is a student who did a poster on the history of gays in the military. She structured her entire poster, as she told me, to look like a paper. So the whole thing was structured to read like a paper; you started on one end and ended up at the bottom. Visually it was very striking and it was a terrific poster, probably the one most students commented on in their evaluations of the poster session. When I talked to her about it, she was concerned that she could not represent the richness of her research into four squares of the poster and expressed a little bit of dissatisfaction with that part of the process. She loved doing the poster. She actually enjoyed it, but as she talked about it, "I couldn't really describe all of my findings." She wrote narratives and then put them on the poster, so you could literally read all the sections and get the gist of her argument.*

For Takayama's students, the more unsettling thing was moving beyond the confines of a laboratory notebook where everything is recorded so as to be reproducible by others, a central aspect of the scientific method. When asked to create an open-ended Bug Book, a place for reflection and connection outside the protocols of a laboratory notebook, the results were mixed. And some of the students' discomfort reflected, in part, their lack of expertise.

KT: In a laboratory notebook, the analogy would be a recipe. You have to know exactly how many tablespoons of sugar to add and there is a set of instructions that follows. It's really focused on what has been done and what's going to happen next, or even drawing in previous data that have now been illuminated whereas there was something confusing about it earlier. It's not linear, but there is always a trajectory in terms of what's happening. They didn't know what the ideas and reflections meant. Were they about your experiments? About the bug? About what?

DR: *So that reflection part was the most confusing?*

KT: Most confusing, very, very unsettling for them. Now, the first year we were pretty structured. I note in the Bug Book instructions, "You must have a concept map." Perhaps this was my intent at scaffolding, because I thought,

"Maybe this will help them to start to formulate what they're going to do." We even stipulated what this was going to do. "It's going to help you draw relationships between your bug and anything you deem relevant to its story." So even though we're saying that you should have a concept map, this is not the concept map that they know. We were talking about stories. What story? Bugs don't have stories.

DR: *Creative writers would say so.*

KT: That's right. The terms we were using were just so wacky for these science students that they did not make sense. We're giving them some structure but still there are untidy aspects to it that are quite unsettling. Then, the year after that, there were no instructions. It was just, "This is your Bug Book and you are free to write anything about your bug."

DR: *Did you have Bug Book guidelines the second year?*

KT: The second year had a page that said, "Bug Book Guidelines," and then it said, "The guidelines are, that there are no guidelines. This is a blank book in which you are welcome to document anything you'd like to about your bug."

DR: *So, my sense is that the second year you threw out the conventions.*

KT: We did. As a scientist, I thought that the format with only the grids in the first year was loose, but I realized that's because I'm an expert in the discipline. My thinking was that this is so unconventional that surely it should free them, but since they weren't experts yet—they are still first- or second-year students—in the first year they just selectively read the guidelines and said, "Okay, all right, it has grids and I'm just going to do the same thing that I usually do but this time at least I know I don't have to write down every single chemical or everything that goes into this experiment. I don't have to sign every page." I realized I needed them to really just jump off the cliff, to really free them.

Cross-disciplinary Collaboration in SOTL as Signature Practice

As the selections from our ongoing conversation suggest, we contend that cross-disciplinary collaboration is a signature practice of SOTL. In our case, the conversations have focused on the practice of doing SOTL work, reflecting the value of such collaboration for identifying what to investigate in terms of student learning (the kinds of questions one might ask), the methods to use in SOTL research (how to make choices from a range of initially unfamiliar methods), or the audience(s) we hope to reach (beyond the usual disciplinary suspects). The following exchange illustrates how our cross-disciplinary collaboration produced such dynamic results:

KT: SOTL really allows people to think about and draw upon some of those shared commonalities. One does not necessarily have to be concerned about what the product is going to look like at the end of that collaboration, which I think is often what has to drive collaborative research, because there does have to be something to show—the fruits of the collaboration and what the data look like, so to speak, and what the evidence and the conclusions are. But SOTL creates an opportunity for engagement purely in the process of thinking about teaching and learning and how our students are or are not learning. That in itself defines the nature of cross-disciplinary collaboration. I think when you and I started talking several years ago, we weren't thinking in formal terms about a collaboration, or that there would be a product at the end, but we really were trying to understand what this process looks like. And I think through those shared conversations, commonalities and contrasts started to emerge that nucleated some ideas about, "Well, wouldn't it be nice if we could go public with this. We've so much enjoyed having these conversations, but we would like to share some of these ideas with a broader audience."

DR: *What's interesting to me is that the collaboration is more than the research. Let me back up for a minute. You mention this idea that it starts as a conversation and so this idea that my engagement with a scientist sparked interest in what we have in common as teachers. That conversation gave me the opportunity to ask new questions about what's going on in my classes for students. It propelled me in a new direction. For example, I could easily have looked at what and how do students demonstrate their research skills in a history class and look at their papers. But by learning from scientists how a different discipline presents their work, a new idea emerged for me about looking at the research process by having students present their work in a visual way. It actually mirrors an important element of how I teach history, using visual evidence. Our conversations raised all these questions for me about the impact of visual representations and the teaching and learning of history, and what happens when students use visual means to demonstrate what they know about their research projects. That's an unexpected place for me. I never expected that I would be measuring or thinking about what students do with posters in a history class. My involvement in collaborative SOTL raised these questions for me, propelled me in new directions, helped me to think about the process of the research design and then interpret what I found. What SOTL is for me as a professional, as an historian, is the richness of cross-disciplinary collaboration.*

KT: Picking up on what you said about new questions and new directions, I think had I not been having these conversations with you, my ideas about visualizations and visuality would be very limited to my own context of teaching science students. Now I'm thinking about visuality in a much broader sense and taking into consideration what visual literacy looks like across the disciplines. So there are branches that come out of these cross-disciplinary collaborations that I could not even have designed had I wanted to because they only arose through learning about unfamiliar territory for me. When I have the opportunity to engage in conversations that bring me to unfamiliar territory, it forces me to reconsider paradigms that I have about what learning is for my students, which have been limited to sort of "small-box" scientific thinking and doing. I think the cross-disciplinary conversations allow for unexpected ideas to present themselves and these small paradigm shifts challenge you to think about what you thought you knew about student learning and the context within which they are learning.

As other authors explore in this collection, what constitutes SOTL "research" has emerged frequently in our conversations, especially how to select the best methods to investigate student learning (see Poole; Grauerholz and Main in this volume). Cross-disciplinary conversations like ours help to alleviate such "methods anxiety," a common issue among SOTL researchers, especially those who are new to this kind of work.[9] The following exchange illustrates:

DR: *The value of those cross-disciplinary conversations is that you take a fresh look at something you've done in the past and it might propel you in a new direction either through a new research question or a new teaching strategy, either way. For me, it was a little bit different in the sense that I—because of the cross-disciplinary encounter of SOTL—I deliberately inserted something different into the curriculum to measure what happens when a student encounters something new and unfamiliar in a history class, but I would not have done that without the collaboration that SOTL provides. What I find really interesting is this idea that the interactions themselves can produce very different kind of results.*

KT: What you just said is important because if I did not have an audience (as you're my audience right now), where I could come back and talk about what happened, then sometimes trying something new in the classroom is limited to just that. That's it. There isn't an opportunity to share, to think about, to dissect and to analyze. In the context of SOTL, an activity where students are placed in unfamiliar territory may have broader implications in terms of the ways of thinking about student learning, the ways I'm thinking about my discipline. SOTL provides a forum for understanding what I'm doing at a much deeper level and understanding what my students are doing when they entered into unfamiliar territory.

DR: *I think what distinguishes an SOTL forum from another kind of forum is that the audience is a much different audience than you might be used to in terms of discussing your research. You have to really think about what is an essential*

*understanding of the discipline and how do I communicate that to someone
else. I mean, we have to do this all the time for students, to teach students how
to think in a disciplinary sense. In SOTL you have to do it for each other. You
have to decode your discipline for someone who's not in your discipline [Pace
2004b; Shopkow et al. in this volume]. The process of doing that raises all kinds
of questions, for me, about what is essential about doing historical research.
Then those questions raise questions about you as a researcher. "Now I'm in
unfamiliar territory, analyzing posters." Then you have to figure out "How do
I draw my disciplinary training to do this visual analysis?" Certainly this kind
of historical research is not completely unfamiliar. But for me, trained as an
historian of the nineteenth century, having to interview students was new. The
cross-disciplinary nature of SOTL has strengthened my ability to enter into
those unfamiliar territories as a researcher. I don't think I would've done it
without the support of learning from other people who have used such methods.*

Journeys to SOTL involvement are equally important, laying the
groundwork for being willing to engage in cross-disciplinary collaboration.
Takayama described her journey, and working with researchers from a variety of disciplines in SOTL, this way:

KT: I don't think I even thought about the notion of learning. During my entire
training, I enjoyed the material, and I obviously enjoyed research, but I never
thought meta-cognitively. Perhaps, on my own, outside of the lab, I would
have these ah-ha moments, but you never make those connections and
extend them to the academic realm. But, having said that, I had a very, very
focused, narrow trajectory where I didn't go to a liberal arts college. When
I was in grad school, I had no opportunity to interact with students outside
of my discipline. In my personal life, I really appreciated learning about
unfamiliar territory, which seemed quite exotic and exciting to me because
I was not an expert in these things. I mean, I volunteered at a food co-op
during my postdoc years and I got to know people who were majoring in
the arts and in psychology. . . . I even got to know people in soil science and
farming. I really enjoyed reading outside of my discipline in a very uninformed, naïve way, but what really got me engaged in recognizing the value
of cross-disciplinary conversations was SOTL. When we were all at CASTL,
it really was deeply a defining moment.

DR: *Was this your first experience of working with people that closely from other
disciplines at CASTL?*

KT: It was. I think once I tasted the nectar, that was it. It was almost as if this was
what was missing in my life and I didn't know what it was, but I immediately got it. And from that point on, once I got back to my campus, I really
tried to get involved with as many opportunities for engaging with these

communities as I could. It's as if I felt cheated all those years of my academic life. I intuitively seemed to be moving toward this direction but I never saw it, you know, I was never immersed in it. And so what would probably have been a very disruptive experience for my colleagues (because many of them really only focused on engaging in scholarly discourse with other biologists), was for me truly, truly liberating. In the same sense that perhaps some of my students felt liberated. All of a sudden here is a Bug Book whereas throughout all these years they had to adhere to laboratory notebooks, the scientific method, and the formal way in which science is communicated. This Bug Book just hits them in the face. So I guess those students that really embraced it were kind of like me when I landed.

For Reichard, despite being a faculty member in an interdisciplinary humanities and communication program, working with colleagues from a variety of disciplines in a research context was new. He reflected on his experience with the unfamiliar this way:

DR: *Well, for me, despite coming from an interdisciplinary department, having conversations about my research in an interdisciplinary context was very unfamiliar. Working with people outside of the humanities was unfamiliar. So there are layers to this. In my own training, having gone to law school first and then back to graduate school, I had learned to think like a lawyer and then came back to the humanities. It was a very jarring first semester in graduate school. Now I am in an interdisciplinary humanities and communication program, where my colleagues are from many disciplines, and there are only two historians in the group alongside colleagues in such areas as creative writing, ethics, politics, philosophy, literature, and ethnic studies. But we generally would talk about teaching. When you have to turn that research eye back to what you're working on in a SOTL project, you have to draw on what you know and suddenly the discipline doesn't provide all the answers. So I was almost primed for such a venue. Given these life experiences, and interest, you're sort of primed for the kind of unfamiliarity you're going to find. But if you don't come to SOTL from that kind of experience, I would imagine it's a lot more jarring. As I've noticed, it can be jarring when you're confronted with methods you don't understand. It was that way for me too.*

This cross-disciplinary exchange between an historian and a microbiologist highlights what can happen when SOTL scholars from different disciplinary traditions exchange ideas and find common ground. What may seem implicitly obvious to one needs further explanation to the other, as core assumptions are deconstructed and reexamined in multiple ways. Being able to exchange ideas with researchers working in disciplines that are "unfamiliar" allows for an expansion of how to think about ways to investigate student learning and engage students in our own classes with fresh eyes. Such exchanges between and among faculty across disciplines are signature practices of a "field" like SOTL and a core element of its strength. By asking common questions (like "what happens when students work in unfamiliar territory?"), scholars can bridge their differing disciplinary traditions and approaches, open the possibility for the creativity needed to sustain this work, challenge assumptions, and hone understandings. Such collaboration expands the audience for what we do. SOTL provides a venue for scientists, mathematicians, historians, literary scholars, artists, and others to find something useful for their own research in unexpected places. Sustained dialogue across disciplinary divides, like the one represented here, is crucial if SOTL research is to speak to multiple kinds of audiences.

An ongoing dialogue like ours has been made possible by embracing the idea of a *teaching commons,* a "space in which communities of educators committed to inquiry and innovation come together to exchange ideas about teaching and learning, and use them to meet the challenges of educating students for personal, professional, and civic life" (Huber and Hutchings 2005, 1). Entering into and sustaining the dialogue in such a conceptual space requires receptivity to the unfamiliar: to be willing to ask new questions not typical of one's discipline, to test our new methods of inquiry, to share one's work with a new and different audience, and ultimately take some risks. As this chapter suggests, taking such risks has enhanced our understanding of student learning in our respective disciplines and made us into more creative teachers and scholars, a critical by-product of SOTL's embrace of cross-disciplinary dialogue and collaboration.

NOTES

1. Kevin Dunbar (1997) argues that naturalistic studies of scientific practice (that is, cognitive studies of how scientists think and solve problems) require the process to be examined in an authentic setting. By this he means settings in which scientists solve complex, extended scientific problems as they interact with colleagues and with resources in their research environment. The challenge in scaffolding critical thinking processes through such extended, authentic (and we would add "iterative") experiences is a crucial consideration in fostering creativity.

2. Lendol Calder (2006) suggests similar possibilities in rethinking the ways we teach history in an undergraduate classroom. His call for adopting a new approach to the typical history survey course, one rooted in "uncovering" the meaning of historical inquiry, could help students see the creativity of historical thinking. Such creativity might also be fostered through encouraging students to present their research in new ways.

3. Lee Shulman (2005) describes signature pedagogies as the ontologies of teaching that organize the ways in which future practitioners are educated for their

professions. Examples include the case-dialogue method in law, or the critique, or "crit," in art and design. Shulman has described signature pedagogies as sharing four distinctive features: they are pervasive, routine, habitual, and deeply engaging for students.

4. Velda McCune and Dai Hounsell describe how the characteristic ways of thinking and practicing in the biosciences are evident in students' efforts to master the requirements and conventions of the subject for written and oral discourse. In these ways, these habits seem to be deeply embedded and are connected to their experiential and epistemological underpinnings.

5. The study of history is only one part of the wider Human Communication (HCOM) major, an interdisciplinary degree combining traditional humanities disciplines with more interdisciplinary areas including ethnic studies, media studies, and communication studies.

6. The skill of selecting historical evidence from an array of possible sources is a critical one for students of history. These skills in close reading are equally important in approaching secondary sources, learning to distinguish the "essential" from the "nonessential." Such skills distinguish the "expert" from the "novice" historian, as Sam Wineberg (2001) and David Pace (2004a) (2004b) have also explored.

7. Japanese comics genre.

8. Kathy's Bug Book project was conducted during the years she was at the University of New South Wales in Australia.

9. For one historian's journey working in unfamiliar methods territory, eventually choosing those that best suited his disciplinary training and audience, see Michael B. Smith (2010). For the importance of disciplinary methods and audiences to the practice of SOTL, see Mary Taylor Huber and Sherwyn Morreale (2002).

REFERENCES

Berry, Chad, Lori A. Schmied, and Josef Chad Schrock. 2008. "The Role of Emotion in Teaching and Learning History: A Scholarship of Teaching Exploration." *History Teacher* 41, no. 4: 437–52.

Calder, Lendol. 2006. "Uncoverage: Toward a Signature Pedagogy for the History Survey." *Journal of American History* 92, no. 4: 1358–70.

Dunbar, Kevin. 1997. "How Scientists Really Reason: Scientific Reasoning in Real-World Laboratories." In *The Nature of Insight*, ed. Robert J. Sternberg and Janet E. Davidson, 365–96. Cambridge, MA: MIT Press.

Huber, Mary T., and Pat Hutchings. 2005. *The Advancement of Learning: Building the Teaching Commons*. San Francisco: Jossey-Bass.

Huber, Mary Taylor, and Sherwyn P. Morreale. 2002. "Situating the Scholarship of Teaching and Learning." In *Disciplinary Styles in the Scholarship of Teaching and Learning: Exploring Common Ground*, ed. Mary Taylor Huber and Sherwyn P. Morreale, 1–24. Menlo Park: Carnegie Foundation for the Advancement of Teaching.

McCune, Velda, and Dai Hounsell. 2005. "The Development of Students' Ways of Thinking and Practicing in Three Final-Year Biology Courses." *Higher Education* 49, no. 3: 255–89.

Pace, David. 2004a. "Review Essay: The Amateur in the Operating Room: History and the Scholarship of Teaching and Learning." *Journal of American History* 92, no. 4: 1171–92.

———. 2004b. "Decoding the Reading of History: An Example of the Process." *New Directions for Teaching and Learning* 98: 13–21.

Shulman, Lee. 2005. "Signature Pedagogies in the Professions." *Daedalus* 134, no. 3: 52–59.

Smith, Michael B. 2010. "Local Environmental History and the Journey to Ecological Citizenship." In *Citizenship Across the Curriculum,* ed. Michael B. Smith, Rebecca S. Nowacek, and Jeffrey L. Bernstein, 165–84. Bloomington: Indiana University Press.

Wineburg, Sam. 2001. *Historical Thinking and Other Unnatural Acts: Charting the Future of Teaching the Past.* Philadelphia: Temple University Press.

CHAPTER 10

Talking Across the Disciplines: Building Communicative Competence in a Multidisciplinary Graduate-Student Seminar on Inquiry in Teaching and Learning

JENNIFER META ROBINSON, MELISSA GRESALFI, APRIL K. SIEVERT, KATHERINE DOWELL KEARNS, TYLER BOOTH CHRISTENSEN, AND MIRIAM E. ZOLAN

Although the scholarship of teaching and learning has its origins in disciplinary research on teaching and learning, the field distinguishes itself from this more traditional research by also seeking an audience in other disciplines. Instead of being reported solely in the instruction sections of disciplinary conferences and journals, many people in SOTL also seek multidisciplinary forums because they assume that benefits accrue from having scholars from diverse fields with varied intellectual histories and core pedagogical practices share scholarship about postsecondary education. They assume that teaching in higher education has qualities that both transcend disciplinary boundaries and are rooted in disciplinary differences. The convergence of fields that occurs in such forums has been described as a "trading zone" (Gallison 1997; Huber and Morreale 2002; Mills and Huber 2005). In this lively conceptual space, "scholars are busy simplifying, translating, telling, and persuading 'foreigners' to hear their stories and try their wares. In this zone, one finds scholars of teaching and learning seeking advice, collaborations, references, methods, and colleagues to fill in whatever their own disciplinary communities cannot or will not provide" (Huber and Morreale 2002, 19). Amid this hopeful activity, however, the challenges posed by multidisciplinarity can be underestimated. Disciplinary languages—with their tacitly referenced priorities, epistemologies, methodologies, traditions, and literatures—may, in effect, create mismatched expectations and misaligned use of terminology (see also the chapter by Poole in this volume). As sites of such multidisciplinary conversations multiply and increase—both asynchronously in print sources, such as journal articles and listservs, and also synchronously through campus venues and disciplinary and interdisciplinary conferences in the United States and abroad—attention to the nature of the dissonance created among such languages becomes important for the future of the field.

The Teagle Foundation–funded Collegium on Inquiry in Action at Indiana University responds in spirit to the call that Mary Taylor Huber and Pat Hutchings (2005) make: "For the scholarship of teaching and learning to deliver on its promises, campuses (and graduate schools) will need to become places that can nurture and support this work through appropriate programs, structures, and rewards" (30). The collegium is designed to be a modular program that replicates, in a more controlled and scaffolded manner, the multidisciplinary and inquiry-oriented bases of larger discussions in the scholarship of teaching and learning. Based on three cycles of design, implementation, and refinement in working with a diverse group of students and faculty from four disciplines, this learning community offers a process for generating shared meanings in scholarship of teaching and learning. The process includes three parts: introduce new ways to describe and interpret teaching and learning activities that create a need for a shared vocabulary to represent teaching concepts and experiences, engage participants with this framework so that they can recognize the need for a shared language, and establish a sufficiently safe space for interactions that build such a common language. The lessons of the Collegium suggest ways of improving communication in both multidisciplinary learning communities and multidisciplinary fields, such as the scholarship of teaching and learning.

Literature and Theory

The Collegium on Inquiry in Action exhibits many philosophical and structural aspects of a cohort-based faculty learning community (FLC; Cox 2004). Characterized by trust, collaboration, challenge, enjoyment, and empowerment, faculty learning communities promote teaching development, scholarship, and community as they engage scholars from multiple disciplines in a year-long staff development program. As Martha Petrone and Leslie Ortquist-Ahrens (2004) highlight, FLCs offer faculty "time and opportunity to reflect on their teaching, their discipline, their institution, and themselves" (68). By Milton Cox's (2004) definition of a faculty learning community, the participants decide upon the outcomes, curriculum, and daily agenda of the FLC. However, a structured curriculum established by the facilitator(s) can provide a common grounding in theory as well as models and practice that encourage participants to explore these theories in their own classes (Middendorf 2004). Whether in a structure decided upon by the participants or facilitator, FLC members share the goal of creating student-centered practice; participants may pursue that goal with individual or group teaching interventions.

While the ultimate beneficiaries of the faculty learning community are students, faculty of the FLC reap many benefits from their participation. Through cross-disciplinary discussions and tackling relevant classroom challenges in a safe, collaborative environment, members acquire deeper understanding of their own discipline, self, and multidisciplinary perspectives and increased sensitivity to students' needs and learning (Middendorf 2004). Participants also develop scholarly teaching approaches as they take on course (re)design projects (Richlin and Cox 2004). Faculty learning communities are particularly successful models for engaging faculty in the scholarship of teaching because they provide support for risk-taking and innovation, mentoring, multiple perspectives, and forums for presentation and publication (Richlin and Cox 2004). Such investigations address "signature pedagogies," the instructional methods central to each discipline that, when well designed and well executed, support students' engagement with disciplinary practices and habits of mind (Chick, Haynie, and Gurung 2009).

The socializing work of faculty learning communities can be especially useful for graduate students as a means of helping them develop professional teaching identities, teaching knowledge and skills, interpersonal abilities, and attitudes toward ongoing professional development and networking (McDaniels 2010). In this community of practice about teaching, graduate students exchange knowledge and engage in critical reflection about values, assumptions, beliefs, definitions, and practices (Brower, Carlson-Dakes, and Barger 2007; Kasworm and Bowles 2010). Discussions among graduate students in different fields can help these future faculty to examine, critique, and reframe their disciplinary understandings, leading to new insights (Golde 2010; Kasworm and Bowles 2010), steps which can be particularly valuable as graduate students increasingly undertake interdisciplinary work (Holley 2010). As graduate students develop their disciplinary language and skills in their academic homes (Nyquist and Wulff 1996), participation in a multidisciplinary learning community helps them develop a language about teaching and tools for talking with faculty in other disciplines. Participation in a learning community can also support graduate students' successful transition to faculty life as they develop realistic expectations and become acquainted with the breadth of support available for their teaching and research endeavors (DeNeef 2002; Olsen 1993; Olsen and Crawford 1998; Smith and Kalivoda 1998).

The collegium seeks to help participants become reflective practitioners who make deliberate decisions about their teaching so they might direct classrooms in ways consistent with their philosophy of teaching and learning as well as what is known about how students learn. One of the challenges novice instructors face is being able to make and justify instructional decisions in order to "teach on purpose" rather than simply teaching in ways that mirror their personal instructional history. Taking advantage of opportunities for reflection can empower teachers to take ownership over what happens in their classrooms (Simon 1987), improve their teaching efficacy (Prieto and Altmaier 1994), and systematically examine what is going well in their teaching and what is not, ultimately helping them reconceptualize their teaching practice.

Graduate students participating in the collegium reflect critically and collaboratively in multidisciplinary discussions, an online discussion forum, and classroom observations. Their prior assumptions about teaching and learning are brought into question through this reflective process and solutions to teaching problems are explored as a community of learners. Reflection has been described as "helping teachers to think about what happened, why it happened, and what else they could have done to reach their goals" (Cruickshank and Applegate 1981, 553). It encourages the teacher to become more intentional in the design and instruction of the course and, when done well, can promote student-centered classrooms and inquiry learning, and transform school culture (Gordon 2008). While reflecting in isolation can certainly assist new instructors in becoming more intentional in their teaching, collaborative reflection, as can occur in a learning community, is more likely to initiate change as teachers' assumptions about teaching and learning are challenged and other perspectives and approaches to teaching are explored (Gordon 2008; Hatton and Smith 1995; Pugach 1990; Sparkes 1991). Critical reflection should be collaborative in order to leverage the experience and wisdom of others while contributing to the collective knowledge of the group or discipline.

The multidisciplinary interactions among members of the collegium help to reveal some of the challenges that discipline-based knowledge building presents to the scholarship of teaching and learning as a field. In what follows, we delineate how the collegium is structured and how we have implemented collegium curriculum, and we then describe an interaction that we found to be particularly revealing of the challenges faced by members of the SOTL community. The conversations, reflections, reports, and interviews of the collegium members document that they come to this multidisciplinary environment with their own learning experiences and disciplinary assumptions that can be built upon (Bransford, Brown, and Cocking 1999), that superficial politeness and cooperation may belie more fundamental misunderstandings, and that learning communities can be designed to facilitate mutual understanding. For the fields of graduate student development and the scholarship of teaching and learning, our experience with the collegium learning community provides models for activities that promote multidisciplinary exchange and collaboration in ways that are complementary to disciplinary ways of knowing.

Identifying a Tricky Trading Zone

The collegium brings together faculty and graduate students from four departments (the departments of anthropology, biology, communication and culture, and learning sciences) with different knowledge domains and diverse teaching traditions in a year-long seminar. The goals of the collegium include supporting graduate students to gain a deeper understanding of (1) how people learn; (2) core instructional practices central to their disciplines; and (3) how to effectively assess student learning. Each of the first three departmental teams is composed of four graduate students and one faculty mentor who together consider how to teach in ways that are framed by theory about learning and instruction and that build fundamentally on student thinking. The fourth team, from the learning sciences, is composed of a professor and a graduate student who provide expert perspectives on educational research. All four teams work within their disciplinary contexts and share across departmental lines with their colleagues in a dozen meetings of the full collegium. The meetings are facilitated by an instructional consultant who specializes in issues of graduate student preparedness for teaching and whose familiarity with the scholarship of teaching and learning and experience working with multiple disciplines across the university adds cohesion and balance. Graduate student members of the collegium discuss selected scholarly readings about learning, design and implement new teaching practices in their classrooms, assess student learning in response to those innovations, and share their results and plans for the future with the full collegium and in other public venues, including through electronic course portfolios and scholarly conferences. In these ways, they provide sound feedback and review for their peers and move toward the common goal of sharing evidence-based teaching practices within and across disciplines. The faculty advisors and graduate assistants support the development of the fellows by responding to their posts in the online forums, facilitating collegium discussions, and debriefing together about collegium meetings, with the goal of planning for future meetings and making needed revisions to the curriculum. The advisors also meet with individual students apart from the regular collegium meetings to consult them one-on-one in their own teaching conundrums and to plan, design, and assess the fellows' teaching innovations.

In addition, the faculty mentors and learning sciences participants collect and study data on the collegium as a whole using modified ethnographic methods. Our methods target knowledge, attitudes, and behaviors by tracking members' reflections on readings, their contribution to discussions, and their actual teaching. Every full collegium meeting is audiotaped, and portions of those meetings are transcribed for later analysis. Students' responses to forum postings are collected across the entire year. In addition, we observe students' teaching and collect information about their reflection on their teaching. This "teaching set" includes three components: a lesson-planning document that is collected before an observed lesson, an observation of a lesson (documented through notes and audio recordings), and reflective interviews that follow the observed lesson. These teaching sets occur a minimum of twice a year. Finally we review student-generated portfolios that are submitted at the end of the year, thereby adding a level of analysis beyond what the students generate in their classes.

Creating a model learning community among members of four disciplines is tricky. While Huber and Hutchings (2005) have described the teaching commons as "a conceptual space in which communities of educators committed to inquiry and innovation come together to exchange ideas about teaching and learning and use them to meet the challenges of educating students," David Mills and Mary Huber (2005) recognize that such a space is difficult to achieve even within a field. They note that anthropology, even with its culturally relativistic outlook, is unable to sustain a coherent connection between the research and teaching domains within that field. Indeed, most anthropology departments include scientists who study human biology and evolution, archaeologists who use science to interpret past cultural phenomena, and cultural and linguistic anthropologists who use a wide range of methods to illuminate human phenomena. If this experience of disciplinary dissonance is generalizable, then a multidisciplinary collegium that includes members from the humanities, social sciences, and natural sciences may have some trouble developing the positive trading processes that support a teaching commons.

Communication in the collegium, and indeed in the academy, depends on establishing a common language about teaching and learning among scholars from disciplines that vary widely in research methods and publication styles, and, as we discovered, in ways of looking at their fields of inquiry. If members of the collegium are going to succeed in applying inquiry-based innovations to teaching settings, it becomes critical for all members of the group to understand the methods and meaning of inquiry in their own fields first (that is, anthropology, biology, and communications). However, it is also crucial for members of the collegium to form a common language that allows for meaningful communication across disciplines. One set of questions driving the design of the collegium was "Do the disciplines really differ to an extent that makes communication difficult, and if so on what level? What specific issues are misunderstood? What does successful cross-disciplinary communication look like?" Shortly after the collegium convened in the first year, it became clear that, although we had established a space for trading among four departments, we had not yet established a language for communicating. As early as our third meeting of the first year, we found that multidisciplinary interchange could be problematic and that an ostensible trading zone can resemble unfamiliar and wary parties meeting for the first time on a territorial boundary.

A debate between the students emerged as students were engaged in a discussion about the difference between "learner-centered" versus "knowledge-centered" environments, terms that were introduced in required reading for the week from *How People Learn* (Bransford, Brown, and Cocking 1999), which focused on the design of learning environments. The goal of assigning the reading was to help the fellows distinguish between different kinds of learning environments (learner-, knowledge-, assessment-, and community-centered), become more thoughtful about the "centeredness" of their classrooms, recognize whether their current teaching practices were aligned with the kinds of centeredness described in the reading assignment, and identify what kinds of learning environments would be most advantageous for their own teaching. The day began with the fellows discussing the assigned reading as a large multidisciplinary group. As the discussion unfolded and graduate student fellows started sharing pedagogical strategies from their own teaching, some fellows became defensive about the pedagogical strategies they were most familiar with and the discussion became quite heated. Conversation developed into a debate about how scholars perceive the nature of reality, particularly between those who study the natural and cultural worlds.

The transcription of the audio recording of this meeting showed that the graduate students registered surprise at the ways in which other disciplines operate, sometimes due simply to the silo nature of the academy. Said one humanist, "I never actually have the chance to have a conversation with biologists." As an example, graduate-student teachers from communication studies recognized differences between the way they and the biologists present viewed the realities of what it is they study. Communication and culture students recognized that "in science there is something that you are investigating" but also commented, "You can never say something is 'the' reality without also discussing what it is you're doing by saying that." The exchange became a small version of the classic "nature/nurture" debate. One of the scientists commented about the constructed nature of cultural understanding with the following: "but when you're talking, it sounds like you're saying that you're purely about nurture." On the other hand, a communications student said,

> Because I feel like—and correct me if I'm off—but from what I know about biology is biology; at the heart, scientists are very interested in figuring out how things are. Like, this is, this is a thing that happens. And the thing is somehow real and apparent and is really out there. And for us, looking at culture, culture isn't really something that you have. I don't have my culture. But it's the thing that I'm doing. It's a process. It's something you choose or you yourself effect or you enact. I'm performing white middle-class Midwestern woman right now. . . . It's something that I'm doing.

The anthropology students split along the lines of their subdisciplines, with bioanthropologists being more aligned with the biologists and the cultural anthropologists aligned with students from communication and culture. While such divisions may not be surprising in and of themselves, it is notable that one of the more vocal and defensive students on the "side" of science was a biological anthropologist coming from a department that prides itself on taking a holistic approach to understanding and studying people. While scholars from the Department of Communication and Culture do not have much opportunity to interact with biologists, cultural and biological anthropologists at Indiana University do so all the time. Sievert, the faculty mentor from anthropology, expected the biological anthropologists to temper the discussion and to have the language necessary to do so, when in fact the stances they adopted served to deepen disciplinary lines.

During the conversation, we traversed a territory that included recognition of the unfamiliar and difficulty situating the origin and character of difference, along with mild contretemps and defensiveness. It appeared that the graduate student instructors desired to make things "correct" through politeness strategies skirting the interpretation of actual differences at first. Although the conversation was tinged with defensiveness in tone, students added polite cues such as "correct me if I'm wrong" and "hopefully I've misinterpreted."

This debate had a desired effect of inspiring students to come to grips with the fundamental differences that hindered understanding between graduate students of science and cultural studies. A student summarized this understanding: "Whereas I would say in biology even though there's a sociology to how science gets done and whose ideas are considered important—

and I mean, there's a lot of that in there!—the ultimate goal is really, is a, it's a non-union goal. It's . . . figuring out how the mechanism works." After this session, a graduate student in biology wrote, "I think the discussion today was very interesting and while understanding differences in our fields may not directly relate to our individual classrooms, I think it is really important to understand how we think and teach differently." This student clearly recognized the value of seeing difference but was uncertain how that understanding relates to what happens in the classroom. She was still unclear about how fundamental assumptions inculcated through her disciplinary training influenced the pedagogies she had experienced in her field. Without that awareness, she was in a disadvantaged position for seeing the relevance and possibilities for revising her teaching methods. In other words, disciplinary differences were recognized but sequestered from the day-to-day practice of teaching.

What This Is a Case Of: Connecting The Collegium to SOTL

The above episode foregrounds the kind of disconnect that consistently emerges between members of the SOTL community; it is unique in that the different understandings and interpretations of new terms did not go unnoticed or were not simply glossed away. Instead, the members of the collegium began to interrogate the differences between their disciplines, their assumptions about the nature of knowing, and their consequential differential interpretations and understandings of a set of novel terms.

It was clear that the graduate students varied in their understanding and usage of specific terminology that typifies the learning sciences and education literature. This is to be expected, as graduate students tend to start teaching without having much exposure to literature that comes out of either learning sciences or SOTL. On a more specific level, collegium participants used such terms as *knowledge-centered* and *student-centered* in somewhat different ways. Specifically, most students described their own practice as being student-centered, although observations of their classroom practice suggest that this was not necessarily the case. The point is not that some students were misrepresenting themselves, however, but rather that their interpretations of these terms were shaped by their previous ideas about teaching and what good teaching practice looks like *in their discipline*. It was the discipline grounding that became an important topic of conversation and an eventual resource in supporting students to communicate effectively with each other. Our analysis of this conversation makes it clear that students' personal experiences affect their interpretation of terms, leading to conversations that are ostensibly about the same thing but which in fact carry multiple, unseen contradictions.

A key question is what supported this more revealing conversation and whether the activity that led to this productive displacement might be useful in other circumstances. The debate that emerged among the collegium participants was, as previously mentioned, spurred by the introduction of a new framework: the distinction among learning environments organized around learners, knowledge, assessment, and community (Bransford, Brown, and Cocking 1999). Perhaps because of their lay definitions, the meaning of these terms seemed straightforward. Indeed, in response to the pre-meeting writing prompt to "Analyze [a recent lesson] in terms of the four 'environments' advanced in Chapter 6 of *How People Learn*," students easily identified an aspect of their lesson that they saw as corresponding to one of the four environments. However, it was clear even from these initial posts that students were interpreting the same concepts slightly differently. As an example, one biology student characterized a learning environment as both knowledge- and learner-centered: "He [the professor] demonstrated the skills and techniques while bringing up real life anecdotes regarding the dangers of contamination. He, often, reminds the students how they may one day be in the instructor or manager positions where proper technique could save lives." In contrast, a student from communication and culture also characterized her approach as being learner-centered:

> I started out a class last week going over "muddiest points" my students submitted to me the class before. A couple of them asked really thoughtful critical questions that applied to key concepts that are addressed over the content of the course. I felt bringing those questions into the classroom was a way of starting to get at a learner-centered environment through informal assessment. The questions allowed me to "discover what students think in relation to the problems on hand" and then attempt to give "them situations to go on thinking about the critical concepts."

The biology student seemed to understand the notion of "learner-centered" as characterizing instruction that was relevant or interesting to the learners. In contrast, the communication and culture student understood the term as meaning that she needed to understand what the students in her class were thinking as a factor in her instruction. It was in attempting to analyze these examples in discussion—and later, about an example from a video that everyone watched together—that these very different understandings and visions of the notion of "learner-centered" instruction emerged. It seems that these new terms, and more importantly, the need to talk across examples of these terms, served to displace the fellows from their prior conceptions of teaching, so they all had to adapt in order to create some kind of common meaning.

This process of creating common meaning was in no way easy or quick. In the course of the discussion described above, students began to discuss the different epistemologies of their disciplines and the assumptions that each discipline made about what it means "to know" (see also Poole chapter in this volume). This was a difficult discussion to have, because there are, at times, dramatic differences between the values of different disciplines, and some fellows clearly believed that their home discipline's way of seeing the world was more valuable than others. As a consequence, in the meetings following, we adapted our plans so that we began discussions within discipline-based groups to establish, first, the core concepts and the core processes that were valued in each group's home discipline. We then moved into cross-disciplinary groups to compare and contrast these core issues. Once again, in being asked to frame their disciplines through a common framework that was novel to all, students were presented with the need to clarify their terms and their disciplinary standpoints before they could talk together in ways that used terms consistently and meaningfully, before they could effectively contribute to the collective conversation about teaching.

This plan for subsequent meetings allowed a safe space to emerge that made growth of an effective trading zone of ideas possible. In addition to the disciplinary and cross-disciplinary groups, the safe space was supported through multiple forums for interaction: disciplinary mentors who were available for information and advocacy, a graduate assistant who was available for off-the-record discussions, and online pre-meeting writings where students were able to organize their thoughts for the day's discussion and preview others.'

• • •

Interactions among members of the collegium open to examination the challenges that multidisciplinary learning communities face. These findings highlight the importance of communication and indicate a process for generating shared meanings in such communities: introduce new ways to describe and interpret teaching and learning activities that create a need for a shared vocabulary to represent teaching concepts and experiences, engage participants with this framework so that they can recognize the need for a shared language, and establish a sufficiently safe space for interactions that build such a common language.

For the multidisciplinary field of SOTL more broadly, the experiences of the collegium members indicate the power of discipline-based learning experiences and assumptions, even accompanied by politeness and cooperation skills intended to make such a group functional. They suggest the utility of introducing activities into face-to-face and electronic meetings that provide new frameworks and displace prior conceptions so that participants have clear incentive to create common meanings. Preconference, newcomer, and graduate-student forums designed on these outcomes could build a base of common understanding and goodwill among participants. Participants in such activities would benefit from establishing disciplinary affinity groups and other safe spaces that can provide a base of support before moving into multidisciplinary discussions. Regular opportunities to check back in with these groups as well as to foray out into new multidisciplinary ones will facilitate risk taking inherent in departing from prior understanding. Involving mentors from a variety of disciplines who are experienced in such discussions along with learning science experts who can draw authoritatively on research in a variety of contexts will also help to make a productive and safe space. Finally, providing time for individual writing as a means to organize thoughts and preview the thinking of others provides a more thoughtful and prepared basis for communication. In this way, SOTL communities in higher education can move all participants *outside* of easy default understandings about teaching and learning so that they can engage respectfully as they build new zones for multidisciplinary exchange and collaboration in ways that are also complementary to disciplinary ways of knowing.

REFERENCES

Bransford, John D., Ann L. Brown, and Rodney R. Cocking, eds. 1999. *How People Learn: Brain, Mind, Experience, and School.* Washington, DC: National Academy Press.

Brower, Aaron M., Christopher G. Carlson-Dakes, and Shihmei Shu Barger. 2007. *A Learning Community Model of Graduate Student Professional Development for Teaching Excellence.* Madison: Wisconsin Center for the Advancement of Postsecondary Education (WISCAPE). http://www.wiscape.wisc.edu /publications/WP010.

Chick, Nancy, Aeron Haynie, and Regan A. R. Gurung. 2009. "From Generic to Signature Pedagogies: Teaching Disciplinary Understandings." In *Exploring Signature Pedagogies: Approaches to Teaching Disciplinary Habits of Mind,* ed. Regan A. R. Gurung, Nancy L. Chick, and Aeron Haynie, 1–18. Sterling, VA: Stylus.

Cox, Milton D. 2004. "Introduction to Faculty Learning Communities." *New Directions for Teaching and Learning* 97: 5–23.

Cruickshank, Donald, and Jane Applegate. 1981. "Reflective Teaching as a Strategy for Teacher Growth." *Educational Leadership* 38, no. 7: 553–54.

DeNeef, A. Leigh. 2002. *The Preparing Future Faculty Program: What Difference Does It Make?* Preparing Future Faculty Occasional Paper No. 8. Washington, DC: Association of American Colleges and Universities.

Gallison, Peter. 1997. *Image and Logic: A Material Culture of Microphysics.* Chicago: University of Chicago Press.

Golde, Christopher. 2010. "Entering Different Worlds: Socialization into Disciplinary Communities." In *On Becoming a Scholar: Socialization and Development in Doctoral Education,* ed. Susan K. Gardner and Pilar Mendoza, 79–96. Sterling, VA: Stylus.

Gordon, Stephen P. 2008. *Collaborative Action Research: Developing Professional Learning Communities.* New York: Teachers College Press.

Hatton, Neville, and David Smith. 1995. "Reflection in Teacher Education: Towards Definition and Implementation." *Teaching and Teacher Education* 11, no. 1: 33–49.

Holley, Karri. 2010. "Doctoral Student Socialization in Interdisciplinary Fields." In *On Becoming a Scholar: Socialization and Development in Doctoral Education,* ed. Susan K. Gardner and Pilar Mendoza, 97–112. Sterling, VA: Stylus.

Huber, Mary Taylor, and Pat Hutchings. 2005. *The Advancement of Teaching and Learning: Building the Teaching Commons.* San Francisco: Jossey-Bass.

Huber, Mary Taylor, and Sherwyn Morreale. 2002. *Disciplinary Styles in the Scholarship of Teaching and Learning: Exploring Common Ground.* Washington, DC: American Association of Higher Education and the Carnegie Foundation for the Advancement of Teaching.

Kasworm, Carol, and Tuere Bowles. 2010. "Doctoral Students as Adult Learners." In *On Becoming a Scholar: Socialization and Development in Doctoral Education,* ed. Susan K. Gardner and Pilar Mendoza, 223–42. Sterling, VA: Stylus.

McDaniels, Melissa. 2010. "Doctoral Student Socialization for Teaching Roles." In *On Becoming a Scholar: Socialization and Development in Doctoral Education,* ed. Susan K. Gardner and Pilar Mendoza, 29–44. Sterling, VA: Stylus.

Middendorf, Joan. 2004. "Facilitating a Faculty Learning Community Using the Decoding the Disciplines Model." *New Directions for Teaching and Learning* 98: 95–107.

Mills, David, and Mary Taylor Huber. 2005. "Anthropology and the Educational 'Trading Zone': Disciplinarity, Pedagogy, and Professionalism." *Arts and Humanities in Higher Education* 4 (February): 19–32. http://ahh.sagepub.com /content/4/1/9.abstract.

Nyquist, Jodi D., and Donald H. Wulff.1996. "Recognizing and Adapting to Stages of Graduate Teaching Assistants' and Graduate Research Assistants' Development." In *Working Effectively with Graduate Assistants,* ed. J. D. Nyquist and Donald H. Wulff, 18–32. Thousand Oaks, CA: Sage.

Olsen, Deborah. 1993. "Work Satisfaction and Stress in the First and Third Year of Academic Appointment." *Journal of Higher Education* 64, no. 4: 453–71.

Olsen, Deborah, and Lizabeth A. Crawford. 1998. "A Five-Year Study of Junior Faculty Expectations about Their Work." *Review of Higher Education* 22, no. 1: 39–54.

Petrone, Martha C., and Leslie Ortquist-Ahrens. 2004. "Facilitating Faculty Learning Communities: A Compact Guide to Creating Change and Inspiring Community." *New Directions for Teaching and Learning* 97: 63–69.

Prieto, Loreto R., and Elizabeth M. Altmaier. 1994. "The Relationship of Prior Training and Previous Teaching Experiences to Self-Efficacy among Graduate Teaching Assistants." *Research in Higher Education* 35, no. 4: 481–97.

Pugach, Marleen C. 1990. "Self-Study: The Genesis of Reflection in Novice Teachers." Paper presented at the annual meeting of the AERA, Boston, April.

Richlin, Laurie, and Milton D. Cox. 2004. "Developing Scholarly Teaching and the Scholarship of Teaching and Learning through Faculty Learning Communities." *New Directions for Teaching and Learning* 97: 127–35.

Simon, Roger I. 1987. "Empowerment as a Pedagogy of Possibility." *Language Arts* 64, no. 4: 370–82.

Smith, Kathleen S., and Patricia L. Kalivoda. 1998. "Academic Morphing: Teaching Assistant to Faculty Member." *To Improve the Academy* 17: 85–102.

Sparkes, Andrew C. 1991. "The Culture of Teaching, Critical Reflection, and Change: Possibilities and Problems." *Educational Management Administration and Leadership* 19, no. 4: 4–19.

CHAPTER 11

Getting at the Big Picture through SOTL

LAUREN SCHARFF

Context, such as the specific disciplinary content material, instructor characteristics, and classroom environment, is crucial to acknowledge when we are attempting to understand the learning process (Gibbs 2010). But are there not general principles related to human learning that will transcend context, for example, motivational influences, attention, and memory processes? (See also Gurung and Schwartz in this volume for discussion of learning principles that transcend context.) Why do we try things in our classes that we have heard "worked" in other colleagues' classes? We do so because we assume and hope that they may also work in ours. Sometimes they do seem to work in our classes and thus, perhaps, we've tapped into a more generalizable principle. But other days, these borrowed ideas don't work and we must ask how our classroom context differed from our colleague's and how that impacted the success of the approach. Context specificity and generalizability each have value as SOTL research goals, and both must be understood prior to us fully appreciating the "big picture" of student learning.

A second realm in which SOTL uncovers the big picture results from the push within institutions of higher education to state and assess learning outcomes at the institution, department, and course levels. Outcomes such as communication skills, information literacy, and critical thinking clearly have context specificity, but they also imply some amount of generalizability because we expect them to be developed in courses across many disciplines. Accreditation bodies require learning experiences that are aligned with the outcomes and data that allow them to determine whether the outcomes are being achieved. These pressures follow from public calls for accountability in higher education, and they have been one of several factors that focus attention on teaching and learning (Huber and Morreale 2002).

Therefore, there are a multitude of interdisciplinary SOTL research opportunities to get at the big picture, both to better understand the generalizable and context-specific aspects of learning, and to support assessment of learning outcomes that are shared across courses and departments. Unfortunately, the latter type of research opportunity may be avoided by faculty due to unpleasant associations with assessment techniques that have been put into place in order to meet accreditation requirements. While some such techniques have merit, they are often developed in isolation by persons other than the faculty who are required to use them, and frequently the faculty who use them do not collaborate or communicate between departments about what they are doing.

This chapter explores two SOTL projects at the U.S. Air Force Academy (USAFA).[1] Both involve efforts across core courses in multiple departments and both illustrate the unfortunate tendency for departments to work independently and without collaboration, even when they have common goals. They also demonstrate how SOTL efforts can break down those barriers and foster cross-disciplinary conversations about teaching and learning, that is, they exemplify what can result from interactions within an "educational trading zone" (Mills and Huber 2005).

Exploring Underlying Learning Principles with SOTL

The first project serves as an example of looking for underlying principles to explain student behaviors when using a common pedagogical technique (pre-flight/pre-class assignments as part of just-in-time teaching, or JiTT) in freshmen-level math, physics, and behavioral sciences courses. Specifically, we examined motivational factors, which we believe are largely independent of discipline. Thus, our findings could be applicable to a wide range of instructors at other institutions and across many disciplines.

This study fits Mary T. Huber's (1999) definition of interdisciplinary research in that common methodologies were used across all departments to collect data from students. However, the different pre-flight implementation approaches used by the different departments had developed independently rather than in a collaborative way to allow investigation of their impact. Thus, this study also has some features that might better fit what Carmen Werder in this volume describes as multi-disciplinary, that is, those "that simply tap multiple disciplinary perspectives without any deliberate attempt at integration." As part of the scholarly process, results from the study were shared with the departments and used to support rich conversations among the faculty. Part of the richness came from learning about what other departments had been doing and how it impacted the student behaviors.

This project came about as a result of a conversation in an educational trading zone during the 2009 conference for the International Society for the Scholarship of Teaching and Learning (ISSOTL). A colleague from physics and I (representing behavioral sciences) were talking about how courses in our two departments implemented the use of pre-flights. We discovered both similarities and differences in implementation. Courses in both departments followed the basic JiTT procedure: students completed pre-flight assignments prior to class and submitted them electronically so that the instructors could review the responses prior to class and use them to tailor the class session (for example, modify what was covered based on the patterns of responses or use responses to initiate class discussions).

There were two differences in implementation that caught our attention, the latter becoming the focus of the project. First, the *type* of questions was different in the two departments. While the goal of the physics questions was to allow the instructors to assess students' ability to understand and solve problems using physics concepts, the goal of the behavioral sciences pre-flight questions was to systematically develop students' critical thinking abilities (although the questions placed the critical thinking exercises within the context of content for each day). While not the main focus of the project, by being aware of this difference, we were later able to share it when talking to colleagues in other departments who were interested in incorporating pre-flights but who had not considered variations in implementation to better suit their disciplinary approaches (pre-flights were originated in physics by Novak and Patterson 1998).

The difference that led to our study was how each department used points to motivate student completion of the pre-flights assignments. In the physics courses, 20 percent of the course points were allotted to pre-flight assignments. In the behavioral sciences course, no points were given during that fall semester, while during the following spring semester 10 percent of course points were allotted to the pre-flight assignments. We also learned that in two core math courses, pre-flights were used and they had no points associated with them. Each course had a different logic for their use of points (or no points), but no data had been collected on actual completion rates and factors influencing those rates.

In physics, where the pre-flight process had been used the longest and was most integral to the course design, they were willing to give a large number of points in order to increase completion rates. In math, students were told that they should complete the assignments "because it was the right thing to do and was expected of them as part of their development into leaders of character."[2] In behavioral sciences, the pre-flights were incorporated as part of an inter-teaching technique[3] during the fall semester, but no points were given to students for pre-flight activity. By the spring semester, the course director modified the course design and point structure so that those instructors using the pre-flights could allot points for completion. The number of points allotted in the spring was based on data from the fall semester of this study, and the impact was studied during the second part of this study.

Regardless of the logic behind the assigned points, we agreed that the potential benefits of increased student preparation for class and more efficient use of class time only occurred if students actually completed the pre-flights. Thus, we decided to do an interdisciplinary study in which we investigated the influence of several factors on students' reported likelihood to complete their pre-flight assignments. The study did not investigate disciplinary differences in question type, as the focus was motivational factors influencing completion rates—something we believed transcended the disciplines themselves.

Exploring Motivations that Might Influence Completion of Pre-flight Assignments

Once we focused on the topic of motivational factors, we opened up our discussion to include factors beyond simply the points allotted to the assignments. These factors included how long it took students to do the work, how the instructors used the pre-flight responses, and the perceived value of the assignment for learning. Based on our personal experiences and discussions with colleagues, we knew that there would be variation along all these factors within all three departments. For example, some instructors in each department gave systematic feedback to each student's pre-flight responses each lesson and clearly used the responses during each lesson, while others occasionally gave feedback or used the responses, and a few rarely or never gave feedback or clearly used the responses in class.[4]

As we discussed these factors, we thought about how they fit with established theories of motivation.[5] For example, motivation can come from intrinsic factors or extrinsic factors. With respect to these dimensions, awarding students points for pre-flight activity is clearly an extrinsic factor. Extrinsic factors can be good initially to motivate behaviors, especially if a person doesn't start with an intrinsic desire to do the task. However, solely relying on points in a learning environment can lead to a greater likelihood that students will focus on performance goals such as obtaining high scores rather than mastery goals of deep learning. USAFA has very clear ranking of students based on grades, fitness tests, and military training performance. Thus, our students tend to be extremely performance oriented. As instructors, we want them to move beyond their performance orientation and develop an appreciation for what they are learning. Other factors related to the JiTT process fit with these motivational constructs. Intrinsic motivation can be tapped if the pre-flight questions have personal value. Personal value might occur due to a student's preexisting interest in the subject matter. This is why students often admit to working harder and being more diligent in their major's courses. Intrinsic motivation might also be due to an instructor's ability to show relevance and applicability of the material. Intrinsic motivation is more clearly linked with mastery goals.

How an instructor uses the pre-flight responses in the classroom may impact several aspects of motivation. If an instructor highlights a student's response during class, this recognition can serve as an extrinsic motivator and it can reinforce performance goals. It can also support a type of motivation that instructors don't always acknowledge as an important influence in our classrooms: social motivation—the desire to appear socially responsible and to develop relationships with classmates. Finally, by taking time to read the responses and use them to support learning in class, an instructor signals his/her value of the process, which can in turn increase the value students perceive for the process.

These examples are not exhaustive with respect to how components of the pre-flight process might interact with various theories of motivation. Additionally, the time it takes to complete the pre-flights will interact with the above factors and also interact with time-pressure demands beyond the individual course. However, we believed that by assessing even this constrained list of pre-flight variables, we would capture a good first-level understanding of how they interact with respect to student completion of pre-flights and, perhaps, other assignments as well.

Brief Overview of Our Methodology and Findings

At the end of the fall semester, we asked all students in the freshman physics courses (N = 683), the calculus courses (mostly freshmen, N = 805), and all students in the Introduction to Behavioral Sciences courses that implemented pre-flights (all freshmen, N = 318) to complete an in-class feedback form.[6] This form contained closed-ended scale responses asking them to indicate the percentage of pre-flight assignments that they had completed during the semester, how much time they took to complete a typical pre-flight assignment, and whether their instructor had made good use of the pre-flight responses (for example, used the responses to modify class discussion or the lecture material on a given day). At the end of the spring semester, we asked students in the Introduction to Behavioral Sciences courses where pre-flights were implemented to complete an in-class feedback form containing the same questions, along with questions that asked them to rate whether the pre-flight assignments helped them prepare for exams, get more out of the textbook, prepare for class discussions, and structure their study time. These latter questions were designed to assess perceived student value of the pre-flight assignments with respect to factors that might more directly impact their learning.

Not surprisingly, the use of points was significantly related to the reported completion rates. Completion was indicated using the following scale: 1 = 95–100%, 2 = 75–95%, 3 = 50–75%, 4 = 25–50%, and 5 = less than 25%. Students in physics had pre-flights worth 20 percent of course grade. Their mean completion rate was 1.71. This was a higher reported completion rate than the students in the courses giving no points for the pre-flight assignments: the math mean completion rate was 2.91, and the behavioral sciences fall semester mean completion rate was 2.90.

Based on this data, the behavioral sciences department was encouraged about allotting points for completion of pre-flights in the spring semester. Scott Simkins and Mark Maier (2004) found that by allotting 5 to 10 percent of the course grade, student completion of their pre-flights averaged 80 to 90 percent. Thus, we allotted 10 percent of the spring semester course grade to the completion of pre-flights, noticeably less than the established practice in the physics department. This change impacted the reported completion rates that spring. They were significantly higher than in the courses that gave no points, but lower than the completion rates reported in the physics courses (spring semester mean completion rate = 1.89).

The amount of points was associated with other factors. The time taken to complete assignments was significantly different for the four groups. Students in physics where points counted 20 percent (mean = 2.05) and behavioral sciences spring semester where points were 10 percent (mean = 2.03) took significantly more time than math (mean = 1.7) and behavioral sciences fall semester (mean = 1.8) where there were no points on each assignment, where a rating of 1 = 0–30 minutes, 2 = 30–45 minutes, and 3 = 45–60 minutes. In this case, there was no statistically significant difference between the physics and spring behavioral sciences groups. The lack of difference between these two groups could be due to a variety of reasons. Perhaps the assignments were such that students didn't need longer to finish them, or given their very busy schedules, 30 to 45 minutes is the maximum that most freshmen are willing to spend on any given homework assignment.

The data became more interesting when we analyzed the impact of instructor use of student pre-flight responses during class time. This analysis suggested that more than points matter. During the fall semester, instructor use was significantly correlated with completion rates for the behavioral sciences course and for the math courses (both giving zero points for completion), but *not* for the physics courses. Specifically, the more strongly the math and behavioral sciences students agreed that their instructors put their responses to good use, the higher the completion rates. But instructor use did *not* impact completion rates in physics. This suggested that the allotment of 20 percent of the course grade to pre-flights overwhelmed the influence of instructor use. This was the second factor that led to our choice of 10 percent for completion of pre-flights in the spring semester behavioral sciences course. We wanted to know whether we could match the physics completion rates using fewer points plus good instructor use of responses.

Was there still an impact from instructor use when we allotted 10 percent of the course grade for completion of pre-flights? Yes. Of most interest to us was that we could match the completion rates of physics students in those cases when students were at least neutral in their agreement that their instructor made good use of their responses, as shown in figure 11.1.

Going back to our earlier discussion of motivational factors, one of the reasons that good instructor use influenced student completion rates could be that good use increased students' perceived value of the pre-flights. By taking time before class to read the responses, thinking about how to use them to enhance learning and then clearly doing so in class, an instructor indicates that the responses are an integral part of the learning process. The student effort is acknowledged and the assignments are less likely to be perceived as "busy work." Some instructors even took time to explain the pre-flight process to the students, along with clear statements of the value of the pre-flights.[7] Thus, we predicted that instructor use would also significantly correlate with the student ratings of the potential benefits of the pre-flights (only measured during the spring semester in behavioral sciences). Indeed, that was the case. The better the instructor use, as perceived by students, the more strongly students agreed that the pre-flights helped them prepare for exams, get more out of the textbook, prepare for class discussions, and structure their study time.

Departmental Response to the Results

As part of the scholarly process, not only did we disseminate our project to external colleagues at the ISSOTL conference in 2010 (Scharff, Lee, Rolf, and Novotny 2011), but we also scheduled times to present the results to each of the three departments. In math and physics, both faculty who taught the courses as well as other departmental faculty attended the presentations and discussions. In addition to presenting the methodology and results of

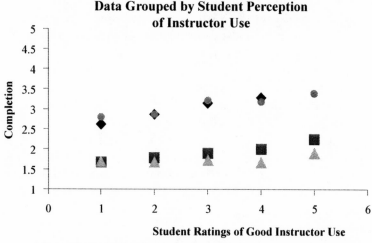

FIGURE 11.1. Impact of the number of points and reported instructor use of pre-flight responses on student completion rates (lower completion values represent higher completion rates; 1 = 95-100% and 5 = less than 25%). Physics (20% of grade) and Behavioral Sciences spring semester (10% of grade) had significantly higher completion than Math or Behavioral Sciences fall semester (zero points for pre-flight completion). For all courses except Physics, ratings of instructor use (lower ratings indicate better use) correlate significantly with completion. By allotting 10% of points and achieving at least neutral agreement of good instructor use (ratings = 1, 2, or 3), Behavioral Sciences was able to match completion rates to Physics.

the project, we provided background on several theories of motivation and time for discussion so that the faculty could brainstorm about how different things they did might tap different aspects of motivation. We felt this was particularly important for the math and physics faculty because theories of motivation were not part of their disciplinary background. In fact, several faculty members commented that they appreciated that component of the presentation and that it led them to think in more complete terms about what might motivate student behaviors in their classes.

In math, much of the discussion focused on the pros and cons of allotting points for pre-flight completion. This matter had been discussed at length prior to this study, and the decision had been made to not allot points because successful college students and developing leaders of character should not need to be reinforced for fundamental class preparation behaviors. However, during this discussion, there were data available to better inform the discussion. The point was made that many freshmen students may not yet have developed the self-initiation and time management skills that would lead them to regularly complete the pre-flights if no points were assigned to them. Further, the math faculty were keenly aware that math (calculus in this case), is often not a topic for which students have preexisting intrinsic interest. Thus, extrinsic motivators would have enhanced influence.

Of course, the data also showed that aspects of good instructor use would increase completion rates (for example, showcasing student responses will serve as extrinsic motivators, and clear use can increase perceived value). Further discussion along these lines led to the realization that the variation in instructor use may have been due to poor communication with new instructors[8] about the value of the pre-flight process. It became apparent that instructors could do a better job of communicating the benefits of pre-flights to the students. While no final decisions about how many (if any) points to allot to pre-flight completion in future freshmen core calculus courses were made during the presentation and discussion, the conversation was collegial and it was clear that additional conversations would occur.

In physics, the conversation also centered strongly on the allotment of points; however, here the "new" possibility put on the table was to decrease the number of points for pre-flight assignment completion. Some instructors thought that some of the points could be used for other student work in order to increase likelihood of its completion. Other instructors pointed out that high completion was essential for the way the courses were designed, and by having a large percentage of the grade allotted to completion of the pre-flights, there could be less concern about instructor use. However, while a large number of points can lead to high completion rates, students can resent the work rather than appreciate it as part of the learning process (for example, Cookman, Mandel, and Lyons 1999). Thus, as with the math department, there was clear realization that there would be value to better informing new faculty about the pre-flight process and encouraging them to communicate value to their students.

In behavioral sciences, there was rapid agreement that, if pre-flights were used, a 10 percent allotment of points was good. Instead, the majority of the discussion centered on the benefits of pre-flights and the logistics of implementing them within a course. Unlike in math and physics, the Introduction to Behavioral Sciences course director did not require that all instructors incorporate the pre-flights. Only about half of the instructors in recent semesters incorporated pre-flights, some of them just trying it for one semester and then moving away from them due to the instructor load and the difficulty of being able to read all the responses prior to the start of class and meaningfully incorporate them into the class lesson. By learning more about the JiTT process (which hadn't been clearly communicated to all of them prior to the presentation due to instructor turnover), some additional instructors seemed interested in trying pre-flights in their courses. Knowing that other instructors in other departments were implementing pre-flights communicated additional value of the JiTT process.

Further, one of the instructors who had tried pre-flights and then moved away from them due to workload shared that, when she stopped using the JiTT process, there was an obvious decrease in student learning of the critical thinking skills that were the focus of the pre-flights. This instructor had implemented alternate assignments to develop the skills, but rather than occurring each lesson (as with pre-flight approach), they occurred twice during the semester. This helped with instructor load but reduced the amount of practice the students received at developing the skills. Another instructor shared some modifications to the pre-flight process that she used in order to manage the logistics of reading and responding to all the student responses. She felt that with her modifications (for example, reading and responding to a subset each lesson), she was still able to communicate the value of the process to the students and recognize individual student responses (as an extrinsic reinforcement). As with math and physics, the process of sharing the results of the study with this department led to meaningful and informed discussion.

Summary

We could have tried to manipulate the number of points given for pre-flight completion within one department using separate classes. And to an extent we did this in the behavioral sciences classes by comparing the difference in points across two semesters. However, by using classes in three departments/disciplines, we greatly increased our participant pool and the number of instructors/topics involved, which increased generalization. Possibly of most value was that the different departments, all nominally using the same pedagogical technique, were able to see data and consider options that they may not have been willing to try themselves. For example, faculty in the math department had been reluctant to give any points for pre-flights, and the physics department allotted 20 percent of the points to pre-flight completion; hearing about the procedures in other departments made them willing to question their own. Further, by presenting an overview of motivational theories in addition to sharing the data, there was a neutral scaffold that allowed the rich conversations involving multiple factors. The discussions did not center on "which department's approach was the best." Instead, in each department the faculty used the data as well as the theoretical background to focus on possibilities that made sense for them within their discipline and their departmental zeitgeist. Current follow-up studies are expanding data collection to other courses (for example, upper-level math courses where intrinsic motivation might be higher than in the lower-level, required core math courses) and are also assessing impact on learning of the material and student perceptions of pre-flight assignments' value for learning rather than focusing on completion rates.

Using SOTL to Coordinate and Revitalize Outcome Assessment

Our second interdisciplinary SOTL effort (still in an early stage) provides an example of a new approach to accomplishing and assessing our institutional outcomes, and one that we hope will more enthusiastically engage a larger percentage of our instructors across multiple disciplines/departments. It illustrates several challenges that will likely resonate with faculty at other institutions as well as outlines strategies that might be of interest to those facing similar challenges.

Approximately five years ago, the USAFA determined nineteen outcomes spanning multiple degree programs and cadet training, identified classes and training programs that should target each outcome, and formed outcome teams to lead the assessment of each outcome. While initial institutional outcome assessment efforts were well intended and were founded in good practice (for example, use of standardized rubrics, collaboration between representatives of targeted departments), in most cases they failed to receive "buy-in" from the faculty teaching the identified courses. In fact, many faculty members were not even aware of the existence of the rubrics. Not surprisingly, after an early push for incorporation of the outcome assessment measures, the efforts lost steam.

Independent of the formal outcome team structure of the institution and as part of the SOTL program discussion groups during the late spring of 2010, freshmen-level core course directors from the departments of history, English, and behavioral sciences began conversations about a common challenge they faced with their students: poor critical thinking and writing abilities across the curriculum. The discussion moved beyond the traditional focus of what content to deliver in their individual courses, although discipline-specific content was also seen as important (Rotherham and Willingham 2009). Instead we strategized about how we might work together to create educational experiences and common resources to support the development of our students' critical thinking skills, one of the institutional outcomes. As an example of the greater appeal of this approach, faculty from the First Year Experience Program learned of these discussions and asked to become part of the group (in contrast to being assigned by upper administration).

Even though our focus narrowed to the development of critical thinking skills within freshman core courses, those of us involved in this new effort realize that it will take months or years to fully implement. However, we hope that some of the early stages presented below serve as a useful model for an interdisciplinary SOTL effort aimed at supporting and assessing institutional outcomes.

Designing an Interdisciplinary Effort to Develop Foundational Critical Thinking Skills

Central to building a cohesive effort was coming to agreement on a common definition of "critical thinking." While the term is familiar to most people in academia, a precise definition of the term has not been converged on in the literature. Further, there are many theories, models, and descriptions of critical thinking and how to teach it (for example, Barbour and Streb 2010; Halpern 1996; Paul and Elder 2006). However, these approaches consistently recognize that critical thinking is comprised of many underlying skills and attitudes (for example, identifying underlying assumptions, generating and evaluating alternative solutions, skepticism, and curiosity). Based on examination of the literature and deep discussion, the group developed a common definition that specifically targeted a small number of foundational critical thinking skills that fit well with existing discipline-specific objectives of their various freshman-level courses: "Critical thinking is the process of questioning and analyzing assertions, in order to make an informed judgment or propose solutions. Three essential components of this process are the evaluation of relevant evidence, identification of biases and assumptions, and consideration of multiple perspectives." We hope the students, who also suffer from varying notions of critical thinking, will be unified by this simple and accessible definition.

Beyond the need for a unifying definition of critical thinking, the group also recognized the need to address terminology that differed between disciplines (and instructors) for similar aspects of the critical thinking process. (Note a similar acknowledgement of multi-disciplinary terminology and communication challenges in the chapter by Robinson et al. in this volume.) Unfortunately, based on feedback from students and shared instructor observations, it seems common that students compartmentalize their learning into courses and often show little transfer even within their major. Compartmentalization is even more likely when instructors use different terminology, unaware of what other instructors are doing.

The recognition of differing terminology also revealed that we did not really know *what* was being done in other departments to support the development of critical thinking in our students. Thus, we were missing out on opportunities to reinforce each other by working together and explicitly acknowledging what was happening in other classes when we discussed critical thinking applications in our own classes. If addressed, the explicit acknowledgment of other instructor/course efforts and activities communicates an important message to the students: they cannot escape or compartmentalize the critical thinking lessons. Importantly, we hope they will come to regard the development of those abilities across different courses as *intentional and purposeful.* Likewise, the message to the instructors is that development of strong critical thinking skills will not happen through one or two activities in a single course. Rather, each of the underlying skills that support critical thinking requires multiple opportunities for practice and feedback in order to achieve mastery (Bensley 2010; Svinicki 2004).

If we do not help students understand why we build these multiple opportunities across courses, they will be likely to classify them as redundant and not useful, and perhaps resent them. This is a natural tendency that goes beyond the development of critical thinking or other academic endeavors—everyday observation shows most humans become frustrated if they do not understand why they are being asked to do something that requires effort. Therefore, clear and compelling communication about our objectives and reasons for class lessons and activities should increase student ownership. However, in order to do this effectively in our interdisciplinary case, we needed to establish a convenient means of communication among instructors across several departments and disciplines.

Thus, in addition to face-to-face group discussions among the course directors (who then disseminate information to the instructors teaching their course), we will encourage and maintain communication among all involved instructors by using a discussion board on our Sharepoint site. Instructors have begun to post the dates and brief descriptions of critical thinking activities in each of the involved core courses. This allows instructors across departments to more easily know what is going on in the other freshman core courses, make reference/links to those activities in their own courses, and perhaps build on them. The discussion board is open to all USAFA instructors, so other course instructors could also use the information. For example, instructors for more advanced courses would be able to better understand what critical thinking experiences the students had had in their lower-level classes.

An additional effort (beyond the common definition and terminology, and the communication of critical thinking activities) is the development of some common resources that will be explicitly used by the identified freshmen core courses but also available to all other USAFA instructors. The common resources (posted on the same Sharepoint site mentioned above) will include a list of critical thinking terms and a critical thinking guide that contains very brief chapters explaining criteria for component parts of the critical thinking skills.

The list of terms includes short descriptions of how those terms are used in the different disciplines. What we desire to accomplish with this list is a means by which to identify and link common critical thinking elements that might seem different due to discipline-specific terminology. For example, the term "explication" figures frequently in English courses, but rarely in behavioral sciences courses. It refers to a close study of a text combined with an analysis of background information (for example, extratextual clues) that might help readers better understand the functioning of the work as a whole. Although distinct in many ways, explication nonetheless brings the reader to recognize and assess alternate perspectives, a common practice in behavioral sciences. If alternate perspectives are fully explored, then characteristics of people who express alternate perspectives should be taken into account (for example, their education, family history, current situational pressures). As another example, the term "thesis" in history is analogous to the term "hypothesis" as used in behavioral sciences, chemistry, and Introduction to Engineering (course directors from the latter two departments joined the effort in early Spring 2011). By identifying such parallels and explicitly linking them both in the common resources and through student interaction, we hope to help faculty and students understand the parallels and increase the likelihood that students apply the skills beyond a specific course.

The critical thinking guide is conceptualized to be a collection of guidelines and criteria that unify the efforts of instructors and simplify the learning process for students. While it contains links to more comprehensive references such as writing manuals, our brief chapters focus on explicit criteria and examples to guide students while they engage in using critical thinking skills and also provide possible grading criteria for instructors. Chapters explicitly relate different skills to one another and how they can build on each other. The primary chapters focus on the skills identified in the common definition and subsequent chapters will include topics that might be discipline-specific with respect to assignments in the core courses during the freshmen year. For example, students in freshman history are more likely to read primary sources than students in freshman behavioral sciences. During the Fall 2010 semester, the history department debuted several "chapters" that included the topics of critically analyzing sources of evidence, constructing sound arguments, making connections, inspecting a book, reading and listening for understanding, and historical questioning. We built on these resources during the Spring 2011 semester and released them to all USAFA students and instructors during the Fall 2011 semester.

A final aspect of this interdisciplinary effort that warrants mentioning due to possible transferability to other institutions is the benefit of working with the Freshman Year Experience (FYE) Program. Instructors for the FYE Program come from all departments across the USAFA. Thus, as we work with the FYE instructors, we are able to reach beyond the initial departments involved through the freshmen core courses, and we have learned about efforts to develop critical thinking in other courses. Therefore, as we post the various critical thinking activities on the Sharepoint site, we will be sure to encourage inclusion of activities occurring outside the freshmen core courses.

Assessing the Impact of Our Preliminary Efforts and an Early Lesson Learned

SOTL endeavors are not simply about trying new things to enhance learning (based on previous literature and scholarly discussions) but also are about collecting data that will allow us to assess the impact of those initiatives on student learning and behaviors known to influence learning and then disseminating what we learned. The assessment component is also what most directly links our efforts to institutional, cross-discipline outcome assessment efforts. At this point in time, our efforts have primarily been focused on understanding the individual initiatives that had been occurring in each department and developing resources that allow instructors across multiple disciplines to more systematically and intentionally support the development of critical thinking in our freshmen students. Our early assessments are focused on baseline measures of student awareness and understanding of these critical thinking efforts and their perceived value of the activities. We hope that, over time, as our efforts become more transparent and integrated, students will better understand and appreciate critical thinking assignments and will show increased ability to transfer their critical thinking skills across classes and beyond. As implementation progresses, we will shift the assessment focus to include measures of student critical thinking skills.

With that said, we do have some useful preliminary data based on initial, mostly independent departmental initiatives to develop critical thinking.

During the 2009–2010 academic year, the department of behavioral sciences implemented the use of pre-flights and the JiTT process as part of an explicit effort to develop critical thinking skills in freshmen students enrolled in their core course. By having students answer critical-thinking-related, pre-flight questions prior to every lesson, they had multiple opportunities for practicing targeted critical thinking skills and multiple opportunities for feedback. During the Fall 2010 semester, the department of history redesigned its freshmen core course to explicitly include the development of critical thinking skills as part of the course objectives, and consistently incorporated the critical thinking mini-chapter resources.

End-of-semester feedback from students in both courses illustrated a mix of responses about how the course developed their critical thinking skills and the value/motivation they had for the critical-thinking-related activities. Variation in student awareness of the multidisciplinary efforts also was clear from baseline feedback gathered from all freshmen through the FYE course early in Spring 2011. Neither of these results were surprising given that, at that point, the resources and explicit linking of efforts across the core courses have not yet been put into place, and instructors varied in their efforts to transparently incorporate the critical thinking exercises. We hope that follow-on feedback efforts will indicate increased student awareness and appreciation of the multidisciplinary efforts to develop their critical thinking skills.

Of immediate use was that the pattern of student responses indicated that much of the variation was linked to instructor differences in implementation. These data provide us with a meaningful early lesson learned: without widespread instructor buy-in, implementation will occur with different levels of enthusiasm and emphasis. Realistically, increasing and maintaining instructor buy-in across the different courses and through the years will necessitate ongoing and explicit buy-in from department heads and other senior administrators. Finding an effective balance between instructor autonomy and student achievement of institutional outcomes will require ongoing leadership and teamwork. Fortunately, because the course directors, who are faculty themselves, are choosing to take an active role in this project, there is more widespread buy-in from the other instructors.

The Way Ahead:
Integrating with the Institutional Assessment Teams

News of this freshmen core-course SOTL effort to develop critical thinking reached the administration in charge of outcome assessment and was received positively. In fact, the senior outcome administrator suggested that a new approach to outcome assessment might be to create an SOTL project for each outcome by having some of the faculty teaching the targeted courses work together to come up with a question of common interest related to the outcome. By allowing the instructors to develop their own research and assessment questions (although guided by the institutional outcomes), we should have higher levels of interest and participation in the process (Ryan and Deci 2000). This linkage between SOTL and institutional interests is similar to the strategy reported in this volume by Cheryl Albers at Buffalo State College, where they specifically linked "the SOTL work of individuals . . . to common pedagogic issues of priority to campus leaders." Currently, the freshmen-level critical thinking SOTL group is building a partnership with the formal critical thinking outcome team, which includes course representatives from all course levels. This SOTL research group will not replace the outcome team but will become an integral part of the outcome assessment by sharing resources they develop and data that is collected. As an indication of the appeal of the developmental approach we are taking (focusing on a few foundational components at the freshman level), members of the critical thinking outcome team who represent upper-level courses have formed sophomore, junior, and senior course groups. Course instructors within these groups have begun to share their critical thinking efforts and discuss how to build on critical thinking skills beyond those targeted by the freshmen core courses. Further, the group responsible for our respect for human dignity outcome has begun using the critical thinking approach as a model for their own efforts.

General Summary

The above two examples of interdisciplinary SOTL research illustrate aspects of both synthetic interdisciplinarity and transdisciplinarity as defined by Lisa R. Lattuca (2001). A primary distinction between the two types of research is the extent to which "the contributions or roles of the individual disciplines are still identifiable" (82). In the pre-flight/motivation study, the details of the implementation approaches were different in the different departments; however, we argue that the different choices made for implementation were often not grounded in disciplinary differences per se but rather were due to historical ways of doing things in those departments and the specific persons involved. More specifically, the choices about how many points to allot to the pre-flight assignments (0 percent, 10 percent, or 20 percent) were not based on learning math versus physics or behavioral sciences. The *type* of pre-flight questions in each department varied based on more disciplinary considerations, but that was not the focus of the study. Thus, with respect to understanding motivational factors that influence students to complete the pre-flight assignments, the study transcended the disciplines, and the specific departmental settings simply provided the conditions needed to investigate the big picture of motivational factors.

The critical thinking SOTL effort also transcends the disciplines in that the multidisciplinary group will investigate the impact of developing a common definition and resources. However, some items in the resources will be clearly discipline-specific (for example, terms such as *exposition* and the brief chapter focusing on historical questioning). As we move from assessing the impact of the initiative on student awareness of and motivations about critical thinking efforts across the disciplines to actual critical thinking abilities, disciplinary differences will likely play a more influential role.

Regardless of which type of research description best fits the two studies, the inclusion of multiple disciplines will ultimately lead to both a broader understanding of the underlying factors that transcend the disciplines and a clearer realization of contextual factors that make the findings less generalizable. (See Grauerholz and Main's chapter in this volume for an in-depth discussion about the challenges of generalizability.) When designing an interdisciplinary study, it is not necessary that the efforts in each department be identical. There needs to be enough commonality (for example, underlying factors such as motivation or goals such as critical thinking) so that it makes sense to treat departments as comparison groups or to investigate transferability of efforts. However, it is helpful if the assessments are identical in whole or part so that better comparisons can be made across the disciplines. This necessitates an open, noncompetitive attitude from departmental administrators and good communication among those conducting the research.

As mentioned by many others, opportunities to take part in an "educational trading zone" (Mills and Huber 2005) provide an excellent means by which to bring together faculty and promote the exchange of ideas that might lead to interdisciplinary research. However, without some guidance, faculty from different disciplines might have a hard time finding common ground that would lead to an interdisciplinary project. For example, faculty in physics and math were not familiar with the motivational theories that provided the structure for the interdisciplinary pre-flight project (additional examples are given in Poole's chapter of this volume). Thus, it can help to have facilitators with backgrounds in educational research, teaching pedagogy, human learning and cognition, and so forth.

It is also important to disseminate results not only at professional meetings but also at the university and departmental levels. The intra-institutional discussions serve several purposes. At USAFA, they allowed results and implications to be discussed within the specific context of the departments, they allowed recognition of those who conducted the research, they led to improved communication across departments and an increased appreciation for the efforts of colleagues in other departments, and, finally, they inspired other faculty to engage in SOTL research.

The process of earning a college degree is a multidisciplinary effort for the student. Interdisciplinary SOTL research is one means by which we can work together to better understand the "big picture" and more systematically create meaningful learning environments and experiences for our students.

NOTES

I would like to acknowledge the following persons for meaningful contributions to the projects and feedback on chapter drafts: Dr. Richard Hughes, CDR Stephen Sprague, Dr. Andrea VanNort, Dr. Jim Rolf, Lt. Col. Steven Novotny, and Maj. Damian McCabe.

1. Distribution A, approved for public release, distribution unlimited. The views expressed in this document are those of the author and do not reflect the official policy or position of the United States Air Force, Department of Defense, or the U. S. government.

2. "Developing leaders of character" is the overarching mission of the U.S. Air Force Academy.

3. The interteaching method (introduced by Boyce and Hineline 2002) involves sending students probing questions about the material to be covered the following day in class. Students are required to read the chapter with the questions in mind so that they are prepared to discuss the material and questions in class. Following small group discussions, they write a summary of their responses and indicate any points of confusion. Instructors present mini-lectures to introduce and/or clarify misconceptions, but otherwise they facilitate discussions among the small groups to encourage high-level processing of the material and so the students stay on task.

4. Some instructors included pre-flight assignments although they didn't use them/follow the JiTT procedure because, at USAFA, the core courses are designed by the course director and all sections of the course have common assessments, some with little or no individual instructor flexibility. Thus, individual instructors might have to require the students to complete the pre-flight assignments as part of the course but then not fully engage in the JiTT process themselves.

5. A short but nice overview of several motivational theories can be found in *McKeachie's Teaching Tips: Strategies, Research, and Theory for College and University Teachers,* 13th edition by McKeachie and Svincki (2010).

6. The procedure and surveys for this study were reviewed and approved as educationally exempt by the Institutional Review Board.

7. This is a noted best practice for incorporating pre-flights. See Camp, Middendorf, and Sullivan 2010.

8. The challenge of keeping new instructors fully informed is a significant one at USAFA. Every academic year, there is 30 percent turnover of faculty as military faculty members rotate in and out of three-year positions.

REFERENCES

Barbour, Christine, and Matthew J. Streb. 2010. *CLUED in to Politics: A Critical Thinking Reader in American Government.* Washington, DC: CQ Press.

Bensley, D. Alan. 2010. "A Brief Guide for Teaching and Assessing Critical Thinking in Psychology." *Association for Psychological Science* 23: 49–53.

Boyce, Thomas E., and Philip N. Hineline. 2002. "Interteaching: A Strategy for Enhancing the User-Friendliness of Behavioural Arrangements in the College Classroom." *Behaviour Analyst* 25: 215–26.

Camp, Mary E., Joan Middendorf, and Carol Sullivan. 2010. "Using Just-in-Time Teaching to Motivate Student Learning." In *Just-in-Time Teaching,* ed. Scott Simkins and Mark Maier, 25–38. Sterling, VA: Stylus.

Cookman, Claude, Sara Mandel, and J. Michael Lyons. 1999. "The Effects of Just-in-Time Teaching on Motivation and Engagement in a History of Photography Course." In *Just-in-Time Teaching: Blending Active Learning with Web Technology,* ed. Gregor Novak, Andrew Gavrin, Wolfgang Christian, and Evelyn Patterson, 1–16. Upper Saddle River, NJ: Prentice Hall.

Gibbs, Graham. 2010. "The Importance of Context in Understanding Teaching and Learning: Reflections on Thirty-five Years of Pedagogic Research." Keynote presented at the International Society for the Scholarship of Teaching and Learning, Liverpool, October.

Halpern, Diane F. 1996. *Thought and Knowledge: An Introduction to Critical Thinking,* 3rd ed. Mahway, NJ: Lawrence Erlbaum.

Huber, Mary T. 1999. "Disciplinary Styles in the Scholarship of Teaching and Learning." Paper presented at the Seventh International Improving Student Learning Symposium, University of York, UK.

Huber, Mary Taylor, and Sherwyn P. Morreale, eds. 2002. *Disciplinary Styles in the Scholarship of Teaching and Learning: Exploring Common Ground.* Washington, DC: American Association of Higher Education.

Lattuca, Lisa R. 2001. *Creating Interdisciplinarity: Interdisciplinary Research and Teaching among College and University Faculty.* Nashville: Vanderbilt University Press.

McKeachie, Wilbert, and Marilla Svinicki. 2010. *McKeachie's Teaching Tips: Strategies, Research, and Theory for College and University Teachers,* 13th ed. Belmont, CA: Wadsworth.

Mills, David, and Mary T. Huber. 2005. "Anthropology and the Educational 'Trading Zone': Disciplinarity, Pedagogy, and Professionalism." *Arts and Humanities in Higher Education* 4: 9–32.

Novak, Gregor, and Evelyn Patterson. 1998. "Just-in-Time Teaching: Active Learner Pedagogy with WWW." Presented at International Association of Science and Technology for Development.

Paul, Richard, and Linda Elder. 2006. *A Guide for Educators to Critical Thinking Competency Standards: Standards, Principles, Performance Indicators, and*

Outcomes with a Critical Thinking Master Rubric. Foundation for Critical Thinking, http://www.criticalthinking.org.

Rotherham, Andrew J., and Daniel Willingham. 2009. "Twenty-first Century Skills: The Challenges Ahead." *Educational Leadership* 67: 16–21.

Ryan, Richard M., and Edward L. Deci. 2000. "Self-Determination Theory and the Facilitation of Intrinsic Motivation, Social Development, and Well-Being." *American Psychologist,* 55: 68–78.

Scharff, Lauren, Robert Lee, Jim Rolf, and Steve Novotny. 2011. "Factors Impacting Completion of Pre-class Assignments in Physics, Math, and Behavioral Sciences." In *Improving Student Learning: Eighteen Global Theories and Local Practices—Institutional, Disciplinary and Cultural Variations,* ed. Chris Rust. Oxford: Oxford Centre for Staff and Learning Development.

Simkins, Scott, and Mark Maier. 2004. "Using Just-in-Time Teaching Techniques in the Principles of Economics Course." *Social Science Computer Review* 22: 444–56.

Svincki, Marilla. 2004. *Learning and Motivation in the Postsecondary Classroom.* Bolton, MA: Anker Publishing.

CHAPTER 12

Growing Our Own Understanding of Teaching and Learning: Planting the Seeds and Reaping the Harvest

CHERYL ALBERS

Cross-disciplinary scholarship of teaching and learning provides many challenges but also holds much promise. One of these challenges stems largely from our disciplinary silos from which we gain both our academic identity and the tools with which we conduct our scholarship. These silos can be the cause of competition, misunderstanding, and devaluing (Poole, this volume). The promise of SOTL is that its focus on teaching and learning can penetrate these silos. The dilemma of respecting and also infiltrating these disciplinary differences can be addressed through bringing together a range of individuals to explore a common concern. However, this approach often raises a second challenge, which is not unique to cross-disciplinary SOTL but is certainly amplified through collaborative work. This is the highly contextualized nature of classroom-based investigations. It is one of SOTL's strengths that it probes not just how students learn in general but rather how specific students learn specific content under the guidance of specific teachers. Yet it is precisely this contextualized nature that can be a barrier to undertaking work around a central problem.

This chapter reports on ways that faculty and staff from a variety of disciplines and units used SOTL to better understand the issue of student engagement. Data from interviews, reports, and meeting minutes are analyzed to identify the difficulties and benefits that were encountered. Specifically examined are three ways of categorizing the questions asked by or problems that drove these SOTL studies, common methodological barriers that were encountered and how they were overcome, and what has been learned by undertaking cross-disciplinary SOTL at Buffalo State College.

Planting the Interdisciplinary Seeds: SOTL Fellowships

All of the SOTL studies reported in this chapter were conducted by the SOTL/Carnegie Academy for the Scholarship of Teaching and Learning

(CASTL) Fellows at Buffalo State. Administrators instituted fellowships in 2002 to provide financial inducements for individual scholarship while at the same time ensuring that these systematic investigations focused on topics that strengthened the academic milieu of the college. These fellowships were one of several initiatives toward creating an institutional culture that valued SOTL. However, our approach was distinctly different from that at other institutions where promoting change involved "getting more people to do SOTL or hoping to develop a critical mass that will eventually change the institution" (Schroeder 2007, 4). Our goal was to promote change by tying fellowships to the change agendas of our campus leaders. This was a deliberate strategy on the part of the CASTL campus coordinator and supportive administrators who understood that "when the scholarship of teaching and learning speaks to such pressing institutional agendas as student achievement and success, it is likely to receive more support and recognition" (Hutchings, Huber, and Ciccone 2011, 6).

The high-priority and high-visibility institutional priorities that fellowships addressed cut across disciplines, departments, and other units on campus. These priorities emerged in a number of ways, such as through accreditation reviews, standardized testing results, funding initiatives, and strategic planning. The most recent round of strategic planning began in 2008 with a stakeholder's conference that determined that the primary focus for the 2009–2013 strategic plan would be the creation of quality learning experiences for students. The National Survey of Student Engagement's (NSSE) five benchmarks of effective educational practices, level of academic challenge, active and collaborative learning, student-faculty interaction, enriching educational experiences, and a supportive campus environment formed the framework for most initiatives aimed at achieving this goal.

The CASTL Advisory Committee in conjunction with campus administrators had already been using these benchmarks in the call for fellowship submissions. Embedding them in the strategic plan strengthened the tie between the SOTL studies undertaken by fellows and campus-wide priorities. Conducting SOTL work around these benchmarks moved the fellowship initiative toward what Lisa Lattuca (2001) refers to as synthetic interdisipinarity. In the introduction to this book, Kathleen McKinney notes that this form of interdisciplinairity is driven by the exploration of teaching and learning questions that bridge the disciplines. Thus our unifying concern among fellows' work became "How do we use SOTL to better understand and promote student engagement at Buffalo State?"

Documenting and Analyzing Our Growing Understanding of Student Engagement at Buffalo State College

To illuminate the connections among these cross-disciplinary studies, a number of data sources were reviewed. These included interviews conducted with fellows, final reports written by fellows at the conclusion of their project, published results of fellows' projects, and minutes of the CASTL Advisory Committee meetings.[1]

The author and a research assistant developed a thirteen-question interview protocol to evaluate the impact of the CASTL Fellowships. The questions were prompts to encourage participants to reflect on the impact of their fellowship on their classroom practice, their professional careers, and the campus as a whole (for example, What do you believe are the short-term and long-term benefits of the college putting resources into the CASTL Fellowships? How have your departmental colleagues reacted to your SOTL work?). The first three cohorts of Fellows (n = 8) were contacted for the first wave of interviews. The research assistant conducted half-hour interviews with six participants over a two-month time frame in 2006. Despite several attempts to schedule interviews with two additional fellows and offering them alternative methods for submitting answers to the questionnaire, no arrangements could be made. One of these fellows was eventually interviewed in the second wave.

In 2008, a second research assistant used a similar protocol and procedure to conduct the next round of interviews. Six fellows from the next two cohorts were contacted. Four of these individuals were interviewed. One professor who had retired declined for medical reasons, and time constraints eliminated one other individual.

Research Questions:
Three Frameworks for Finding Connections Across Disciplines

In this section three frameworks are used to find common threads across disciplines in the problems posed or questions asked by fellows in their SOTL studies. First, the projects were categorized by the NSSE benchmarks of student engagement. Then the same projects were analyzed using two different SOTL taxonomies (Nelson 2003; Hutchings 2000).

From 2002 until this chapter went to press, the campus has awarded twenty-five fellowships over nine years. These individuals are from sixteen academic departments and units. At the time of receiving the fellowship, two of the awardees were professional staff, fifteen assistant professors, seven associate professors, and one full professor; at time of publication, eight fellows had received promotions. The twenty-five fellows who make up the sample conducted a range of projects focused on the five indicators of student engagement identified by the authors of the NSSE and based on a review of the literature on factors that promote student learning. Categorizing each of these projects according to the benchmark of engagement reveals that seven SOTL projects focused on level of academic challenge, nine on active and collaborative learning, two on student-faculty interaction, five on enriching educational experiences, and one on supportive campus environment.

This predominance of fellows' studies in three of the indicators of engagement parallels campus reactions to the results of the NSSE. When the results from the initial benchmark study were made public, two outcomes generated a lot of buzz. First, there was pride in the numbers of students who indicated involvement in enriching educational experiences. This result confirmed a perceived strength in engaging significant numbers of students in undergraduate research, service learning, and internships. Involvement in such extension activities are often paired with active and collaborative classroom practices, providing a second popular focus for study. Third, there was concern that results pointed to lower-than-desired ratings on level of academic challenge. This quantified an issue of longstanding concern to many on campus and also raised questions regarding how to increase academic challenge in a way that would result in more student learning, not just more student work.

The CASTL Advisory Committee was asked by the assessment officer to see whether there were ways that SOTL could be used to better understand the NSSE results. Committee members indicated that many of the past fellowship projects could shed light on the interplay among these benchmarks and student learning as illustrated in the final section of this paper.

Several authors offer other taxonomies for studies in the field of the scholarship of teaching and learning. Craig Nelson's (2003) taxonomy is based on levels of analysis used in SOTL studies: reports on particular classes, reflections on many years of teaching experience, comparisons of courses or students across time, learning science, and summaries and analyses of sets of prior studies. Nineteen of the studies done by Buffalo State fellows fall under Nelson's first category. One study attempting to identify aspects of courses that have a long-term impact on students could be considered "reflections of many years of teaching." A liberal interpretation of Nelson's third category might include a project based on interviews with faculty from many departments to identify effective strategies for capitalizing on diversity in the classroom, an investigation of the development of global awareness in prospective teachers, and a third project that identified significant issues faced by faculty teaching in first-year student learning communities. None of the studies involved Nelson's categories of learning science or summary/ analysis of prior works. Two SOTL studies are difficult to classify in this taxonomy.

This difficulty in applying taxonomies to SOTL work reflects the fact that some studies fall into more than one category, a fact acknowledged by Pat Hutchings (2000). She proposes a taxonomy of four categories that, when applied to these studies, reveals slightly more diversity of focus. Six SOTL projects could be categorized as attempts to identify the following: "What is/are" effective multidisciplinary strategies for capitalizing on diversity, significant issues in first-year student programs, the impact of service learning on achieving the goals of diversity classes, factors that facilitate the persistence of underrepresented students, student understandings of plagiarism, and the impact of participation in a Saturday morning Global Book hour in a diverse community. Eighteen of the fellows' studies come under the "What works" category, which involves proving or disproving the effectiveness of an intervention. Hutchings's third category, "Visions of the possible," could describe the development of a model for establishing academic networks to foster learning in the field. None of the fellows took on the kind of work that Hutchings describes as the "Formulation of new conceptual frameworks" that shape thought about practice.

These analyses suggest that although fellows brought a variety of disciplinary perspectives to their SOTL work, the questions they asked fell into three categories crossing disciplinary boundaries. First, how can we better understand the ways that enriching experiences such as service learning, undergraduate research, or internships promote student learning? Second, can we identify the impact of active and collaborative learning strategies on students' cognitive and affective engagement with course content? Third, what classroom activities provide a level of academic challenge appropriate for engaging students in authentic learning? To answer these questions, fellows gravitated toward studies of a single classroom, seeking to illuminate what transpires there or what facilitates the learning process. The design of these studies involved selecting methods most appropriate for the question posed.

Methods: Familiar and Unfamiliar Territory

From its inception, leaders of the SOTL movement have promoted the use of research methods that are appropriate to the question under study. In their seminal work *Scholarship Assessed,* Charles Glassick, Mary Taylor

Huber, and Gene I. Maeroff (1997) suggest that methods chosen should be appropriate to the goals of the study, applied effectively, and modified in response to changing circumstances and the discipline of the researcher. This final point of using methods familiar to the discipline is further developed by Mick Healey (2000): "For most academics, developing the scholarship of teaching will only bring about change in their priorities if it is embedded in disciplines and departments" (172–73). He attributes this to the fact that most academics' sense of identity lies with disciplines and that "there is a strong perception among staff that there are significant differences among disciplines in what academics do and how those activities are described and valued" (173).

Huber and Sherwyn P. Morreale (2002) tie this disciplinary perspective to both the production and the valuing of knowledge about teaching and learning in higher education.

> For good or for ill, scholars of teaching and learning must address field-specific issues if they are going to be heard in their own disciplines, and they must speak in a language that their colleagues understand. This language, which we are choosing to call a discipline's "style," is made up of, at its core, what Joseph Schwab (1964) so elegantly distinguished as substantive and syntactic structures: the "conceptions that guide inquiry" and the "pathways of enquiry [scholars] use, what they mean by verified knowledge and how they go about this verification." (20–21)

However, as the following fellow found, conducting SOTL within accepted disciplinary styles is no guarantee of acceptance:

> For example, I am a criminologist. People will want information about the teaching of criminology—fine. But if that information is produced by criminologists, they say that criminologist is not being a good criminologist [because he or she focuses on SOTL rather than disciplinary research]. And if that information is being produced by an education professor, then they say it means nothing to criminology. So, there is this real fundamental disconnect about the valuing of SOTL within the disciplines that I felt—that's why I found SOTL to be where people were willing to toss aside that strange place in which so many people exist. (Johnson, interview)

Huber and Morreale (2002) recognize that conducting SOTL from within one's disciplinary comfort zone can be a double-edged sword. "The applicability of one's discipline to problems of teaching and learning can be an effective argument for the rightness and importance of this work. On the other hand, the resistance of these problems to the discipline's familiar modes of inquiry, conceptualization, and research procedures can limit interest in the scholarship of teaching and learning and even undermine its legitimacy" (16).

The use of methods that are familiar to the discipline serves at least three purposes. First, the majority of those involved in the production of SOTL are doing so in addition to maintaining an active research agenda within their discipline. Under these conditions, spending time to learn new research techniques seems an unrealistic demand. It is more expedient to suggest, if appropriate to the research question, that practitioners apply methods already in their research tool kit to the study of classroom practice. Second, while there are several academic journals devoted to the publication of SOTL, faculty may prefer to submit manuscripts to the discipline-based pedagogic journals. Reviewers for these journals are likely to be more comfortable with articles that use familiar methods. Third, at the local level, the first gatekeepers of academics' productivity are often the departmental renewal and promotion and tenure committees. While faculty members are increasingly familiar with SOTL work, they may still be unsure of how to assess its quality. Using familiar methods helps committee members see how classroom study can be linked to a disciplinary research agenda.

In theory, these reasons for using discipline-based methodological tool kits make good sense, but in practice, choosing techniques appropriate to the question under investigation often requires that a researcher adopt unfamiliar techniques. This section provides examples from our work that illustrate both the adaptation of disciplinarily familiar techniques to SOTL and the challenges of learning new techniques that fall outside of the fellows' disciplinary training.

Associate Professor of Sociology Gary Welborn designed his study of the relationship between service learning and diversity based on his informal observations of the impact of service learning on his students' attitudes about diversity and social justice. As a sociologist, he used his familiarity with survey methods to develop a measure of the perceived change that students undergo as a result of taking a diversity course. In its final form, the survey was administered to students in diversity courses, some taught with traditional methods and others that included a service-learning component. Although he used a familiar research technique, its development became a learning experience as he shared drafts with members of the service-learning community including faculty from a range of academic departments and units. "The process of developing the survey questionnaire provided me with an opportunity to dialogue with colleagues about issues related to diversity and social justice. This has been very rewarding and has helped me broaden my understanding of both the issues and some of the strategies and tactics colleagues have developed to help deepen student awareness and sensitivity to diversity and social justice issues" (Welborn, interview).

Associate Professor of Elementary Education and Reading David Henry was interested in documenting the impact of engaging pre-service teachers with hands-on experience in conducting clinical interviews on their knowledge and beliefs about the role of assessment in teaching. His class provided both information on the theory behind clinical interviews and practice in conducting interviews in the field as well as in assessing what the interviews revealed. Similar to Welborn, Henry's training and experience as a social science researcher provided him with the skills necessary for designing the qualitative and quantitative surveys used in his pre- and post-testing of science and math teaching-methods students.

Other fellows faced greater methodological challenges as they became aware of the fact that the studies they proposed suggested measurement, data analysis, or sampling issues that required refining or adding to their existing skill set. Fellows who pursued methods that were outside of their familiar tool kit entered "unfamiliar territory" similar to that described by Reichard and Takayama, Poole, and Robinson et al. in this volume. The following examples illustrate ways that fellows at Buffalo State met such challenges.

In designing her study, Associate Professor of Music Lisa Hunter found that most of the literature on learning communities substantiated their benefits for engaging first-year students with the campus culture and thus improving retention. However, Hunter was interested in investigating to what degree intellectual growth accompanied involvement in learning communities. She wanted to use an established and validated measure; this is not a standard part of training in music education. Her search led her to the Measure of Intellectual Development based on William Perry's (1970) Model of Intellectual and Ethical Development, which consists of an open-ended essay in response to a prompt administered in a pre/post-test format. Hunter engaged professional raters from the Center for Intellectual Development to score each essay. Due to the complicated nature of the way the data is reported, she sought assistance from the Scholarship Support Center on campus to ensure the validity and reliability of her analysis. This analysis allowed her to report the results in a way that documented differences in the intellectual development positions between learning community and non-learning-community freshmen.

Assistant Professor of Business Diane McFarland also had difficulty analyzing the quantity of data she collected for her study of the impact of structured engagement with community agencies on students' mastery of course material, their ability to apply this material, and their attitudes toward civic and social responsibility. Reflective essays, pre- and post-tests on marketing theories, and surveys on civic and social engagement were some of the data she gathered to assess the impact of service learning. Questionnaires were also administered to the community groups to determine whether and how such collaboration aids the organization. Most of these data were collected in hard copy.

During the year in which she conducted her study, McFarland attended several meetings with others working on SOTL projects based in other disciplines, where she talked about her growing distress at the amount of data piling up and her concerns about how to analyze the qualitative data. "I can't tell you how many times I've gone through the data just to come up with a single conclusion. And there's much more data to be mined" (McFarland, interview). Colleagues suggested she begin to collect qualitative data in digital form in order to use software analysis programs. After doing so, she attended a campus training session on the software program she eventually used. "Some of the reflections are on disks and some are only hard copy, so I read through the hard copy to come up with the plotting of this . . . what I'm calling 'culture-shock' on the marketing plan. But I will need to spend more time" (McFarland, interview). Part of what was so time-consuming was finding how to come up with the most useful analysis. Again, colleagues from disciplines such as education and sociology were influential in providing examples of how they develop coding rubrics for this purpose.

Methodological Issues Across Disciplines: Analysis and Interpretation

Two other methodological issues that have not been easily resolved have arisen in several studies. First is the analysis of the results of SOTL studies with small sample sizes. This is most restricting to those who are more familiar with large quantitative data sets. Second is interpretation of results of studies using multiple measures when some measures indicate positive change while others do not. These issues cut across disciplines and indicators of engagement. The experiences of three fellows exemplify the challenge found in working with small numbers.

Assistant Professor in the International Center for Studies in Creativity John Cabra evaluated the use of technology on student recall of and reactions to psychometric statistics. A secondary goal of his intervention was to reduce apprehension about the level of academic challenge involved in the use of statistics. Cabra taught the same set of statistics in two ways, once to a class in Fall 2007 (n = 9) and then to a class in Spring 2008 (n = 8). This small sample restricted the use of the most common tests of statistical significance. Cabra settled on gathering qualitative data to support the results of the Mann Whitney U test.

Associate Professor of Social Work Ronnie Mahler also studied the use of technology to help students understand statistics. Rather than a focus on the level of academic challenge involved in learning statistics, however, she focused on the impact of active and collaborative learning. Students participated in workshops of differing duration on conflict and the role of mediation in conflict resolution. In 2005, twelve students participated in an abbreviated three-hour workshop using the same content and format that had been given in the previous year. After receiving course material on statistics, students in both groups used Excel to work together in class to evaluate the effect of the educational workshop. In 2004, ten students participated in a two-day educational intervention on conflict mediation. Again, the benefits of using data on student learning were inhibited by the fact that the small sample restricted the statistical procedures Mahler traditionally used in her research. Instead she reported her results as descriptive statistics and trends.

Associate Professor of Psychology Jill Norvilitis assessed the impact on student learning of enriching experiences through awarding undergraduate research fellowships. The study involved comparing the results of students who received a fellowship to those of two comparison groups with differing levels of involvement in scholarly activity. There were fifteen student fellows, nine advisees, and ten students with some research experience who participated with a faculty mentor. With this small sample, Norvilitis could not rely on many of the statistical tools of her discipline; instead she looked for trends that were supported by qualitative data.

A second methodological issue that cuts across many disciplines and indicators of engagement is trickier to define than the analysis of small samples. This issue arose when data analysis indicated little difference between students who received an intervention and those who did not, or between pre- and post-tests. What puzzled the fellows doing these studies was a contradiction between results gathered through quantitative measures, such as grades, indicating no significant differences and those gathered through qualitative measures, such as narrative final course evaluations, indicating a positive impact. The studies of Pacheco and Draeger, which are detailed below, illustrate this problem.

Assistant Professor of Chemistry Maria Pacheco investigated the impact of redesigning traditional chemistry experiments to include "real life" applications such as soil testing in a community garden in a low-income area of inner-city Buffalo. The research design involved the comparison of two lab groups: a treatment group and a control group that shared a common lecture experience. Quantitative measures indicated little difference between treatment and control groups in achievement. The treatment group, however, indicated more positive attitudes toward science. When presenting her results to members of the campus community, Pacheco was encouraged by faculty from the social sciences to think beyond the limited differences she found in achievement to explore ways to capture the changes she saw intuitively.

Initially, fellows working together to interpret this situation decided that possibly the wrong quantitative measures had been chosen to capture the particular changes resulting from this intervention. In an interview, Pacheco reacts to this collaborative effort:

> It's a good feeling to know that you can corroborate your feelings if nothing else—this works or it doesn't. And sometimes it doesn't and you do have to go back and change, but it's nice that you're getting support for what you're doing and you can have people who can give you feedback—like I said, when I gave the presentation, it was very good, I got excellent feedback in terms of how to look at the data in terms of maybe follow the students for a few more years, see what their careers are and all of those things that I might not have necessarily thought of until they brought it up. I think that thing of community, exchanging ideas is very good.

Assistant Professor of Philosophy and Humanities John Draeger studied two introductory philosophy classes, each consisting of approximately forty students. The first group wrote long papers in which they were asked to demonstrate competence in three elements of critical thinking. The second group wrote a short assignment on each element before writing the longer paper. Students completed questionnaires throughout the project to assess anxiety and student comprehension while papers were assessed with a critical thinking rubric. Contrary to initial assumptions, the incremental writing assignments did little to clarify perceptions, calm anxiety, or improve writing. However, data did suggest that small assignments focused student attention on the critical thinking elements and thus may turn out to be a more efficient way of teaching these skills.

Working together to unravel these situations, fellows suggested several alternatives to the inadequate measures explanation for conflicting results. The second possibility was that the measures were not inadequate at all but instead provided evidence that the interventions had an impact on variables in the affective domain that were typically measured qualitatively, while the intervention had no effect on cognitive outcomes, typically measured quantitatively. The third alternative is that with SOTL, as with any study of human behavior, it is possible that students were exhibiting a Hawthorne effect. In other words, the simple act of participating in the study affected the scores of students in control groups or before exposure to the treatment. Grauerholz and Main, in their chapter in this volume, present a fourth possibility: that it is impossible to construct a true control group in classroom-based research, thereby negating its usefulness in measuring the impact of an intervention.

In summary, some fellows at Buffalo State have conducted SOTL projects by employing methods that parallel those they use in their disciplinary research. The predominance of interviews and questionnaires as measures within SOTL provides an advantage for those in the social sciences or fields of study where qualitative methods are commonly used. Often the methods that faculty members use in their discipline-based research are ill-suited or insufficient for their SOTL questions. Fellows who found themselves in this position encountered the need for a fast acquisition of new skills to use the tools most appropriate for classroom study. This acquisition was often self-guided, requiring substantial investment in time and effort learning new methods. However, most fellows did not tackle this alone. The resources they used included informal discussions with each other; campus-run workshops; campus research support staff; peer feedback from local, national, and international presentations; and outside experts.

While some fellows grappled with the issue of analysis of small samples, others were challenged with interpreting data to identify "what worked." This problem was especially evident when the research design divided the class into experimental (or quasi-experimental) and traditional treatment groups. Multiple measures sometimes presented differing results; most commonly questionnaires or interviews indicated positive student reaction to an intervention that produced no difference in measures of achievement.

These issues around analysis and interpretation are most likely to impact individuals who are more familiar with the use of statistical tools for data analysis. Fellows whose disciplinary research is grounded in large data sets struggled more than those familiar with field methods and case studies, usually social scientists who commonly use multiple measures to understand experiences in a small group. In addition to differences in familiarity with research styles, a second distinction in confronting these methodological issues is evident in fellows' experiences. The drive to find consistent evidence through instruments that measure different aspects of learning is underpinned by the conviction that students' attitudes and their cognitive understanding are so intertwined that positive change in one should be paralleled with positive change in the other. As fellows pushed beyond attributing these outcomes to the probability that the measures of achievement were not capturing the changes indicated in self-report, more fundamental assumptions about learning emerged.

Seeking answers to these questions raises more fundamental concerns about SOTL in general. Has the push to see SOTL as having impact on student learning resulted in a reluctance to accept the value of changing students' attitudes and values, even when they are not related to cognitive change? When studies report no differences between control and treatment groups, does that mean the treatment was not effective, or that the control group was affected by simply engaging students in SOTL, regardless of its focus? Or, as Grauerholz and Main challenge in their chapter in the book, is the use of control groups even appropriate for SOTL?

Outcomes: Reaping the Harvest

One of the lauded strengths of SOTL is the fact that it is contextually bound (Gibbs 2010). By most definitions, SOTL studies involve systematic investigation informed by the nature of the specific classroom, institutions, and communities in which they are situated. A more expansive definition offered by Carolin Kreber (2002) suggests that "scholars of teaching . . . draw on formal and personal sources of knowledge construction about teaching, effectively combine this with their knowledge of the discipline to construct *pedagogical content knowledge,* continuously further this knowledge through self-regulated learning processes, and validate their knowledge through peer-review" (18). Kreber's definition of SOTL implies that it is inseparable from the context in which it occurs.

Building a Knowledge Base from Contextually Bound Work

This focus on context cautions us about using the results of these studies to draw conclusions or make recommendations about the best ways to foster student engagement. While Stephen Gareau found no difference in student recall between content presented digitally and that presented in print, might the results be different in another community, on another campus, in another discipline, or for that matter with a different class that Gareau taught? There would be little dispute that the answer is "of course."

It is sometimes difficult to reconcile this context-dependent characteristic of SOTL with the call to use SOTL to build an intellectual commons

(Huber and Hutchings 2005), or what Scharff (this volume) refers to in this text as The Big Picture of student learning, for to do so implies generalizing from one context into many others. In their contribution to this volume, Grauerholz and Main argue against the implicit assumption that findings from SOTL research are generalizable from one setting to another. McKinney (2006) reminds us that SOTL has the potential to "move us further along a path to understanding the bigger picture of learning in a discipline, including pedagogical content knowledge and signature pedagogies" (40). But in order to realize this potential, we must use SOTL as an "opportunity to develop new and stronger forms of collaboration across institutions and across disciplines" (41).

The quandary lies in how to use context-rich SOTL work to build a body of knowledge that influences practice. Our experience builds on the idea that the body of knowledge we are trying to accumulate through SOTL takes many forms. Kreber (2003) suggests "we engage in the scholarship of teaching as we construct knowledge through reflection in three different domains of teaching knowledge" (31–32). Lee Shulman (1987) has labeled these domains of knowledge: content (understanding of subject matter within the discipline), pedagogic content (including both a general understanding of human learning as well as how this takes place within the discipline), and curricula (familiarity with the range of materials and strategies available within the discipline, the ability to select the most appropriate, and awareness of how one's course relates to other aspects of a student educational experience). Kreber and Patricia Cranton (2000) label these domains instructional (instructional design), pedagogical (how students learn and how to facilitate learning), and curricular knowledge (goals, purposes, and rationales that guide practice).

All of the studies conducted by fellows at Buffalo State make contributions to instructional or pedagogic content knowledge within the disciplines. However, only one of the studies seems limited to disciplinary context. It is difficult to generalize the impact of using context-rich chemistry labs outside of the natural sciences. With this exception, these studies could inform practice within other disciplinary and cultural contexts. However, this is not achieved through generalizing the results of context-bound investigations. Rather, it is achieved through transference that occurs in collaboration. Hearing a creative studies professor describe his investigation of the use of technology to reduce student anxiety over learning statistics may stimulate a colleague who teaches statistics in another department to consider whether this might work within his or her context. The result of the philosopher's use of structuring writing assignments to reduce student anxiety over writing can be useful to any professor who assesses learning through papers. However, making this transfer from one group of students to another or from one setting to another needs to consider the highly contextualized nature of SOTL.

Transference and SOTL: Conditions and Benefits

Our experience at Buffalo State has been that this intra-institutional transference can happen in two ways and under two conditions. Cross-disciplinary initiatives can build pedagogical content knowledge and curricular knowledge. First, in order for this transference to take place, studies need to include extensive information about the contexts in which they occur. This includes both demographic information and what field researchers refer to as "rich description," which paints a detailed picture of the conditions of the study, allowing others to compare it to their own context. Shulman's comments on the importance of rich description of context when sharing SOTL across institutions are equally important in the kind of synthetic interdisipinarity undertaken at Buffalo State. "We do so by documenting as comprehensively as necessary the characteristics of the individuals whom we have studied and the procedures we have used. . . . More specifically, the reader must judge whether the findings we report for the individuals whom we have studied should be considered applicable to any other group of individuals regarding whom our reader might be interested" (Shulman 1981, 9).

Second, there need to be opportunities for colleagues to learn about each other's work that go beyond written documents and formal presentations. Some of these are highly structured as is the Teagle Collegium at Indiana University at Bloomington (Robinson et al., this volume). Yet it seems that informal working groups are where much of the building of this intellectual commons takes place. "So often it is difficult for junior faculty to meet and work with people from other departments and deanships; I looked forward to the meetings and the chance to forward the work that is important to all of us" (Eastman, interview).

One of the most elegant descriptions of the way the Buffalo State fellowship program provides opportunities for such transference comes from the creative studies professor who studied the role of technology in learning statistics.

> I gained from people's personal experiences with teaching because that interaction, that camaraderie, that I have with my colleagues in this group help to test my thinking around teaching. So I'll hear somebody say something they do in their class and I say, "Wow, I never thought of doing that and I thought that this would be a better way to go." They're having some success. And I start questioning

> my own paradigm about teaching and so I start to ask them a lot of questions about what they're doing, and then I start to experiment. And, so, you know, CASTL helps me to question my own paradigm around what's the best way to teach, what's the best way of reaching out to the learners. Through CASTL I learned that, wow, there is rigor. There are ways in which you can really think about teaching that you can engage in metacognition. (Cabra, interview)

We have found that in addition to transference of pedagogical content knowledge, there is a second type of knowledge built through our cross-disciplinary work. This is exposure to and appreciation of diversity of research designs. Cross-disciplinary work provides models that encourage individuals to expand the ways that they question and study their practice. "Selecting the method most appropriate for a particular disciplined inquiry is one of the most important, and difficult, responsibilities of a researcher. The choice requires an act of judgment, grounded both in knowledge of methodology and the substantive area of the investigation" (Shulman 1981, 11). This chapter illustrates ways that the fellowship program at Buffalo State accomplishes the "cross-fertilization" that results from viewing other pedagogies and research methods argued for by Poole in this volume.

Moving toward Transdisciplinarity

Up until now, the greatest benefits derived from this work have involved expanding pedagogic content knowledge and research knowledge of fellows. We believe these studies and the dissemination of their results have moved us closer to understanding student engagement within specific classroom contexts. Our next goal is to begin to look for patterns among the results of various studies addressing each of the NSSE benchmarks. As the diversity and number of classroom-based projects in each category expands, we are accumulating a better picture of factors that influence student engagement within our institutional context. To expedite this process, the CASTL Advisory Committee has decided to focus on academic challenge during the next round of fellowships. We hope to use systematic study to build an intellectual commons where SOTL studies promote individual growth in pedagogical and curricular knowledge while addressing systemic institutional priorities. In doing so, we will be reminded of Shulman's (2011) wise observation that "SOTL is an area of scholarship that does not solve problems once and for all. The challenges of teaching are persistent. . . . These are problems that are not cured, but managed" (6).

NOTES

1. Fellows as of 2011 include: Assistant Professor of Adult Education/ Educational Foundations Susan Birden received a Reflective Practice grant in 2002–2003, Associate Professor of Criminal Justice and Coordinator of African and African American Studies Scott Johnson received a Collaborative Teaching grant in 2002–2003, Associate Professor of Hospitality and Tourism Lori L. Till received an Applied Learning grant in 2002–2003, Lecturer of Hospitality and Tourism and Director of Campus House Kathleen O'Brien received an Applied Learning grant in 2003–2004, Assistant Professor of English Gloria Eastman received an Assessment grant in 2003–2004, Assistant Professor of Computer Information Systems Sarbani Banerjee received an Assessment grant in 2004–2005, Associate Professor of Social Work Ronnie Mahler received an Inquiry and Action grant in 2004–2005, Associate Professor of Chemistry Maria Pacheco received a Promoting Persistence grant in 2004–2005, Assistant Professor of Computer Information Systems Stephen Gareau received a First-Year Students grant in 2005–2006, Assistant Professor of Elementary Education and Reading David Henry received a Research as Pedagogy grant in 2005– 2006, Professor of Educational Foundations Frederick Howe received an Assessment grant in 2005–2006, Assistant Professor of Philosophy John Draeger received a Liberal Arts grant in 2006–2007, Assistant Professor of Business Diane McFarland received an Integrating Inquiry and Action grant in 2006–2007, Academic Skills Center Coordinator Tom Renzi received a First-Year Students grant in 2006–2007, Assistant Professor at the International Center for Studies in Creativity John Cabra received a Pedagogical Research grant in 2007–2008, Assistant Professor of English Adrienne Costello received a Pedagogical Research grant in 2007–2008, Associate Professor of Sociology Gary Welborn received a Supporting Student Learning grant in 2007–2008, Assistant Professor of Elementary Education and Reading Pixita del Prado Hill received a Pedagogical Research Faculty grant in 2008–2009, Assistant Professor of Music Education Lisa Hunter received an Active and Collaborative Learning grant in 2008–2009, Associate Professor of Psychology Jill Norvilitis received an Enriching Student Learning Experiences grant in 2008–2009, Assistant Professor of Communications Ann Hsiang-Liao received an Active and Collaborative Learning grant in 2009–2010, Assistant Professor of Educational Foundations Reva Fish received an Academic Challenge grant in 2009–2010, Assistant Professor of Music Victoria Furby received a Student-Faculty Interactions grant in 2009–2010, Assistant Professor of Computer Information Systems Ruth Guo received an Active and Collaborative Learning grant in 2010–2011, and Associate Professor of Elementary Education and Reading Kim Truesdell received an Enriching Student Learning Experiences grant in 2010–2011. Note that academic level and departmental/unit affiliations listed are those occupied at the time of receiving fellowship. Eight fellows have been promoted to a higher rank since the completion of their fellowship.

REFERENCES

Gibbs, Graham. 2010. "The Importance of Context in Understanding Teaching and Learning: Reflections on Thirty-five Years of Pedagogic Research." Keynote presented at the International Society for the Scholarship of Teaching and Learning, Liverpool, UK, October 19–22.

Glassick, Charles E., Mary Taylor Huber, and Gene I. Maeroff. 1997. *Scholarship Assessed: Evaluation of the Professoriate.* San Francisco: Jossey-Bass.

Healey, Mick. 2000. "Developing the Scholarship of Teaching in Higher Education: A Discipline-Based Approach." *Higher Education Research and Development* 19, no. 2: 169–89.

Huber, Mary Taylor, and Pat Hutchings. 2005. *The Advancement of Learning: Building the Teaching Commons.* San Francisco: Jossey-Bass.

Huber, Mary Taylor, and Sherwyn P. Morreale. 2002. "Situating the Scholarship of Teaching and Learning: A Cross-disciplinary Conversation." In *Disciplinary Styles in the Scholarship of Teaching and Learning: Exploring Common Ground,* ed. Mary Taylor Huber and Sherwyn P. Morreale, 1–24. Washington, DC: American Association for Higher Education.

Hutchings, Pat. 2000. "Approaching the Scholarship of Teaching and Learning." In *Opening Lines: Approaches to the Scholarship of Teaching and Learning,* ed. Pat Hutchings, 1–10. Menlo Park, CA: Carnegie Foundation for the Advancement of Teaching.

Hutchings, Pat, Mary Taylor Huber, and Anthony Ciccone. 2011. "Getting There: An Integrated Vision of the Scholarship of Teaching and Learning." *International Journal for the Scholarship of Teaching and Learning* 5, no. 1: 1–14.

Kreber, Carolin. 2002. "Teaching Excellence, Teaching Expertise, and the Scholarship of Teaching." *Innovative Higher Education* 27, no. 1: 5–23.

———. 2003. "Challenging the Dogma: Towards a More Inclusive View of the Scholarship of Teaching." *Journal on Excellence in College Teaching* 14, no. 2/3: 27–43.

Kreber, Carolin, and Patricia Cranton. 2000. "Exploring the Scholarship of Teaching." *Journal of Higher Education* 71, no. 4: 476–95.

Lattuca, Lisa R. 2001. *Creating Interdisciplinarity: Interdisciplinarity Research and Teaching among College and University Faculty.* Nashville: Vanderbilt University Press.

McKinney, Kathleen. 2006. "Attitudinal and Structural Factors Contributing to Challenges in the Work of the Scholarship of Teaching and Learning." *New Directions for Institutional Research* (129): 37–50.

Nelson, Craig E. 2003. "Doing It: Examples of Several of the Different Genres of the Scholarship of Teaching and Learning." *Journal on Excellence in College Teaching* 14, no. 2/3: 85–94.

Perry, William. 1970. *Forms of Intellectual and Ethical Development in the College Years: A Scheme.* New York: Holt, Rinehart, and Winston Press.

Schroeder, Connie. 2007. "Countering SOTL Marginalization: A Model for Aligning SOTL with Institutional Initiatives." *International Journal for the Scholarship of Teaching and Learning* 1, no. 1: 1–9.

Schwab, Joseph. 1964. "Structure of the Disciplines." In *The Structure of Knowledge and the Curriculum,* ed. G. W. Ford and Lawrence Pugno, 6–30. Chicago: Rand McNally.

Shulman, Lee. 1981. "Disciplines of Inquiry in Education: An Overview." *Educational Researcher* 10, no. 6: 5–23.

———. 1987. "Knowledge and Teaching: Foundations of the New Reform." *Harvard Educational Review* 57, no. 1: 1–22.

———. 2011. "The Scholarship of Teaching and Learning: A Personal Reflection." *International Journal for the Scholarship of Teaching and Learning* 5, no. 1: 1–7.

CHAPTER 13

Navigating Interdisciplinary Riptides on the Way to the Scholarship of Integrative Learning

CARMEN WERDER

> *Riptide: a strong surface current flowing outwards from a shore and occurring when two tidal streams meet, can be turbulent and dangerous.* (Merriam-Webster Online 2011)

Increasingly, scholars call for grounding the study of teaching and learning in ways that cut across disciplinary boundaries (McKinney 2009). At least one scholar has even challenged any preference for a scholarship of teaching and learning that relies solely on a single discipline, saying that such a limited grounding risks it going unread and ignored (Weimer 2008). In this volume, Robinson et al. urge us to view the cultivation of interdisciplinary dialogue as essential communicative work if the scholarship of teaching is to be understood beyond our own disciplinary conversations. Even earlier, while calling attention to the value of recognizing *Disciplinary Styles in the Scholarship of Teaching and Learning*, Mary Taylor Huber and Sherwyn P. Morreale (2002) urged us to gravitate toward the "borders of disciplinary imagination" (2), similar to what Peter Galison (1997) had termed the "trading zones" where we can transcend disciplines and learn from each other.

While these calls tend to cast interdisciplinary scholarship as a constant good ever to be pursued, the invitations frequently omit specifics as to what *we*—as active scholars in research on teaching and learning—mean when we reference the scholarship of teaching and learning using that language. In reviewing the history of this language in higher education, Julie Thompson Klein (1990) synthesized the data in proposing "interdisciplinarity" as the larger term and then delineating it in terms of the degree of interaction demonstrated between disciplines. In this synthesized scheme, she defined "interdisciplinarity" as a continuum based on the extent of interaction observed: from "multidisciplinarity" (more than one discipline addressing the same problem, but with little or no interaction between them), to "pluridisciplinarity" (interaction based on disciplines using methods and findings from other disciplines), to "transdisciplinarity" (interaction across disciplines and unified by some overarching vision or theme that goes beyond disciplinary interests).

Lisa R. Lattuca (2001) advanced the study of this use of interdisciplinary language by interviewing thirty-eight faculty from two universities and two liberal arts colleges doing this kind of research and teaching. As a result, she offers a new taxonomy shifting the basis of the categorization from the degree of interaction observed to the kinds of questions being asked and thus suggests another lens for defining and delineating scholarship that somehow cuts across or around disciplines. This taxonomy (also referenced in Kathleen McKinney's introduction to this volume) outlines four types of research and teaching, though the first one (informed disciplinarity) doesn't really count for our purposes as it refers to work responding to questions springing from one discipline and simply informed by scholarship from other disciplines. The second kind (synthetic interdisciplinarity) refers to work responding to questions that spring from more than one discipline, questions that bridge disciplines. The third kind (transdisciplinarity) highlights work based on questions not grounded in any particular discipline, and the fourth kind (conceptual interdisciplinarity) points to work on questions that have no discernible disciplinary basis (112).

Noteworthy in Lattuca's scheme, the taxonomy points to a focus on the *origins* of the work (that is, the questions), rather than on the resulting performance (such as the degree of interaction in Klein's scheme) or on the resulting product. At the same time, Lattuca does note that interdisciplinarity can be discussed in terms of the ends achieved, saying that "interdisciplinary approaches result in less distorted forms of knowledge and thereby redistribute power to individuals who would otherwise be powerless" (16). Ultimately, though, Klein's taxonomy highlights the *process* of interdisciplinarity (interaction), and Lattuca's taxonomy privileges its *origins* (questions).

So how might these definitional frames advance the overall goals of the scholarship of teaching and learning? They both seem useful to a degree but ultimately limiting. In reflecting on how they might limit the advancement of SOTL, I would suggest that both conceptual frameworks emphasize dimensions other than what we seek to accomplish with this research in the first (and last) place: optimal student learning. If we can assume that the way *we* talk about the work is telling and reveals our implicit values and goals (and I believe we can), then examining how we are using interdisciplinary language in the context of our professional conversations might point to an even more helpful linguistic framing.

Putting aside for the time being the definitions themselves, I wonder to what extent those of us active in SOTL have been characterizing our work as "interdisciplinary" in our professional contexts. To gain some sense of the language we have been using, I reviewed the International Society for the Scholarship of Teaching and Learning (ISSOTL) Conference programs for two years: 2004 (the first year of the conference) and 2010 (a recent year).

At the first ISSOTL Conference in 2004, participants gathered in Bloomington, Indiana, around the theme of "The Scholarship of Teaching and Learning: Perspectives, Intersections, and Directions." While the conference's theme itself does not explicitly point to crossing disciplinary boundaries, the language of *intersections* suggests that it might invite presentations on interdisciplinary work. However, out of the 234 conference titles—including all plenaries, posters, roundtables, and concurrent sessions—only six titles included a word or phrase explicitly pointing to interdisciplinarity. Here are the six titles with my added emphasis of the interdisciplinary words/phrases:

1. "Service Learning: A Not-so-New Pedagogical Initiative *Across Disciplines*" (Marilyn Simons, roundtable)
2. "Negotiating *Multi-disciplinary* Collaboration (Ginny Saich, concurrent session)
3. "*Interdisciplinary* Undergraduate Research at Oakton Community College" (Mark Walter, concurrent session)
4. "Facilitating *Interdisciplinary* Team Collaboration" (Linda Carpenter and LaVonne Cornell-Swanson, concurrent session)
5. "Advancing the Scholarship of Teaching in a Research University: Forming a *Cross-Disciplinary,* Instructor-Driven Research-Based Teaching Group" (Pia Marks et al., concurrent session)
6. "Connections: An *Interdisciplinary* Learning Community" (Morteza Shafii-Mousavi and Karen Smith, concurrent session)

Of course, despite the absence of an interdisciplinary word or phrase in the title, other presentations could have, and certainly did, address interdisciplinary research/teaching. For example, some presentations that used cross-institutional language implied that cross-disciplinary work had been involved, in titles such as "Building a Multi-Institutional Collaborative Structure or Process for Advancing the Practice of Teaching through Scholarly Inquiry into the Scholarship of Teaching and Learning" (Renee Meyers and Katrina Lazarides).

Titles also pointed to one discipline borrowing from another with language such as "Teaching and Learning Economics through Student-Centered

Scholarship in the Business Curricula" (Kenneth Fah). Other titles implied work across disciplines in terms of spanning broader academic domains with language such as "Dissemination of the Scholarship of Teaching and Learning Within the Sciences" (Andrew Feig). My point here is not that interdisciplinary research was not going on, but rather that the presenters themselves did not call attention to an interdisciplinary focus by using the language explicitly in their titles.

In sharp contrast, at the same time that the 2004 ISSOTL Conference program contained only six explicit mentions of interdisciplinary work, there was much attention paid to disciplinary-based research. The overwhelming majority of titles for the concurrent sessions (at least thirty-eight) used specific disciplinary terms and emphasized their grounding in one specific discipline, in titles such as "Transforming the Introductory Sociology Course for Diversity" (Patrick Ashton) and "Toward a Poetics of Teaching: Using Scholarships to Inform History Teaching" (Bob Bain). Some other presentations had titles that pointed to the value of a disciplinary-based focus, such as "Decoding the Disciplines: Helping Students Learn Disciplinary Ways of Thinking" (David Pace and Joan Middendorf). Of course, here again we need to be careful in assuming that the title's use of disciplinary language implies an exclusive interest in staying grounded in a particular discipline (as their chapter in this volume clearly refutes). Again, this observation does not reflect to what extent these presentations may have involved interdisciplinary research but rather that the titles chosen to represent the work explicitly highlight a disciplinary-based interest.

What we can safely say is that a review of the words and phrases used in the titles from the 2004 conference program suggests a more explicit focus on disciplinary-based SOTL than on interdisciplinary scholarship. Another indicator of the 2004 ISSOTL Conference program highlighting discipline-based scholarship over interdisciplinary inquiry is the title (and in this case, also the substance) of the final plenary talk delivered by Lee Shulman: "In Search of Signature Pedagogies: Learning from Lessons of Practice." In urging us to consider what we can learn from the pedagogies associated with specific disciplines, Shulman's talk signaled what has continued to be an interest in studying the nature of specific disciplinary-based pedagogies, with Regan R. A. Gurung, Nancy L. Chick, and Aeron Haynie's *Exploring Signature Pedagogies: Approaches to Teaching Disciplinary Habits of Mind* (2009) representing an extension and elaboration of that interest.

In an effort to see whether this discipline-based emphasis persisted, we turn now to the 2010 ISSOTL Conference when participants gathered in Liverpool, England, to examine "Global Theories and Local Practices: Institutional, Disciplinary, and Cultural Variations." Noteworthy is the way that the conference theme itself points to "disciplinary variations," rather than to interdisciplinary relationships, suggesting an even more heightened attention to research grounded squarely within disciplines and a focus on differences rather than on similarities or interrelationships.

Strikingly, of the 265 concurrent sessions listed in this most recent program, the same number of sessions as in 2004—only six—have titles that include specific interdisciplinary words or phrases (emphasis mine):

1. "Measuring Creativity: Approaches to Encouraging and Assessing the Ineffable *Across Disciplines*" (Dannelle D. Stevens, Ellen L. West, and Candy Reynolds)

2. "*Transcending Disciplines:* Students' Perceptions of the Use of Online Learning Objects to Develop Skills, Promote Interaction, and Enhance the Student Learning Experience" (Ruth Matheson, Ian Mathieson, and Ingrid Murphy)

3. "Employability Skills to Operate at the *Inter-Disciplinary* Interface: Combining Virtual Authentic Learning Opportunities with Reflective Assessment" (Sandra Jones)

4. "What Is the Impact of *Interdisciplinary* SOTL Seminar Programs on Faculty Development?" (Marilyn Cohn)

5. "Developing a Pedagogic Portal to Promote Pedagogical Innovation *Across Disciplines*" (Scott Simkins, Kim Marie McGoldrick, and Mark Maier)

6. "Learning Style Preferences *Across Disciplines*" (Patricia Albergaria-Almedia and Rita Mendes)

Alongside these few titles with interdisciplinary language are a larger number of titles with specific disciplinary references—at least thirty-one, which is about the same as 2004 with thirty-eight—including titles such as "Revitalising a Physics Laboratory Program for Non-Physics Majors—Developing a Framework Emphasising Disciplinary Relevance" (Joe Anderson and Robin Clark). Again, I do not mean to say that the titles alone confirm an obsession with discipline-based research on teaching and learning over interdisciplinary research but only that the words and phrases chosen suggest a continued highlighting of the disciplinary rather than interdisciplinary emphasis.

This preference for choosing disciplinary terms over interdisciplinary language in the titles may, and I emphasize *may*, point to an ongoing interest in grounding this research in disciplines rather than across them. As McKinney notes in the introduction to this volume, this disciplinary emphasis was at the heart of the scholarship of teaching and learning when it began as it was motivated by a collective desire to begin in our own contexts, in our own disciplines, with our own courses, and with our own students. So it is logical that this interest would persist.

However, what other factors might account for such a dramatic absence of interdisciplinary language in the ISSOTL program titles? One explanation could be that given the absence of any clear, shared definition for *interdisciplinary research*, scholars would logically resist using it in such a conspicuous position as their titles. Safer to highlight the disciplinary origins of the work than to suggest some interdisciplinary focus if the audience does not share a common understanding of its denotation.

The proportionately low number of lexical references to interdisciplinary research in the record of our main professional conversations may also reflect the challenges, and even barriers, to doing interdisciplinary work. If, in fact, scholars resist entering these murkier interdisciplinary SOTL waters, why might that be? Perhaps the expectations seem too high. Unlike cross-disciplinary studies that tap multiple disciplinary perspectives without any deliberate attempt at integration, Klein and W. H. Newell (1997) contend that an interdisciplinary approach denotes intentionality in bringing together disciplinary perspectives into a newer, fuller understanding. Even Lattuca's (2001) taxonomy, though she says that it is not meant to be hierarchical, notes that informed disciplinarity (with other disciplines simply informing the work) is not true interdisciplinarity and requires something more. In citing Michael Gibbons and his colleagues (1994) in her orientation essay in *Disciplinary Styles in the Scholarship of Teaching and Learning*, Huber (2004) also cautioned that we have real interdisciplinarity only when we have the "explicit formulation of a uniform discipline-transcending terminology or a common methodology" (35–36). Perhaps, then, scholars of teaching and learning perceive the interdisciplinary bar as too high and thus veer away from framing their studies in those terms.

Furthermore, as Myrna H. Strober (2010) insists in her recent analysis of six case studies of *Interdisciplinary Conversations*, dialogues across disciplinary boundaries do not necessarily succeed. She finds that disciplinary habits of mind and cultures, as well as interpersonal habits, confound even the best-intended alliances so that very few interdisciplinary conversations produce positive results. This epistemological confounding reflects what Poole (in this volume) says about differing research paradigms challenging interdisciplinary SOTL work. And if SOTL, even in clearly disciplinary terms, has struggled to gain academic legitimacy because it tends to play by different research conventions than other kinds of research, as Grauerholz and Main discuss (also in this volume), then perhaps the stakes of doing interdisciplinary scholarship on teaching and learning are simply too high.

If so, then what are the costs of hiding the interdisciplinary nature of the work? Do we limit its impact if we do not scale out beyond interdisciplinary terms? I wonder what costs there might be of not framing the research in explicitly interdisciplinary terms. Does the advancement of the scholarship of teaching and learning rely on needing to surmount these challenges and boldly talk about our work in interdisciplinary language? Perhaps not. In fact, perhaps talking about this research in interdisciplinary terms represents a risky, even flawed, view.

While those of us who have done teaching/research with colleagues across disciplinary boundaries tend to feel that this border-crossing results in a rich mingling of ideas and methods, little evidence exists to show precisely what is gained in the mix. Certainly, collegial conversations across disciplines can *feel* satisfying. But to what extent are they useful in advancing the scholarship of teaching and learning? Perhaps their primary significance has more to do with their affective benefits. As Parker Palmer and Arthur Zajonc (2010) insist, this collegial correspondence may, in fact, be at the "*heart* of higher education" (emphasis mine) and if we have any hope of "renewing the academy," we need to learn how to facilitate these conversations better. Not to diminish this lofty (and worthy) goal of renewing higher education, nor to suggest that rejuvenating our spirits would not also result in better teaching and learning, but I question framing the scholarship of teaching and learning too much in either disciplinary or interdisciplinary terms. Like a riptide that can be extremely dangerous in the undertow produced, representing this scholarship as either disciplinary or interdisciplinary may be risky. If, as Robert B. Barr and John Tagg (1995) proclaimed years ago, we need to shift from a teaching paradigm to a learning paradigm, then perhaps we err by talking about this work excessively in either disciplinary or interdisciplinary terms. By highlighting the language of *disciplinary* or even *interdisciplinary* in describing SOTL, we risk putting the focus on teaching subject matter since the term "disciplinary" is so closely associated for most of us with discipline-based knowledge, rather than on the resulting learning. While learning can certainly be disciplinary (unique to a discipline) and interdisciplinary (shared concepts or skills across disciplines), we do not talk about learning that way. *Interdisciplinary teaching* and *interdisciplinary research*— yes—but not *interdisciplinary learning*. At least, I found no instances of that collation in any of the conference titles reviewed.

So are we collectively stymied in any efforts to bridge our disciplinary work? Does developing a shared SOTL lexicon or an overarching epistemological paradigm represent such a lofty, even unfeasible, goal that we must stay moored in our familiar discipline-based ports? Or is there some benefit in moving away from *disciplinary* and *interdisciplinary* language altogether to some other lexical framing?

Perhaps turning back to the language we are using in our professional conversations at ISSOTL conferences can reveal more about how we are representing our work. What else do the titles suggest about the focus of our collective attention? In terms of pervasiveness, the 2010 program includes at least forty-one titles that contain the words or forms of the words *faculty, development, pedagogy, teaching,* or *teaching practices*. If we are to take those terms as linguistic cues, we would deduce a preoccupation with the scholarship of *teaching*. Titles such as "*Teaching* Academics to *Teach*: A Disciplined Approach" (Karen MacKeachern et al.) and "Academic Migration, Disciplinary Knowledge, and Emerging *Pedagogies*" (Colina Mason and Felicity Rawlings-Sanaei; emphasis mine) reflect a focus on teaching rather than on learning. Of course, I am not suggesting that we should ignore a concern with pedagogy. A large part of the work I do at my institution centers on just that, but perhaps our tale—the way we are representing the work in our professional conversations—might be veering towards an overemphasis on the teaching and a slighting of the learning. Certainly, we believe that the "advancement of learning" (Huber and Hutchings 2005a) represents the end-all and be-all of SOTL. As McKinney (2007) notes, "SOTL can serve many functions for disciplines, departments and institutions, faculty, staff, and students. Most importantly, SOTL has the function of improving student learning" (13). While the SOTL literature contains references like these to keeping learning in the forefront, perhaps we need to continually remind ourselves of that priority in the language we choose to talk about our work to each other and, just as importantly, to colleagues not familiar with SOTL and to the public.

So what language might we turn to in emphasizing both our desire to cross discipline boundaries in doing this research and our interest in keeping learning front and center? One candidate could be the language of *integrative learning* since it brings together an interest in connecting learning across differences (disciplinary and otherwise). To what extent are we using this language in our professional conversations? Apparently not much. Alongside the striking paucity in using interdisciplinary language in the 2010 conference program titles is an equally noticeable gap in language that highlights integrative learning with only one title including it: "Establishing *Integrative Learning* in a Sociology of Culture Class" (Siarhei Liubimau). Gilian Gerhard and Jolie Mayer-Smith (2008), who highlight the integrative piece in describing interdisciplinary work by saying that scholars working in this vein focus on "synthesizing (their) insights into a conceptual whole" (2), might say that there is a relationship between the absence of interdisciplinary language and terms pointing to integrative language. Both kinds of omission suggest less interest in bridging, in synthesizing, than in deepening study within one domain.

Before further considering the merits of using the language of *integrative learning* for characterizing our work, let us review how the term is defined. In "mapping the terrain" of integrative learning, Huber and Hutchings (2005b) provide a foundational definition in asking how we might "help students pursue their learning in more intentionally connected ways" (1). How this connected learning is achieved, then, becomes the subject of study.

So what is the significance of these observations? Are we professionally more focused on disciplinary SOTL than on interdisciplinary SOTL, and more preoccupied with teaching than with learning? As far as the first question is concerned, I don't think we can say with any certainty that the lack of explicit references to interdisciplinary studies in the ISSOTL conference program titles over its existence means that scholars are not crossing their disciplinary borders. At the same time, given the many explicit references in conference program titles to disciplinary research, we can safely assume that the discipline-based current of SOTL remains strong.

The answer to the second question is more worrisome. Are we favoring talk of teaching and making it more explicit in characterizing our work than we do learning? Given the increased interest in integrative learning in the last decade, it is surprising that we have neglected highlighting it more in our professional conference presentation titles. However, that might be changing. A case in point: The entire issue of the fall 2010 *Liberal Education* was dedicated to integrative learning. In describing the kind of education needed for the twenty-first century, William H. Newell contends in that issue that "a mixture of integrative learning and interdisciplinary studies, appropriately conceived and well grounded in academic disciplines, constitutes the most effective education for a complex world" (2010, 1). And in describing a trajectory for "Getting There" (achieving maximum benefits from SOTL) as "an Integrative Vision of the Scholarship of Teaching and Learning," Hutchings, Huber, and Anthony Ciccone (2011) frame it conceptually with a title signaling what could be a shift in emphasis in the way we talk about the work. While the term "integrative learning" is certainly not new in SOTL circles, they intimate that perhaps we need to talk about it more that way. Since the concept references an understanding of learning as connected—built across the curriculum and co-curriculum, enabling scholars to make simple connections among ideas and experiences as well as an ability to synthesize and transfer learning to new, complex situations within and beyond the campus—the term is spacious in its reach.

Ever since the American Association of Colleges and Universities (AAC&U) invited proposals for a project called "Integrative Learning Opportunities to Connect" (2004) with 150 institutions responding, we have had access to this term and to its extensive terrain. And yet, if the ISSOTL conference program titles are any indication, we may be slighting it as an object of research and focusing too much on how we are teaching. However, as Palmer and Zajonc (2010) insist, "a philosophy of integrative education cannot be achieved simply by adding up the pedagogical parts, no matter how excellent they might be" (10). We need to focus our work on learning itself. Invoking Barr and Tagg's (1995) lingering call to stay focused on the learning, we would do well to talk about our work less in interdisciplinary language and more in terms of the integrative learning.

In short, to continue to employ disciplinary-derivative terms may be risky. Just as the notion of *signature pedagogies,* first identified by Shulman (2005) and expanded on by Gurung, Chick, and Haynie (2009), initially seemed extremely useful for understanding discipline-based teaching practices and how they might be used across disciplines, the concept tends to highlight not only discipline-based approaches but also to foreground teaching over learning. As long as we are talking about *disciplines* in any fashion, we risk losing our concentrated gaze on student learning.

At the same time, to assume that framing the scholarship of teaching and learning in cross-disciplinary terms represents the only viable response is also problematic. While Maryellen Weimer (2008) has provided a compelling cautionary tale in pointing out that if we talk about this work only in disciplinary terms, we risk it going unread and thus unused, I would add that if we frame the work too heavily in cross-disciplinary terms, we risk shifting our eyes from the real prize: student learning. For example, in saying that "practitioner scholarship on teaching and learning . . . is written to improve practice" (3–4), she implies that the proper object of our scholarly attention is to advance teaching, that is, to improve *practice.* But is it? Several authors in this volume (Poole; Grauerholz and Main; Robinson et al.) have highlighted the challenges to doing interdisciplinary SOTL. I would add that talking about the work too much in either disciplinary or cross-disciplinary terms risks losing sight of why we engage in it at all: to advance student learning.

In revisiting how we talk about our work in professional contexts such as the ISSOTL conferences, we are simultaneously reconceptualizing it. By reminding ourselves to talk the talk of learning, particularly of integrative learning, we also recommit ourselves to working toward it. So what will help us remember to talk this talk and, thus, walk this walk? Perhaps Shulman's (2011) recollection of how the Carnegie Academy for the Scholarship of Teaching and Learning (CASTL) evolved from the Academy for the Advancement of Teaching (only) will help. In reflecting on "how an organization dedicated to 'the advancement of teaching' evolved into 'an academy for the scholarship of teaching *and* learning,'" Shulman acknowledges that it hadn't occurred to him, even though he had been doing SOTL, to "name it" that way (2).

What else might help us to revisit the way we are talking about this work? Perhaps one of the main benefits of engaging students as co-inquirers in SOTL is their ability to remind us of the importance of using language that keeps the focus on learning. Because this co-inquiry process often entails a translation process where students approach "Academese as a Second Language," they expect us to interpret the work in their terms (Werder and Otis 2010). Thus, the more we engage students as full partners in the research, the more we will remember to mind both our linguistic and conceptual Ps and Qs. Engaging students more fully as co-inquirers, including undergraduates who have not yet decided on disciplinary majors, raises the chances that we will talk about the work in their terms—the terms of learning. In this way, the student voices initiative within SOTL has likely helped us recognize the dangers of casting about in the riptide of disciplinary and interdisciplinary SOTL. As Lattuca (2001) insists, "We must judge scholarship on the basis of its contribution to the advancement of knowledge. Any other evaluation privileges the discipline over the enterprise and diminishes both the scholarship and the community that produces it" (266). I would push that contention further in saying that we must judge the scholarship of teaching and learning on the basis of its contribution to the advancement of integrative learning, and any other evaluation diminishes the whole journey.

REFERENCES

Barr, Robert B., and John Tagg. 1995. "From Teaching to Learning: A New Paradigm for Undergraduate Education." *Change Magazine* (November/December): 13–25.

Galison, Peter. 1997. *Image and Logic: A Material Culture of Microphysics.* Chicago: University of Chicago Press.

Gerhard, Gilian, and Jolie Mayer-Smith. 2008. "Casting a Wider Net: Deepening Scholarship by Changing Theories." *International Journal for the Scholarship of Teaching and Learning* 2, no. 1: 1–11.

Gibbons, Michael, Camille Limoges, Helga Nowotny, Simon Schwartzman, Peter Scott, and Martin Trow. 1994. *The New Production of Knowledge: The Dynamics of Science and Research in Contemporary Societies*. London: Sage.

Gurung, Regan A. R., Nancy L. Chick, and Aeron Haynie, eds. 2009. *Exploring Signature Pedagogies: Approaches to Teaching Disciplinary Habits of Mind*. Sterling, VA: Stylus.

Huber, Mary Taylor, and Pat Hutchings. 2005a. *The Advancement of Learning: Building the Teaching Commons*. San Francisco: Jossey-Bass.

———. 2005b. *Integrative Learning: Mapping the Terrain*. Washington, D.C.: Association of American Colleges and Universities and the Carnegie Foundation for the Advancement of Teaching.

Huber, Mary Taylor, and Sherwyn P. Morreale, eds. 2002. *Disciplinary Styles in the Scholarship of Teaching and Learning: Exploring Common Ground*. Washington, DC: American Association for Higher Education and the Carnegie Foundation for the Advancement of Teaching.

Hutchings, Pat, Mary Taylor Huber, and Anthony Ciccone. 2011. "Getting There: An Integrative Vision of the Scholarship of Teaching and Learning." *International Journal for the Scholarship of Teaching and Learning* 5, no. 1: 1–13.

International Society for the Scholarship of Teaching and Learning (ISSOTL) Conference Program. 2004.

Klein, Julie Thompson. 1990. *Interdisciplinarity: History, Theory, and Practice*. Detroit, MI: Wayne State University Press.

Klein, Julie Thompson, and W. H. Newell. 1997. "Advancing Interdisciplinary Studies." In *Handbook of the Undergraduate Curriculum*, ed. Jerry G. Gaff and James L. Ratcliff and associates, 393–94. San Francisco: Jossey-Bass.

Lattuca, Lisa R. 2001. *Creating Interdisciplinarity: Interdisciplinary Research and Teaching among College and University Faculty*. Nashville, TN: Vanderbilt University Press.

McKinney, Kathleen. 2007. *Enhancing Learning through the Scholarship of Teaching and Learning: The Challenges and Joys of Juggling*. San Francisco: Jossey-Bass.

———. 2009. "Lessons from My Students and Other Reflections on SOTL." *International Journal for the Scholarship of Teaching and Learning* 3, no. 2: 1–4.

Merriam-Webster Online. 2011. S. v. "riptide." http://www.merriam-webster.com/dictionary/riptide.

Newell, William H. 2010. "Educating for a Complex World: Integrative Learning and Integrative Studies." *Liberal Education:* 96, no. 4. http://www.aacu.org/liberal education/le-fa10/LEFA10_Newell.cfm.

Palmer, Parker, and Arthur Zajonc. 2010. *The Heart of Higher Education: A Call to Renewal Transforming the Academy through Collegial Conversations*. San Francisco: Jossey-Bass.

Shulman, Lee S. 2005. "Signature Pedagogies in the Professions." *Daedalus* 134, no. 3: 52–59.

————. 2011. "The Scholarship of Teaching and Learning: A Personal Account and Reflection." *International Journal for the Scholarship of Teaching and Learning* 5, no. 1: 1–7.

Strober, Myrna H. 2010. *Interdisciplinary Conversations: Challenging Habits of Thought.* Palo Alto, CA: Stanford University Press.

Weimer, Maryellen. 2008. "Positioning Scholarly Work on Teaching and Learning." *International Journal for the Scholarship of Teaching and Learning* 2, no. 1: 1–6.

Werder, Carmen, and Megan M. Otis, eds. 2010. *Engaging Student Voices in the Study of Teaching and Learning.* Sterling, VA: Stylus.

CONTRIBUTORS

Cheryl Albers is Emeritus Professor of Sociology at Buffalo State College. She is the author of three books and numerous journal articles on teaching and learning. During her tenure as campus SOTL coordinator, Buffalo State became one of twelve coordinating institutions for the international CASTL Leadership program.

Curtis Bennett, a 2000–2001 and 2003–2004 Carnegie Scholar, is Professor of Mathematics at Loyola Marymount University in Los Angeles. His latest publication, forthcoming in PRIMUS, is "An Overview of the Scholarship of Teaching and Learning in Mathematics," written with Jacqueline Dewar.

Jeffrey L. Bernstein is Professor of Political Science at Eastern Michigan University. He is co-editor and contributing author of *Citizenship Across the Curriculum* and has SOTL publications in several pedagogical journals.

Nancy L. Chick is Affiliated Faculty of English and Assistant Director, Center for Teaching at Vanderbilt University. She serves on the ISSOTL board of directors and has published on literary learning and diversity learning as well as SOTL, including co-editing two volumes on signature pedagogies.

Tyler Booth Christensen is an adjunct faculty member of the psychology department at Indiana University–Purdue University–Columbus, and a learning sciences PhD student at the Indiana University–Bloomington Center for Innovative Teaching and Learning. His research focuses on becoming a reflective practitioner through collaborative critical reflection practices.

Jacqueline Dewar is Professor of Mathematics at Loyola Marymount University. She is a 2003–2004 Carnegie Scholar. One of her recent publications is "Helping Stakeholders Understand the Limitations of SRT Data: Are We Doing Enough?" in the *Journal of Faculty Development*.

Arlene Díaz is Associate Professor of Latin American History and served as director of the Latino Studies Program at Indiana University–Bloomington. She is co-author of "The History Learning Project: A Department 'Decodes' Its Students," recently the winner of the McGraw-Hill/Magna Publications Scholarly Work on Teaching and Learning Award.

Liz Grauerholz is Professor of Sociology at the University of Central Florida. She is a past editor of *Teaching Sociology* and has engaged in numerous SOTL projects, including teaching about the sociology of consumption and exploring institutional effects on teaching behaviors and attitudes.

Melissa Gresalfi is Associate Professor of Learning Sciences and Cognitive Science at Indiana University–Bloomington. Her work considers cognition and social context by examining student learning as a function of participation in activity settings. Specifically, she has investigated how opportunities to learn get constructed in elementary and secondary mathematics classrooms.

Regan A. R. Gurung is the Ben and Joyce Rosenberg Professor of Human Development and Psychology at the University of Wisconsin–Green Bay. Recent books include the textbook *Health Psychology: A Cultural Approach and the co-authored book Exploring Signature Pedagogies: Approaches to Teaching Disciplinary Habits of Mind.*

Mary Taylor Huber is Senior Scholar Emerita and Consulting Scholar at the Carnegie Foundation for the Advancement of Teaching. She has written widely on cultures of teaching in higher education, most recently as co-author of *The Scholarship of Teaching and Learning Reconsidered: Institutional Integration and Impact.*

Katherine Dowell Kearns is a senior instructional consultant at the Center for Innovative Teaching and Learning, Indiana University. Her work focuses on the preparation of graduate students for scholarly teaching and faculty careers.

Eric Main is an assistant director at the Karen L. Smith Faculty Center for Teaching and Learning at the University of Central Florida. He works with faculty members from all disciplines on their SOTL projects and organizes events and workshops to support SOTL initiatives on campus and regionally.

Antonio E. Mateiro is a post graduate student in philosophy at the University of Oxford, where he is focusing on moral philosophy. He has an MA from University College of London and a BA from New York University. As a student at New York University, he worked as an undergraduate research assistant for Professor Caroline Persell.

Kathleen McKinney is the Cross Endowed Chair in the Scholarship of Teaching and Learning and Emeritus Professor of Sociology at Illinois State University. She is a 2003–2004 Carnegie Scholar and has numerous SOTL publications, mostly in *Teaching Sociology,* and books, including *Enhancing Learning through the Scholarship of Teaching and Learning.*

Joan Middendorf is a lead instructional consultant at the Center for Innovative Teaching and Learning and Adjunct Professor in Higher Education Administration at Indiana University–Bloomington. She co-developed the Decoding the Disciplines method and is co-author of *Decoding the Disciplines: Helping Students Learn Disciplinary Ways of Thinking.*

David Pace is Professor Emeritus of European history at Indiana University–Bloomington, co-director of the Freshman Learning Project, and co-developer of the Decoding the Discipline method. He is a fellow in the Carnegie Academy for the Scholarship of Teaching and Learning and has received the American Historical Association's Eugene Asher Distinguished Teaching Award.

Caroline Hodges Persell is Professor Emerita of Sociology at New York University. The author of numerous books and articles, she was a Carnegie Scholar and received the American Sociological Association's Distinguished Contributions to Teaching Award in 2005 and the Sorokin Award in 2006.

Gary Poole is Senior Scholar at the Centre for Health Education Scholarship, Faculty of Medicine, University of British Columbia. Poole is past president of the International Society for the Scholarship of Teaching and Learning as well as a 3M National Teaching Fellow.

David A. Reichard is Associate Professor of History and Legal Studies at California State University–Monterey Bay. He is a 2003–2004 Carnegie Scholar and served as a lead scholar for the 2005–2006 cohort of the program. He has shared his research on student learning in seminars and through blogging, and has had students present research at numerous SOTL conferences.

Jennifer Meta Robinson is Senior Lecturer in the Department of Communication and Culture at Indiana University–Bloomington. She is editor of *Teaching Environmental Literacy Across the Curriculum* and she served as president of the International Society for the Scholarship of Teaching and Learning.

Lauren Scharff is Director of Scholarship of Teaching and Learning and Professor of Psychology at the United States Air Force Academy. She is a past president of the Southwestern Psychological Association and co-authored the book *Aviation Visual Perception: Research, Misperception, and Mishaps.*

Beth M. Schwartz is the Thoresen Professor of Psychology and Assistant Dean of the College at Randolph College. She has edited and authored books including *Optimizing Teaching and Learning* and *The Psychology of Teaching: An Empirically Based Guide to Picking, Choosing, and Using Pedagogy*.

Leah Shopkow is Associate Professor of History at Indiana University–Bloomington. She has served as her department's director of Undergraduate Studies. She was a participant in the Course Portfolio Project and in addition to her work in medieval history she has produced several articles and conference papers on the scholarship of teaching and learning in history.

April K. Sievert is Senior Lecturer in the Department of Anthropology at Indiana University. She co-edited *Personal Encounters in Cultural Anthropology: An Introductory Reader*. She explores how future archaeology faculty can contribute to archaeological literacy, and she teaches a departmental pedagogy course for anthropology graduate students.

Kathy Takayama is Director of the Harriet W. Sheridan Center for Teaching and Learning and Adjunct Associate Professor of Molecular Biology, Cell biology, and Biochemistry at Brown University. She is a 2003–2004 Carnegie Scholar. She has shared her research on collaborative inquiry and visualizations in science education through publications and presentations.

Carmen Werder is Director of the Teaching-Learning Academy and the Learning Commons at Western Washington University. She is a 2005–2006 Carnegie Scholar who has written about her related research on personal metaphors in *Citizenship Across the Curriculum*. She is co-editor of *Student Voices in the Study of Teaching and Learning*.

Miriam E. Zolan is Professor in the Department of Biology at Indiana University. Her lab research focuses on mechanisms of meiosis; in addition, she teaches a seminar for graduate students called Mentored Teaching, in which students focus on student learning, observe outstanding teachers, and both develop and present a lesson for introductory biology students.

INDEX

Note: Page numbers in *italics* indicate tables and illustrations.